John Chalow.
2011

THE ACTORS

To dear John
from a Garrick Actor
(of Sorts ....)

John

THE GARRICK COLLECTION

THE ACTORS

Brian Masters

THE GARRICK CLUB

LONDON

First published in 2010 by The Garrick Club
15 Garrick Street, London, WC2E 9AY
Tel: +44 (0)20 7836 1737/ Fax: +44 (0)20 7379 5966
e-mail: office@garrickclub.co.uk
Web: www.garrickclub.co.uk

A catalogue record for this book is available from the British Library.

ISBN: 978-0-95674-360-2

All images from Garrick Club / Art Archive
and are from works in the Garrick Club collections
Richard Attenborough, Baron Attenborough by Godfrey Argent, 30 July
1969, image © National Portrait Gallery, London, NPG x163781.

Typeset and design by Oberon Books London
Printed in Great Britain by CPI Antony Rowe, Chippenham

Acknowledgements

I have been much assisted by the apparently endless knowledge of our curator, Marcus Risdell, which has helped steer me away from some misconceptions; by the extensive theatrical information stored in the joyful memory of Donald Sinden; by the assiduous study of Samantha Wyndham, who is responsible for the database offered in appendix and index; and especially by the confidence shown by Barry Turner, who invited me to attempt this history for the first volume of a series which he conceived.

Brian Masters

CONTENTS

1

FOUNDATIONS

Giving evidence to the 1832 Select Committee of the House of Commons, to inquire "into the State of the Laws affecting Dramatic Literature", William Charles Macready, the undisputed senior actor of the moment, said of his calling, "I think it so unrequiting a profession, that no person who had the power of doing anything better would, unless deluded into it, take it up."[1]

The crusty bitterness of this reply to a perfectly innocent question is shockingly audible down the years, and it is echoed dozens of times in Macready's naively candid diaries, wherein he laments "the low condition of a player" and talks of "my pariah profession" and the "wretched art" or "my degraded art" to which he had grudgingly devoted his entire life.[2]

The fact was, Macready was deeply embarrassed to be an actor, for he craved respect, and actors were heartily reviled in polite society. There were good social and historical reasons for this contempt, and the leading men of the theatre would expend much effort throughout the nineteenth century in their united determination to redress the situation. It had to be admitted that they faced a veritable pile of Himalayan obstacles to overcome, for

---

1 Report of the Select Committee on the Drama 1832, p 133
2 *Mr Macready* by J.C. Trewin (1955), pp 132, 160, 196-7

legal precedent combined with profound prejudice and the evidence of generations of licentious behaviour associated with the theatre and its patrons made it difficult to defend the profession without some prevarication.

On the legal front, until only very recently actors had been included amongst the dregs of the social stratum. The Act of 24 June 1822 (George IV) declared that "all common Stage Players, and all Persons who shall for Hire, Gain or Reward act, represent, or perform, or cause to be performed, any Interlude, or Entertainments of the Stage, or any Part or Parts therein, such Persons not being authorized by Law…shall be deemed Rogues and Vagabonds, within the true Intent and Meaning of this Act." In this miserable condition they kept company with gypsies, pedlars, beggars, and people who abandoned wives and children, as well as people who showed wounds and deformities (presumably to increase success on the streets). While it is true that a subsequent Act of 21 June 1824 no longer referred to actors as "rogues and vagabonds" and repealed some of the harsher punishments to which they were theoretically subjected, the stigma endured, and was to prove tenacious for some years to come. Some idea of the opinions which prevailed in certain quarters may be gleaned from an outburst in the House of Commons during the third reading of the Dramatic Performance Bill (1833), when Mr Rotch MP said a theatre "served the purpose only of bringing together a set of unfortunate outcasts who had no means of existence and it was beneath the dignity of Parliament to legislate for such a class."[3] He caused momentary uproar in the House, but that did not mean he was alone in his views.

---

3   Hansard, 3rd series, Vol xix, p 1220

One reason actors were so distrusted was the very nature of their talent. Their ability to unleash Dionysian forces, to be possessed and dangerous, made them appear ready to risk self-destruction in their grim lunges after truth. One such was the mighty Edmund Kean, still working in 1830, whose passionate displays of overwhelming emotion caused ladies to blush guiltily, for he was able to release passions and urges within the audience which they felt they should suppress. The world was afraid of actors, hence the world looked upon them with distaste. There had always been other more obvious reasons which were advanced to replace this real, subversive and barely acknowledged cause for distrust, and some of them make alarming reading. As far back as the Elizabethan era, a Rev T Wilcocks could declare, "the cause of plagues is sin, and the cause of sin are plays; therefore the cause of plagues are plays."[4] Since theatres were then breeding grounds for contagion, being stuffed with people in unhygienic proximity, the clergyman had perhaps some justification for his ire. But one and a half centuries later, the reputation of the theatre had actually descended further, for the Puritan mentality equated going to the theatre with going to Catholic mass – both forms of idolatry! One reformer affirmed that "the theatre is at present on such a footing in England, that it is impossible to enter it and not come out the worse for having been in it." He deplored the lewdness of the action, the immodesty of the actresses, the impudence of the songs, and another cleric cried, "a Player cannot be a living member of Christ, or in a true state of Grace, till he renounces his Profession." Another publication, during David Garrick's tumultuous ascendancy, asserted

---

4   F P Wilson, *The Plague in Shakespeare's London* (1927), p 52

that "play-actors are the most profligate wretches, and the vilest vermin, that hell ever vomited out; they are the filth and garbage of the earth, the scum and stain of human nature, the excrements and refuse of all mankind, the pests and plagues of human society, the debauchees of men's minds and morals."[5] Strong stuff indeed, and though the indignant MP who fulminated against "unfortunate outcasts" in 1833 was marshmallow in comparison, one sees that his view had a long pedigree, the distant ripples of which were still there to make Macready uneasy about his profession.

There was in addition the awkward fact that the two patented theatres, Drury Lane and Covent Garden, which alone had the right at that time to present the "legitimate" drama, were situated in insalubrious neighbourhoods. Prostitutes lined the streets, hustled playgoers, hung about stage doors. "One would imagine that all the prostitutes in the kingdom had pitched upon this blessed neighbourhood for a place of general rendezvous", wrote one observer. "Here are lewd women in sufficient numbers to people a mighty colony. Slang for a whore was a "Drury Lane vestal" and for a whore's madam, "Covent Garden abbess". Theatreland was an area to satisfy every depravity, and it was moreover blatant. On one occasion a man picked up a whore outside the theatre and forced her into the royal coach which was waiting, had intercourse with her there and then, encouraged by an eager crowd. Even within the theatre, much the same temper might obtain; some of the boxes were known as the flesh market, and the Theatre Royal Covent Garden was sometimes said to be tantamount to a public brothel.[6]

5　John Brewer, *The Pleasures of the Imagination* (1997), p 333
6　*ibid.*, pp 348-350

The behaviour of the audience, even when not salacious, was far from decorous. They regarded the theatres as their playgrounds, a place to let off steam. They would interrupt a performance, quarrel with the actor, fling oranges across the auditorium, people were squashed side by side on benches in the pit, there was general noise and din and disturbance. The French actor Dufresne had been interrupted by a man shouting from the pit, "You are speaking too low", to which he responded, "And you, sir, too loud." The audience would not stand for impertinence from an actor and the whole theatre erupted in tumult. The following night Dufresne was made to apologise for his rudeness, telling the audience how well he realised his lowly position in life.[7]

That was long ago, but audiences still jealously retained their right to indicate delight or displeasure, to stop a performance or to cause a riot if their preferences were not respected. It has been estimated that both the patent theatres had to be entirely redecorated every ten years to repair depredation due to the violence or boisterousness of the audience. Even in recent times, the great John Philip Kemble had been forced to interrupt his performance to remonstrate with a lady in a box who was talking loudly all the way through. A French visitor noted that "the gallery controlled the acting and thanked the players"[8], and even worse, they were not prepared to condone the smallest opposition to their wishes; "on any provocation [they] took an indecent delight in exacting apologies from the players."[9]

---

7   Thomas Davies, *Memoirs of the Life of David Garrick* (1805), in W A Darlington, *The Actor and His Audience* p 51

8   Brewer, *op. cit*, p 350

9   V C Clinton-Baddeley, *All Right on the Night* (1954), pp 77, 144

It was also J P Kemble who had tried to raise the price of tickets (in order to attract a better class of spectator) as recently as 1809, and had been rewarded with sixty-seven consecutive nights of rioting. The people got their way, and Kemble was obliged to yield. These are the Old Price Riots known to the history books.

In view of all this, it is little wonder that Macready was occasionally peeved and dispirited. A man of his intellectual rigour and haughty pride felt humiliated at having to give way to poor quality stuff on the stage when his soul demanded that the great classics should be revived and reinvigorated to the benefit and education of the people. Instead of which, the great hit of the preceding years had been a drama entitled *Black-Eye'd Susan*. Having opened at the Surrey Theatre in June 1829, it ran for 100 performances before being transferred to Covent Garden and eventually to Drury Lane. A nautical drama by Douglas Jerrold with a risible plot, it starred as William, the hero, an actor who had himself been a sailor with the Royal Navy, T. P. Cooke, and became so popular that writers began inserting sailors into the cast of plays which had no nautical theme whatever. More than sixty years later, the play was still being revived, for its simplicity appealed to the new type of audience who made no demands for intelligence or imagination. A vicious landlord ("a rascal with no more heart than a bagpipe") threatens to evict a poor widow and her daughter (the black-eye'd Susan of the title) unless the rent is paid. That is it, until rescue comes from without, and all is well. It was a perfect example of the easy melodrama, and it positively encouraged audience participation. They wanted digestible pap, predictable, safe and unenterprising, and this is what they got.

The melodrama relied upon formula acting. There was a standard set of characters who did not vary from one play to the next – the hero, the heroine, the villain. The hero was good-hearted, natural, dependable; the heroine pure and unsullied, always dressed in white, with a straw bonnet "which at times of stress slipped from her head and was held by a ribbon"[10]; the villain was swarthy, bore a moustache, carried a cane, and dressed in black. With such people you always knew where you were. If you lost grip of the story, there were well-tried clues to help guide you back on track. There was always some misfortune productive of misery and despair, followed by miraculous salvation and the promise of well-deserved contentment. The heroine would often make her first entrance in rags, to indicate she had had a hard time of it, and the villain would remove any doubt about his character with oaths directed to the audience ("Hell and confusion") which are retained in modern pantomime, a living display of nineteenth-century melodrama; now, as then, the audience is expected to hiss and jeer.

Further clues were given by stylised gestures and postures, to indicate grief (wipe the eye with a handkerchief), despair (wring your hands despondently and very visibly), love (drop to your knees), and the cast would routinely freeze to make a *tableau*, with all the characters making their signature gestures at once. The audience loved it. They were further encouraged by the music, which accompanied the action throughout, and manipulated their moods (this tradition survived into the era of silent films, with the deep piano roll from the pit to announce the arrival of the villain), and the climax

---

10   J L Styan, *The English Stage* (1996), p 314

of *Black-Eye'd Susan* erupted into jolly nautical songs. It is easy to sympathise with the fastidious Macready in the face of all this nonsense.

The confluence of all these influences – social, historical, moral, and legal – made it virtually impossible for an actor to be accepted as a normal, reputable person by anybody but the most adventurous iconoclast, and there were not many of those. The notion that actors might be admitted to the austere precincts of the established Pall Mall clubs for gentlemen was intolerable to most, and it was not unusual for an aristocrat to refuse to acknowledge a man who was revealed to be a "player", while his wife and daughters would likely not be allowed in the same room with him.

There were of course exceptions. The great Garrick was the first to break through the barrier of prejudice and be welcomed at a fashionable table, but even he had to be properly considered before the invitation was secure. Joshua Reynolds had proposed a club for gentlemen, called simply "The Club", in 1764, with original members including Reynolds himself, Dr Johnson, Burke, Beauclerk and Goldsmith. They met for dinner and talk at the Turk's Head in Gerrard Street once a week, then transferred to a tavern in Dover Street to dine once a fortnight. Garrick apparently made it known to Reynolds that he would like to join, whereat Johnson exclaimed, "He'll be one of us, how does he know we will *permit* him? The first duke in England has no right to hold such language." The actor was later properly proposed, and supported by Johnson (who had known him, after all, since adolescence together in Lichfield), but not before Boswell had attested to his "social merit" in opposition to another member's fears that he would introduce "buffoonery" into their society.[11] Garrick remained a member until his death, but outside this select coterie he was still held on sufferance. Walpole felt the need to warn his correspondent, who was about to dine with him, "Be a little on your guard, remember he is an *actor*."[12]

The Sublime Society of Beef Steaks (forerunner of today's Beefsteak Club off Leicester Square), was another exception, having a popular harlequin, John Rich, as one of its eighteenth-century founders, but it was somewhat *louche* in those days, and met in taverns and coffee-houses, as well as theatres, in an atmosphere distinctly different from the sombre and hushed rooms in Pall Mall and St James's Street.

Much more significant was the foundation of the new and immediately august Athenaeum Club in 1824, by John Wilson Croker, the editor of Boswell's *Life of Johnson* and secretary of the Admiralty. This was described as "an association of individuals known for their scientific and literary attainments, artists of eminence in any class of the fine arts and noblemen and gentlemen distinguished as liberal patrons of science, literature or the arts." Sir Humphry Davy presided over the first committee meeting, and of the original list of members, eight would become Prime Minister in time. Although the acting profession was not specifically excluded, it was understood that actors would be unlikely to be proposed. Lord Lansdowne warned that the membership would have to be kept select "as we shall otherwise be overrun with all the pretenders to literature and the arts, than whom

11 Boswell's *Life of Johnson*, Vol I, pp 296-297
12 Horace Walpole, *Letters*, ed. Cunningham (1906), 1 September, 1763

there is not anywhere a more odious race."[13] The hint
was hidden, but unmistakeable; acting was not a fine art.
Indeed, Macready himself was to be blackballed by the
Athenaeum only a few short years later, in 1835.

It was against this background that actors would have to
struggle, over the coming century, to gain respectability for
their profession. They would succeed in reforming the two
patent theatres and liberalising the law which made them
subservient to the Lord Chamberlain's department; they
would rescue the texts of Shakespeare from two hundred
years of neglect and corruption; they would subdue
audiences into reverential awe at their poetic sensibilities
and artistic genius. But it was impossible to foresee, when
a few friends drew up a prospectus for a Club "in the
vicinity of the great theatre…dedicated to all the interests
of the drama", that before the end of the century an actor
would be knighted by the monarch, and well into the next
not only would knighthoods proliferate, but actors would
even be raised to the peerage. That original handful of
enthusiasts would have been astonished.

It is nicely appropriate that the man who first conceived
the idea of what would soon become the Garrick Club
was himself born in Covent Garden, very close to where
the club would be housed. This was James Winston,
who owned part of the lease on the Haymarket Theatre
and had himself been an actor and playwright of some
experience but little renown. He was born James Bown,
the son of a hosier, and had from infancy been infatuated
with the theatre. "While other boys were employing their
leisure hours in juvenile sports…at ten years of age he
was proprietor of a Lilliputian theatre, of which he was

13 Anthony Lejeune, *The Gentlemen's Clubs of London* (1979), p 40

architect, carpenter, machinist, scene-painter, and actor for his wooden groupe."[14] There is evidence of his having attempted to establish a private theatre when he was a teenager, although this did not bear fruit.[15] When he was twenty-two his maternal grandfather, James Winston, died without male heir, leaving young James with independent means, whereupon he was granted Royal License to change his surname to Winston. He thereupon launched his career as a strolling player, appearing on various circuits in Horsham, Dover, Brighton, Dorking and Bath, as well as the little theatre off Tottenham Court Road which would eventually be named Queen's Theatre and form the genesis of the glorious management of the Bancrofts; but that is far into the future. From Tottenham Court Road he brought a set of actors to Richmond, Surrey, and bought the theatre there, immediately losing part of his fortune in a series of "losses and disappointments". So off he went strolling again, this time to Cheltenham and Plymouth, having married one of his actresses the while. The Royal Family attended one of his performances, and he was soon giving comic songs as well as dramatic fare. He wrote a farce entitled *Perseverance*, himself playing the five main characters therein, and went on to spend more of his money on redecorating the theatre at Plymouth, but the season there was, again, not successful.

Back in London, Winston took a one-eighth share in the Theatre Royal Haymarket, then under the management of Robert Elliston, an actor at the peak of his career and very popular with the public. When Elliston resigned, Winston

---

14 *The Monthly Mirror*, August 1805

15 this, and most subsequent information about James Winston, is derived from *Introducing Mr Winston*, a paper given at the Society for Theatre Research Jubilee Conference by Marcus Risdell, to which I am wholly indebted.

took over as Acting Manager in his stead, and played ten different comedy parts in the 1806 season. But halfway through the 1807 season he seems to have developed stage-fright, and thereafter passed all his roles on to other actors and never appeared again. His talents were thenceforth devoted to management alone, joining Elliston at Drury Lane from 1819 to 1827. He was indispensable to Elliston, far more than his right-hand man in fact, for Elliston was an absentee manager busy touring the country circuits as the visiting "star" from London, a position he much preferred, leaving Winston in sole charge at Drury Lane.

An anecdote from this period shows Winston busy operating the thunder machine over the stage during the third act of *King Lear* while Edmund Kean was howling out his loneliness below. Otherwise known as the 'thunder run', it consisted of a sloping wooden trough of planks down which iron balls were rolled to simulate a storm. Winston was so energetic in his operations that he drowned out the performers, until Kean shouted, "I don't care how many flashes of lightning you give me, but, for Heaven's sake, Winston, expel your wind and cut out your thunder."[16] That was in 1820.

When Elliston went bankrupt, James Winston stayed on (again!) as acting Manager at Drury Lane, until the management was taken over by the American Stephen Price, never an actor but overly fond of ludicrous effects, such as real horses and tigers on stage. He stayed from 1826 to 1830, but got on so badly with Winston that he literally locked him out of the theatre by confiscating his keys. Winston then endeavoured to offer his services at

---

16 Richard Southern, *The Victorian Theatre* (1970), p 62, and Marcus Risdell, *op.cit.*

Covent Garden, but could not win the co-operation of the carpenters, which was a crucial blow, for with no people to make or shift scenery, there would be no theatre. There must have been some sad defect in Winston's character for him to have alienated people so easily. At the time when he made his transformative suggestion for a new theatrical club, therefore, he was not in employment of any sort.

He had, however, not wasted his time, and there was evidently a good part of his fortune left, which he spent on accumulating theatrical memorabilia including playbills, scrapbooks, correspondence, and some material which he lifted from Drury Lane (which might account for his having the keys removed). These collections, once vast, are now scattered across the world in various deposits; when they were auctioned much later, there were 1076 lots spreading the sale over three days. A fraction of this remains with the club which he founded. In addition, he made some very attractive drawings in and around Covent Garden, some of which are now in the British Museum while others reside with the collections of the Theatre Museum.

It is doubtful whether he realised at the time that his lasting contribution to the theatre would be the club which he so enthusiastically suggested during the summer of 1831. He had retained his part-ownership of the Haymarket Theatre, but convened the original meeting to discuss his idea, not there, but in the committee room of the Drury Lane Theatre (Mr Price had left the previous year, so the keys were presumably restored!). He was joined there on 17 August by Frank Mills, an occasional journalist and picture-collector; Samuel Beazley the architect and playwright, who was soon to build the Lyceum Theatre; John Rowland Durrant of the Stock Exchange (who would turn out to be the club's finest benefactor); Samuel Arnold, both a dramatist and theatre manager (of whom Hazlitt witheringly wrote "Mr Arnold writes with the fewest ideas possible"); Jerdan of the *Literary Gazette*; and the local auctioneer George Robins, brought in to discuss the acquisition of suitable premises. These gentlemen also enjoyed the aristocratic encouragement of the Earl of Mulgrave (later, 1st Marquess of Normanby), a personable young man who had written a number of not very significant novels and was besotted with the theatre.

Subsequent meetings were held in James Winston's lodgings at 3 Charles Street, Covent Garden, and after nine enrolments and nineteen ballots, the club was effectively constituted. The first General Assembly of members took place on 15 October, 1831, on which occasion the purposes, rules and regulations of the nascent club were unanimously approved, and a General Committee appointed, with the Earl of Mulgrave in the chair.

According to the club's first historian Percy Fitzgerald, writing some sixty years later, these gentlemen decided that the club should be a place where "actors and men of education and refinement might meet on equal terms [that being the revolutionary bit]. Easy intercourse was to be promoted between artists and patrons of the drama and its professors, and a rendezvous offered to literary men." The character of the club would be strictly social and conducive to easy and friendly association, therefore any committee would have to be vigilant "for it was clear that it would be better that ten unobjectionable men should be excluded than one terrible bore should be admitted."[17]

---

17 quoted in Geoffrey Wansell, *The Garrick Club: A History* (2004), p 10, and in
    Fitzgerald's history, p.2

That remains the most cherished rule, yet one terrible bore seems able to slip in unnoticed with each generation.

The first open ballot took place one week later, on 22 October, to add to the one hundred and seventy-five gentlemen who had already been installed as Original Members by invitation. They included the Dukes of Beaufort and Devonshire, plus several marquesses and earls and Lord John Russell who only months before had moved the first reading of the Government Reform Bill in the House of Commons, certainly one of the most important pieces of legislation in the country's history. There were also two illustrious publishers - John Murray and Richard Bentley. More pertinently, twelve actors, all well-known and established, were on the original list, headed by William Macready; Charles Kemble, brother of John Philip Kemble and Mrs Siddons as well as father of Fanny Kemble; Charles Mathews; his son Charles James Mathews; George Bartley; William Dowton; John Pritt Harley, an eccentric who lived alone and collected three hundred walking-sticks; Richard Jones, a very popular comedian said to be the best-dressed gentleman on the stage; Tyrone Power, the Irish actor from Waterford and great-grandfather of the Hollywood actor in the next century; James Wallack; Frederick Yates; and Charles Young.

George Robins secured the lease on a small family hotel at 35 King Street, called Probatt's, taking possession on 7 November 1831. The lease cost £1,500, complete with furniture and fittings (a sum negotiated by John Rowland Durrant, who knew a thing or two about money) and Beazley was given a budget of £500 to convert it suitable to club use. Oddly enough, the house had once been the home of the splendid actor known as 'Gentleman' Lewis, who had a long and illustrious career at Covent Garden and the Haymarket, and was said to be the funniest man on the stage. Hazlitt called him "the greatest comic mannerist perhaps that ever lived" and Leigh Hunt wrote that "vulgarity seems totally impossible to an actor of his manners". Moreover, Gentleman Lewis had known David Garrick himself, though he did not die until 1811, twenty years before his house was acquired for the club. It is wonderfully fitting the Garrick Club's first home should carry the memory of such a man, with precisely those qualities and assets which its members would always value.[18]

The clubhouse opened on 1 February 1832, and the Inaugural Dinner was held on the 13th. Barely six months had passed from conception to launch. The dinner, described as opulent and festive, was attended by one hundred and twenty members, and "almost every individual present was more or less connected with literature and the drama."[19] HRH the Duke of Sussex proposed the toast, observing that the main purpose of the new club was "to afford a rallying point for the lovers of the drama." John Braham sang an air composed for the occasion, with everyone joining in the refrain "to bring back the drama to glory again", and Charles Mathews gave more entertainment at the end. If Addison was right to advance the notion that gentlemen's clubs be the essence of good companionship and warmth of feeling, then the foundation of this one was to demonstrate it from the start. "Man is said to be

18 William Thomas Lewis (1748-1811), DNB
19 *The Literary Gazette*, 18 February, 1832, pp 107-108

a sociable animal", he wrote, "and as an instance of it we may observe, that we take all occasions and pretences of forming ourselves into those little nocturnal assemblies, which are commonly known by the name of Clubs. When a set of men find themselves agree in any particular, though never so trivial, they establish themselves into a kind of fraternity, and meet once or twice a week, upon the account of such a fantastic resemblance."[20]

The first list of members published that year shows HRH the Duke of Sussex as Patron, with Lord Mulgrave as President and Sir George Warrender Bt., MP, as vice-president. There were twenty-four on the committee, and both Robins and Durrant were listed as Trustees. Moreover, another three actors joined the list – Charles Farley, Drinkwater Meadows and T. P. Cooke (from *Black-Eye'd Susan*), with Charles Kean, son of Edmund, the following year. James Winston himself is not on the list, for he had been appointed the club's first Secretary. Since it was his idea in the first place, he might as well bear the burden of administration, a task congenial to him anyway. The minutes of that initial meeting in August 1831 are in his hand, and he was central to the shaping of the club's agenda and constitution. He was also the club's first (unofficial) librarian, and immediately began acquisitions to the theatrical library which is now without parallel in the world.

If we return to the parliamentary Select Committee at which Macready made his surly remark about the profession of acting, we shall see that the fledgling Garrick Club assumed a huge role in the proceedings. Not only did club members form one quarter of all those

---

20 *Spectator* No.9

sitting on the committee, but they provided 15 witnesses, out of a total of 39. It might almost have been a family affair. But the importance of this event, both to the club's purpose and to the future of the theatrical art in England, cannot be overrated, and it was to mark the first in a long sequence of historical pivots in which the club played a crucial role. Only two theatres in London were permitted by law to show classical drama, by which was meant in large part the tragedies of Shakespeare in various versions which used only a portion of Shakespeare's actual text. Hence these were always referred to as the 'legitimate' drama, the inference being that any attempt by a smaller theatre to put on such a play would be illegitimate. The two 'legitimate' theatres were the Theatre Royal Drury Lane, and the Theatre Royal Covent Garden. They had been granted exclusive patents by Charles II on 21 August 1660 very soon after his Restoration, the first to Thomas Killigrew and the second to William Davenant, ostensibly to maintain standards and prevent inferior productions from attracting the wrong sort of audience and offering a lower kind of experience. In fact, they achieved the opposite, for without competition, the two patent theatres more or less did what they liked and mounted productions which were ludicrous as well as lightweight, with musical and balletic interpolations, circuses, popular songs, a farce to begin with and an 'afterpiece' in conclusion, the whole lasting several hours, with a bit of Shakespeare in the middle. If any other theatre attempted to put on a play and charge admission, it was in breach of the law and both management and cast could theoretically be fined £50 for each performance so given. Artful dodges were employed to evade the Act, by not calling the performance a play or the venue a theatre, for example, which brought the whole system into disrepute. The Select Committee was told that on one occasion four members of the Kemble family appeared together at the theatre in Wolverhampton and got round the Act by not charging for tickets; instead, the great Mrs Siddons sold tooth-powder "as used by one of the actors".[21] The Strand Theatre took money for admission through a window, to obviate prosecution for illegally charging for entrance "at the doors." Confusion was complete. James Winston, giving evidence, was asked if he made no distinction between a play of Shakespeare's and a pantomime. "Yes" he said, "there is a great distinction, but they all come under the term drama…It is very difficult to say what is the regular drama and what is not."[22]

It was Edward Bulwer-Lytton who had finally pushed events towards reform in an impassioned speech to the House of Commons calling for action. On 22 May 1832 he presented a petition praying for the repeal of all legislative enactments which restricted the performance of drama, saying that it was high time the monopoly were abolished. The loud protestations from the lessees of Drury Lane and Covent Garden keen to protect their rights were voiced by Charles Kemble, who declared that he had "an indisputable right to the exclusive performance of the legitimate drama…on the faith of the royal word."[23] (One wit commented that to examine Kemble on this matter was tantamount to asking the lamb whether the wolf had a right to devour him).[24] Bulwer-Lytton claimed, on the contrary, that these two theatres had betrayed that faith and had been "prolific of amusements of a cheap order", and the

---

21 *Report of the Select Committee*, p 12
22 *ibid.*, p 20
23 *Report of the Select Committee*, p 42
24 Saxe Wyndham, *The Annals of Covent Garden Theatre*, Vol II, p 64

public had a right to ask why they should continue thus.

"Since the legislature had protected the patent theatres in their vast and exclusive privileges, for the sole purpose of maintaining the national drama" he said, "it was the duty of that body [i.e. Parliament] to say to the monopoly [i.e. the theatres], 'Where are the plays to produce and encourage which we gave you the exclusive privilege? Where are the immortal tragedies, where are the chaste and brilliant comedies? You were to preserve the dignity of the drama from being corrupted by mountebank actors and absurd performances; you have, therefore, we trust, driven jugglers and harlequins from the national stage; you have admitted no wild beasts; you have introduced no fire-eaters and sword-swallowers; you have preserved the dignity of the national drama inviolate; you have left it such as it was when you took it from the hands of Ben Jonson or Shakespeare; for if you have not done this, then you have not fulfilled that object for which we took from your brethren those privileges we have entrusted to you.'"[25] It was as a direct result of this bold appeal that the Select Committee was immediately appointed.

The acting profession would have to wait another eleven years for reform to reach the Statute Book, but the impetus was by now irresistible. (It was also belated, for nobody had noticed that the original patents had expired, and both Drury Lane and Covent Garden were operating under temporary and renewable licence from the Lord Chamberlain under the "obnoxious" Licensing Act of 1737, which had given powers of censorship to the office and sealed the exclusive privileges beyond what Charles II had intended).

---

25 Hansard, 3rd series, Vol xiii, pp 239-259, and in *The Struggle for a Free Stage in London* by Watson Nicholson (1906), pp 326-327

A very famous actor who gave evidence was Charles Mathews, likewise one of the original Garrick members. It was he who revealed that the smaller theatres were in the habit of sending short-hand writers to the patent theatres to write down what they heard, and subsequently copy them without permission.[26] But Mathews exerted an influence upon the club which was not less than sensational, and which is celebrated to this day every time members and their guests dine there. For most of the pictures which adorn the walls belonged to him.

Charles Mathews combined great skills to create supreme artistry in comedy which was unique in his day. His psychological subtlety, conquest of timing, use of silence, facial musicality, affectionate satire, above all generosity of spirit, made him hugely popular with audiences. There were some who pointed out that he was more of a mimic than an actor, without pausing to consider that one must be very good as the second before one might venture to attempt the first. The son of a theological bookseller, he was blessed with a face which was malleable to a degree. He said that his nurse had told him that when he was a baby she used to burst out laughing whenever she clapped eyes on him, because he looked so odd, with a crooked mouth off-centre which appeared to slide up towards his ear. This apparent defect he would turn to great professional advantage.

He first discovered a talent for mimicry as a schoolboy, taking off three brothers at the school to the wonder of everyone else. He seemed to be able to crawl into another's skin and adopt his entire past, voice, manner, style and weakness. On leaving the Merchant Taylor's school he

26 *ibid.*, p 169

went to see the venerable old actor Charles Macklin, then nearly 100, who so terrified him that he fled his company after a few minutes. He did, however, succeed in getting on stage, and played a number of well-known parts (including Polonius to John Philip Kemble's Hamlet), attracting praise and building a reputation, above all establishing a loyal public following. Throughout, it was his talent for transformation which astonished, and it was no mere caricature, but a subtle, assertive assumption of another identity. When he played an old man, for instance, he never fell into the trap of doing what a young man would expect an older man to do – stumble, stutter, hesitate. He played the old man as an old man would play himself. Leigh Hunt was full of admiration. "Mathews never appears to wish to be old", he wrote. "Time seems to have come to him, not he to time, and as he never, where he can avoid it, makes that show of feebleness which the vanity of age always would avoid, so he never forgets that general appearance of years, which the natural feebleness of age could not help."[27]

One of his finest roles was Sir Fretful Plagiary in Sheridan's *The Critic*. In the scene where his awful attempts at poetry are mercilessly exposed, he was all subtlety and shifting vision. He contrived to look cheerful enough, and at the same time allow his eyes and that crooked mouth to betray what he was really feeling, so that the audience felt in complicity with him against the other characters. As Sir Fretful gradually lost his self-control, so there was much fidgeting with the buttons of his waistcoat, undoing them and doing them up again, highlighting the humanity as well as the humour of the character; a lesser actor would have made him foolish and pitiable.

---

27 Leigh Hunt, *Critical Essays on the Performers of the London Theatres* (1807)

But it was his solo performances, one-man shows which he called At Homes, which were to make his legacy special. For up to three hours he would assume between a dozen and twenty different characters, each so sharply distinguished from the others that people found it difficult to believe they were all performed by one man. They involved sudden transformations in voice, language, accent, dress and manners, and some ventriloquy as well, for he could "throw" his voice to introduce one character about to make an entrance, while he was busy getting out of the costume of a previous character, and thus run smoothly from one to the other. His muscle control was so fine that he appeared to change the shape of his face, enabling the audience to *see* which character was going to speak before he said anything. He coined a new word for these solo performances – monopolylogues – and used them to satirise the social conventions of the day.[28]

There might be a theme to the evening, Mathews showing the audience a gallery of American "types', or the characters he met in the course of a day in Paris. One entertainment, called *Stories*, took place on three different levels of a lodging-house in Brighton. He represented all the tenants and their visitors in a dizzying display of virtuosity, leaving the audience in astonishment.[29] Sometimes he would impersonate the leading political figures of the day, and did so with such remarkable accuracy that he was reproached by the Government for imitating Lord Ellenborough too well – a good example of the actor's art being subversive. Even Covent Garden and Drury Lane attempted to have the At Homes banned, because they infringed their rights

---

28 Mathews' personal scrapbook, in the library of the Garrick Club
29 *The Drama: Theatrical Pocket Magazine* (March, 1832)

under the patents, but audiences were devoted to him and his kindly, beneficent entertainments. When he performed an At Home, the theatre was "filled to suffocation", and people were turned away in great numbers. "We call him inimitable", wrote one contemporary, "for though he had many followers, he left no successor, while he himself imitated all the world."[30]

There is a portrait of Charles Mathews at the Garrick Club by George Henry Harlow, which depicts him without disguise, sitting in a chair looking upon himself in five different characters, and appearing to be himself bemused at how he was able to do it. The fact was, his was a talent which could not be bridled; he simply couldn't help himself. There was a telling moment at the Select Committee hearings when Mathews was giving evidence. He told the committee what had been John Philip Kemble's opinion concerning the attraction of large theatres, and in so doing, assumed Kemble's voice. Almost apologising for a defect of character, Mathews said, "I can never repeat a conversation without I do it in the tone of the person who gave it."[31] The Report does not divulge whether the remark was greeted with laughter.

Offstage, in social life, Mathews was forever performing. Two anecdotes illustrate this well. A guest in a bachelor's house stayed the night and arose early for breakfast, disturbed by the sound of a little boy having his face washed. He was unaware there was a child in the house at all, but there could be no doubting the sounds of tantrums and tears, mingled with the sounds of a woman scolding and insisting, and after that the sobs of the child being

---

30 J.W. Cole, *Life and Theatrical Times of Chares Kean, FSA,* Vol I. pp 233, 239
31 *Report of Select Committee,* p 168

swallowed up in the thickness of a towel. He could hear the dirty face bawling again when the towel was momentarily removed, then smothered once more. Having sat down to breakfast, he told his host what he had heard and how sorry he had felt for the little boy's ordeal, whereupon in walked Charles Mathews, who had been the urchin, the woman, and the towel. [32]

The second is a story told by the diarist Thomas Raikes. Mathews had a tiresomely insistent fan who made a habit of going uninvited to his house, following him when he went out, seeking to engage him in conversation, which Mathews, being the decent soul that he was, did not refuse as often as perhaps he might have done. On one occasion the admirer tracked him down to the house of another actor, Alexander Pope, and knocked loudly on the door. The servant announced a gentleman in the hall who demanded to see Mr Mathews and would not be deflected. Mathews looked very embarrassed and apologised to the company, saying that the caller was a dreadful nuisance and he would go down and get rid of him immediately. There ensued the most furious row between the actor and the fan which the people assembled in the dining-room could hear, both shouting, the one determined to enter, the other determined he should retreat. The door then opened and in walked the stranger, who sat down in Mathews' place, poured himself a glass of wine, which he declared to be pretty awful, and proceeded to claim acquaintance with everyone present and to share the latest theatrical gossip with them. For a few moments they sat amazed. Then it dawned upon them that the impostor was Mathews himself, who had imitated the argument downstairs to give

---

32 John Timbs, *Romance of London*, Vol II, pp 435-6

himself time to don a disguise (and presumably had made the servant his accomplice in the joke).[33]

One of the At Home entertainments was fashioned around a history of the acting profession. Starting with the attractive idea that, had everybody been as keen on imitations as he, we might have had passed down to us verbal and visual approximations of how Garrick, Betterton, Jonson and even Shakespeare sounded, Mathews then proceeded to assume them all, impersonating John Philip Kemble, Bannister, Cooke, and even Kemble's own impression of Garrick (whom he had known), so that an entire sequence of historical figures was conjured up before the astonished audience. To make it even more vivid, he had a number of framed portraits of the actors he was impersonating on stage with him, by way of illustration. It was more like an informative lecture, delivered with humour, accuracy and panache. Moreover, the pictures were not borrowed for the occasion, they were his own property, for Charles Mathews had long been collecting and commissioning theatrical portraits with the money that he earned from his very successful performances, until he had amassed the finest collection of its kind ever made by one individual. Not only were there some magnificent Zoffanys from Garrick's time, when the great artist was repeatedly commissioned by Garrick to immortalise his theatrical work, but Mathews befriended and encouraged Samuel de Wilde, who specialised in theatrical portraiture of his contemporaries, and sold them as souvenirs, much as today we might buy a picture postcard. Eventually, no less than 185 of the paintings in the collection were by de Wilde.

---

33 *Old and New London*, Vol IV, p 339

Mathews and his wife Anne lived at Ivy Cottage in Caen Wood (now Kenwood), with a generous garden of seven acres. There, he constructed a special building in which to house his collection, and allowed access to the public upon request. One of the most enthusiastic visitors was Charles Lamb, who devoted an article on the "Mathews Gallery" in the *London Magazine* in 1822. But the public as a whole proved, as is so often the case, to be a nuisance, most of them turning up not to see the pictures but to gawp at the famous funny man to whom they belonged. Mrs Mathews later admitted, "So many came, whom to reject would have been personally mortifying to us, that our peaceful retreat was converted almost into a fatigue to us, too often having all the character of a show-place…where we lived more for others than for ourselves."[34]

After some bad investments had depleted his resources, Mathews reluctantly decided that he would have to sell his beloved gallery, and hired the Queen's Bazaar in Oxford Street in which to display them. He hoped to raise £3,500 (with the de Wildes alone being offered at £3 each, and the mighty Zoffanys for £50 and £30), but offers were not forthcoming, and the sale was abandoned. Had he been able to afford it, he would have liked to offer the collection to the National Gallery, but his exigent needs meant he could not donate them. Meanwhile, he lent a good number of them to the nascent Garrick Club in King Street, of which he was an enthusiastic original member. Thus, the club had on its walls some fine pictures from 1833 onwards, while they still belonged to Mathews himself. But the club did not offer to buy them. According to the club's most

---

34 *The Life and Correspondence of Charles Mathews, the Elder, Comedian,* by Mrs Mathews (1860), quoted in Cole, Vol I, p 239

recent historian Geoffrey Wansell, Mathews was "heart-broken."[35]

Mathews died in 1835, and his widow and son, Charles James Mathews (also an original member), had to dispose of his estate. They wanted the matchless collection of portraits and prints to go to the Garrick, but they were forced to accept the derisory sum of £1000 for the lot (representing at most 10% of the true value), some 235 items, which Mrs Mathews ruefully described as "a sad sacrifice".[36]

Indeed it was, and it might have been even worse were it not for the wild generosity of John Rowland Durrant, the stockbroker and original Trustee of the club, who was such a theatre enthusiast that he had his own private box at Drury Lane. He lent the money for the purchase and, when it became obvious that the club could not reimburse him, simply wrote off the debt some seventeen years later and confirmed them all as a gift from himself. So the kernel of the finest collection of theatrical portraits in the world was acquired for nothing at all.

The pictures were delivered on 25 August 1835, and have been the club's property ever since. All that Durrant has, apart from eternal gratitude, is a plaque in the entrance hall honouring his kindness.

---

35 Geoffrey Wansell, *The Garrick Club: A History* (2004), p 19
36 Mathews Papers at Princeton University, quoted in *Pictures in the Garrick Club*, by Ashton, Burnim and Wilton (1997), p LVII

2

MACREADY

The acting profession in the nineteenth century was a parade of giants and jealousies. To get to the top as a tragedian one had to be single-minded, selfish and remorseless, and to stay there, fierce. When one looks at the careers of all the great actors of the period, one is struck by the one quality which they share, that of competitive vanity (there is a lovely exception in Samuel Phelps, who comes later). One after the other, each seems to be more determined to maintain his position of dominance than to serve the demands of the play, which is of secondary concern; indeed, playwrights were only useful in so far as they provided material which allowed the actor to display his art in the most ostentatious manner; they were the actor's servants, in a way, and wrote to order. Once the actor had attained his position, he had to make sure that potential rivals were discouraged by all means available, including forced unemployment if necessary, although banishment to subordinate roles might suffice for the most part.

When the Garrick Club was formed, those in the first rank included Charles Kemble, then fifty-seven and already suffering from creeping deafness; Charles Young, a disciple and imitator of the self-consciously dignified

Kemble school; Charles Kean, ambitious son of Edmund and still only twenty-one; and the over-riding champion of the day, Macready, who did not get on with any of them. Since they were all Garrick members (the young Charles Kean joined in the following year), this simmering distaste must have made for some frosty encounters.

The undisputed conqueror of the previous generation was Edmund Kean, an actor of volcanic power and emotional inspiration. He does not belong to this story, because he was not a Garrick member and, though only forty-five, had but one year to live. He is allowed, however, to slide in sideways, for the example of his style will colour our understanding of that of his various successors, and his brushes with Macready illustrate the passions which this relentless rivalry engendered. When Macready had made his first appearance at Covent Garden in 1816, Kean had been in the audience, and was seen to applaud loudly. But that degree of acceptance and approval did not survive Macready's perceived impertinence in playing *Richard III* three years later, a part which Kean regarded as his. The newcomer from the provinces was thenceforth seen by Kean as a danger to his supremacy. He was right to be worried, for the crown of Top Actor was from that day forward worn by Macready.

He had been exceedingly nervous before going on stage, for he knew as well as anyone that to challenge Kean in this role, above all others, was to tempt Fate; he would either triumph and be carried into glory, or fail miserably and be forgotten forever. As it turned out, that night of 25 October 1819 altered Macready's life in a couple of hours. The audience in the pit were wild with excitement, waving hats and handkerchiefs in the air, and when the curtain came down they bellowed his name and would not leave the theatre. That night history was made, for William Charles Macready became the first actor ever to be called before the curtain at Covent Garden.[1]

Kean made clear that, though he didn't "mind" Charles Young, "I will not act with Macready."[2] The petulance subsided sufficiently in 1832, the year of the club's birth, for them to appear together in *Othello*, Macready taking the role of Iago, but it was an open gladiatorial contest in full public view, and each man complained bitterly about the other's behaviour on stage. Nevertheless, Macready was a pall-bearer at Edmund Kean's funeral a few months later, not by way of contrition, but in answer to pressure from public opinion; he had initially been reluctant.

Likewise, Macready's relationship with Charles Kemble began promisingly well. When he was still only twenty-four and was starting to build his career in London, he attended a dinner for the French tragedian Talma. John Philip Kemble, who had retired in glory shortly before, was also present, as was Charles Kemble. During the evening, the elder Kemble sent a waiter over to invite Macready to take wine with him. Charles leant across to him and said, "You may think very little of this as a compliment, William, but I assure you it is a good deal from my brother."[3] It was a pity that Macready could seldom rise above his sourness, for he was later to dismiss Charles Kemble with the unkind remark that he was only "first-rate in second-rate parts"[4]

That the antipathy was rooted in an almost childish

---

1 J C Trewin, *Mr Macready* (1955), p 58
2 ibid., p 74
3 *ibid.*, p 50
4 *ibid.*, p 66

pride is manifested by a letter from Macready couched in terms of risible haughtiness. Kemble was acting manager at Covent Garden when Macready was to appear there in 1822. He was somewhat dissatisfied with the parts he was expected to play. "My fortunes are surrendered to the single sway of an actor whose aspirations to supremacy in his profession must render my reputation but of secondary moment to him, while he who has the motive is also armed with the power to molest and distress me…No gentleman of talent or feeling can brook so partial an autocracy."[5]

Despite the fact that they had acted together in Sheridan Knowles' *Virginius*, a tumultuous success which remained in his repertoire until the end of his career, Macready never could spot a grudge without rushing to grab it, and if possible feed on its asperity. One wonders what they made of one another at the club's inaugural dinner ten years later; surely Kemble could not have resisted chuckling over the solemnity of that letter, and sharing it with others. They were to remain fellow-members for many years yet.

Kemble had fallen on hard times financially, until he cast his daughter Fanny with him in a new play by Sheridan Knowles, a comedy called *The Hunchback*. She proved a sensation, the public flocked in, and Kemble's fortunes were rescued. But the pleasure in her success was spoilt by a vicious attack on her in a nasty magazine called *The Age*, not unlike some of the daily 'tabloids' published in the twenty-first century, which was edited by a rogue called Charles Westmacott, whose purpose was always frank blackmail if people wanted their names omitted from his journal. He criticised Miss Kemble's figure, and wrote that her voice had "a guttural thickness, tainted with very

---

5 *ibid.*, p 68

strong provincialisms." That was too strong for Charles, who, when he spotted Westmacott at a performance at Covent Garden in October 1830, pounced upon him with a horse-whip and left the editor rolling and howling on the floor.[6] The incident is only worth reporting for the delicious coincidence that the villain's half-brother, the sculptor Sir Richard Westmacott, was also an original member of the Garrick and would have sat at the same table as Kemble for that celebratory dinner a few months later.

The last of Macready's potential rivals, Charles Mayne Young, had retired one month before the dinner, after a farewell performance at Drury Lane in which he played Hamlet while Macready supported him as the Ghost of Hamlet's father. The house was packed, with people jostling for space, and not much of the performance was heard. But Young had been an actor loved as well as venerated, and Macready showed him unaccustomed respect. Even Kean had spoken of Young's "damned musical voice."

It is instructive to examine the two distinct strands of tradition represented by these different actors to see what it was that Macready was inheriting. It could be said that John Philip Kemble and Charles Mayne Young personified the "classical" style with its emphasis on outward form and the beauty of language perfectly spoken, while Kean stood for the adventurous, the surprising, the shocking, revealing truth through chaos. Macready would follow neither example, but inevitably take something from each. His was the scholarly approach, showing on stage the result of long, hard study and thought, of mental striving. He wanted his performances to be classically fine on the one hand and emotionally true on the other, but in order to

---

6 *The Annual Register*, Vol 72, p 170

get there they had to be above all intellectually satisfying. That was different, and that was why he thought himself superior to both Kemble and Kean.

The classical style might usefully be called Apollonian, and the mercurial style Dionysian, and the distinction is fundamental to an understanding of the way in which the actor's art evolved in the nineteenth century. In Greek mythology (and therefore in human life), Apollo and Dionysus are antithesis; the actor's burden is to bring them together in fruitful fusion.

Apollo had care of the earth, of animals, and of man himself. He was also the god of prophecy, and since prophetic signs were usually manifested in song, he came to represent music, and finally the arts as a whole. Apollo is always depicted as the epitome of physical beauty and moral purity, of the perfection of which mankind is capable through order, control, discipline, restraint, the mastery over oneself and over the plastic world. An Apollonian actor is balanced and calm, sculpting beauty in words, harmony in their expression.

Dionysus was the god of vegetation and of wine in particular. In Ancient Rome he was known as Bacchus. His festivals were characterised by orgies and excessive licence, extending to the eating of raw flesh from a just-sacrificed animal, and he represented what human character may achieve when released from inhibition – unbridled, unrestrained, spontaneous and free. He was god of the full expression of desires and instincts normally buried. Hence he was the bringer of madness, anarchy, revolution. Participants at a Dionysian rite were in a state of hypnosis, possessed by their god and behaving like him rather than as themselves. They underwent a profound alteration of personality, entirely losing self-awareness for the period of the festival, and surrendering themselves to the experience.

One may already discern the two strands of theatrical tradition identified by this definition - the one pure, satisfying, the other electric, unnerving. Quite obviously, Kemble was a typical Apollonian, and Macready looked upon that style of acting as superficial and self-regarding. You need a large helping of Dionysus to be able to cope with Lear, Othello or Macbeth, which was why Macready greatly admired the intoxicating (and intoxicated) Kean as an actor, while at the same time calling him "that low fellow" in his personal habits and demeanour. To him, Kemble had manners, Kean had instinct.

There had been predecessors in the classical tradition whose influence was still felt at the time of Macready's arrival. James Quin had long dominated with his manner "which had more of the senate than of the stage in it, he rolled out his heroics with an air of dignified indifference."[7] But not everyone appreciated his static predictable gesticulations. Dr Johnson said, "I cannot believe the man any more because he rolled his eyes, or puffed his cheeks, or spread abroad his arms, or stamped the ground, or thumped his breast, or turned his eyes sometimes to the ceiling and sometimes to the floor."[8] Of much more recent memory was Alexander Pope, whom Leigh Hunt mercilessly ridiculed. "He has but two gestures", he wrote, "which follow each other in monotonous alteration, like the jerks of a toy-shop harlequin; one is a mere extension of the arms, and is

7 T Cole and H K Chinoy, *Actors on Acting* (1949), p 94
8 Boswell's *Life of Johnson*, Vol 1, p 211

used on all occasions of candour, of acknowledgement, of remonstrance, and of explanation; the other, for occasions of vehemence or of grandeur, is an elevation of the arms… if Mr Pope, however, is confined to two expressions in his gesture, he has but two expressions in his look: a flat indifference, which is used on all sober occasions, and an angry frown, which is used on all impassioned ones."[9]

Similarly, John Philip Kemble was noble, clear and impressive, with much less effort and more credibility, but some found a chilling correctitude in his faultless delivery and tone, of having, as someone put it, swallowed a curtain rod. On his recent retirement, Hazlitt wrote that his manner "had always something dry, hard and pedantic in it", and Leigh Hunt referred to "an indiscriminate importance of manner", chiding Kemble for attaching "a kind of loftiness to every sensation that he indulges" and for "a laborious and almost universal preciseness."[10]

There it is! Apollo does not seek to thrill or appal you, but to uplift and enlighten you. Dionysus needs to strike you with awe, and nobody better exemplified this kind of actor than Edmund Kean, a man so cluttered with faults and weaknesses that one rather sympathises with Macready's impatience. He was often abusive and offensive, missed performances, made embarrassing scenes in the auditorium, and was occasionally even drunk during a performance. Excess marked his character and his art, and when he honed it, used it to serve his purpose, he was nothing short of a genius. Though small and far from imposing in life, (before his triumph he was refused entry

---

9 *The Essays of Leigh Hunt*, ed. Arthur Symons (1903), p 291
10 *The Times*, 15 June 1817, and Leigh Hunt, *Critical Essays on the Performers of the London Theatres* (1807)

to the theatre by a protective stage doorman), on stage he assumed, heaven knows from where, a gargantuan power.

It was a matter of luck that he had been noticed at all. His first London performance was as Shylock in *The Merchant of Venice* at Drury Lane on 26 January, 1814. There had been no advance publicity or announcement, and the house was virtually empty. Another actor sitting in the Green Room that night said he wondered how so few people could make so much noise. The luck which attended the unknown Edmund Kean that night was that one of the great men of contemporary literature, William Hazlitt, happened to be in the audience. What the one achieved, the other recorded, thus making this one of the great first nights in theatrical history. Kean was unknown no longer.

Two weeks later, on 12 February, he gave his first performance of *Richard III* , and a month after that his first *Hamlet*. The theatre was crammed every time he appeared, and he seemed to exhaust himself for each audience. He so hurled himself into the part he was playing, stretching and squeezing his strength of mind and body, pushing his emotional endurance beyond the limits, that he was a husk by the end of it. He frequently appeared wild, loose, on the brink of madness, the sheer demonic energy of his performances causing the audience to tremble. A hero for the Romantic Age and the Romantic Temper, Kean could not have arrived at a better time. Meanwhile, the fans of the 'Kemble school' deplored his lack of dignity, and his habit of leaning against the scenery to rest.

Leigh Hunt penetrated the essence of his appeal when he compared him to Kemble's elevation of tone and noted that while Kemble showed the flower, but had no idea about the roots or dirt or stalks or sinews which produced it, "Kean knows the real thing."

And so, when Macready arrived upon the scene, he had to be measured against not only the external poise of the Kemble school, but also the intrepid spitfire flash of Edmund Kean. He did so by patient study to improve his art, by technique in other words. Some critics did not take to his cautious and respectful approach, saying that he was like a machine that one had to wind up before the curtain, whereupon he could be relied upon to make exactly the same moves and utter exactly the same sounds as he had done at every previous performance. What the critic (it was B R Haydon) did not recognise was that Kean could *not* have repeated a performance, because his genius did not spring from classical conceits and infrangible structures, but from the anarchic demon of inspiration, from Dionysian chaos. Though he would always be pathologically worried by criticism, Macready possibly did not consider Haydon's observation to have exposed a fault; he would *rejoice* in the notion that he was reliable, for that is the quality that he spent his entire life trying to attain.

To get there meant that he had perforce to be single-minded and self-centred. He was overbearing in manner, violent in temper, and demanding of attention. Since his arrival in London he had concentrated on assuring his pre-eminence by what can only be called bullying tactics. ("For years they made me starve on melodramatic villains", he would later tell fellow actor and club-member James Anderson, an experience which hardened him). He would only appear in plays that guaranteed all the best scenes be given to him, and would jockey to make sure that the supporting cast were of inferior talent. He was rude to his fellow actors and dismissive of their efforts. He would tinker with the part in a new play to make it more central and dominant, and playwrights learnt to write to order for him, as anything less than overwhelming would earn his scorn. He was difficult to satisfy.

He would further use the pen of his friend and ally John Forster, who was elected to the Garrick Club in 1834, to write fulsome reviews of his every appearance, which was fair enough, and to disparage the performances of other actors, which was not. His tendency to revise the author's work in order to magnify his own role was so perverse and notorious that it was the subject of a farce at Covent Garden in 1826, in which Tyrone Power played Macready and Charles Kemble was the playwright, a piece of casting quite mischievous in its allusiveness. But all this was to a purpose. Macready's gradual assumption of ascendancy was not, paradoxically, for self-glorification, as he still disdained the actor's life and would rather have been doing something more respectable; it was to place him in a position where, as manager one day, he would be able to preside over the rescue of dramatic art from the trough into which it had been allowed to descend. His nature was didactic. He did not like being an actor, but by making himself the best and keeping competitors at bay, he would be able to teach the world how reform could be accomplished. To resurrect true Shakespearean drama, in his way, he had to be beyond the power of others to control. He had to be king.

His torrent of oaths addressed to all and sundry may appear amusing to us now, but it is doubtful if they were so received. "Quack" was mild, "beasts of Hell" frequent,

and "gasconading dust" colourful.[11] After encountering
Charles Mathews at the club, he confided to his diary
that the man was coxcomb, humbug, and quack, and after
Mathews' death, he declared acerbically, "He was a *player*,
and no more." On Charles Kean, with whom he would
have a public and ungenerous rivalry over many years,
he said worse. Seeing Charles Kean's Macbeth, Macready
said that he was so bad in the part, "so idealess, made up
of long pauses, whimpering, rant, and the falsest system
of intonation, all built up on the most offensive imitation
of his father's worst habits and tricks", that he walked out
after the second act.[12]

He was not much kinder to audiences, either. In Dublin
once he faced "one of the most blackguard audiences I ever
encountered...I dislike and despise them."[13]

So what on earth did such an irascible man make of his
own Garrick Club, which he even described in 1833 as
"really a blackguard place"? He would, in later years, have
one richly affectionate friend in Charles Dickens, but with
other actors he was ever on his guard. Two friends were
John Forster and the lawyer/writer, future judge Thomas
Talfourd, but he thought them both far too unselective in
their acquaintance. Talfourd was sitting in the club one
day with Charles Kemble, whom Macready had never
forgiven for what he considered betrayal back in 1822.
Kemble called out to him and took his hand. Macready
quickly spurned the grip, and Kemble exclaimed, "What,
you won't shake hands with me?" That evening, Macready
wrote that to accept his offer of reconciliation would be

---

11 J C Trewin, *op.cit.*, p 102
12 *ibid.*, p 170
13 *ibid.*, p 208

"tantamount to making alliance with fraud, treachery, falsehood, the meanest and most malignant species of intrigue: in fact, with vileness and profligacy of the most barefaced character."[14] The fact that this encounter occurred only four months after he had been blackballed by the Athenaeum might have had something to do with his mood, but, in truth, such moods did not require a trigger.

Three months later he came across Charles Kean, who made a very formal bow (obviously in fun). Macready wrote, "this young man appears very conceited, and surely not amiable in any part of his conduct that has come under my cognizance. He owes me civility."[15] Noticing that he was regarded warily by other members of the club, he coldly remarked, "this will not kill me", and after dinner there on another occasion, he told his diary that the club was full of "only disagreeable and most vulgar persons."[16]

In view of this unattractive prickliness, it is somewhat surprising to discover that other actors treated him not just with respect, but with controlled affection. They had nicknames for him (nobody bothers to invent nicknames for people they do not like), either "Mac" or, with a wink, "The Eminence". Perhaps they knew that this strangely upright, tortured man was essentially a simple soul who wanted to do the right thing but just did not know how to go about it. He was constantly telling his diary that he really must hold his temper and not let loose so freely; every day there was an apology, privately written if not openly expressed, and his comrades, companions, and especially

---

14 *The Journal of William Charles Macready*, ed. Trewin (1967), p 42
15 *ibid.*, p 45
16 *ibid.*, p 106

fellow club-members, perceived that his essentially good intentions were compromised by his horrid attacks of great wrath (irritation or anger are words too banal for such a man). He was too stiff to be at ease socially.

Much later in his career he was enticed into the Green Room at Covent Garden, a place he rarely entered, by three actors – James Warde, John Pritt Harley and Drinkwater Meadows – plus the artist and scene-painter Clarkson Stanfield. There another actor, George Bartley, made a speech on their behalf, in which he praised Mac's sacrifices and hard work and desired to demonstrate their appreciation. They then presented him with a silver salver on which they had engraved their names. For once, this austere man was almost moved to tears. I like to think it significant that four of the five men mentioned above were Garrick members.

A much later instance of his emotional frailty occurred when Dickens performed a private reading of *The Chimes*. "If you had seen Macready last night", Dickens recorded, "undisguisedly sobbing, and crying on the sofa as I read, you would have felt, as I did, what a thing it is to have power."[17]

Other actors were most conscious of the revolution which Macready's approach to acting was in the process of effecting. It was essentially Romantic in its attention to psychological insight and the inner truth of character which could not be revealed merely through the old style of statuesque demeanour. "The actor's art", he wrote, "is to fathom the depth of character, to trace its latent motive, to feel its finest quiverings of emotion, to comprehend the thoughts that are hidden under words, and thus possess

17 Angus Wilson, *The World of Dickens* (1970), p 187

one's soul of the actual mind of the individual man."[18] He would not speak a line that he did not first understand, in all its secret implications. He could not simply "mouth" the words. This was something quite new, and the profession was beginning to recognize its value.

In order to get to this point Macready devoted months and years to study. He was a relentless scholar, to the extent that he absorbed the plays until he could feel Shakespeare's intention. He also demanded much from himself by way of preparing for a role. To exorcise the temptation towards expansiveness, he would recite the most explosive passages from *Macbeth*, *Othello*, or *King Lear* while lying on the floor, standing still against a wall, or with his arms tied to his side. He would pretend to be whispering when uttering blasted rages, so as to protect himself from exaggeration. He had three large mirrors in his room and would spend hours scrutinising his facial muscles as he rehearsed a speech, alert for over-emphasis or grimace, trying to pare expression down to the eyes alone. At the seaside he would address the waves, to give himself confidence. "The easier an actor makes his art appear", he wrote, "the greater must have been the pains it cost him."

He could not go on to the stage cold, but had to work himself up if the text demanded it. He prepared himself for Shylock's notoriously difficult rage and grief at his Act III entrance by standing in the wings cursing to himself, or rattling a ladder against a wall as if it had caused him offence. If he were still not satisfied, he would return to the theatre on Sunday, when it was "dark" and tackle his speeches, his moves, all alone.

---

18 *Macready's Reminiscences and selections from his diaries and letters* (1875)

There is a story that he was playing *Macbeth* when he was thrown by the absence of his servant, who normally stood in the wings ready with a bowl of cochineal for him to smear over his hands to represent blood. Macready had only seconds to think what to do. Standing nearby was a commercial traveller who had been permitted by the stage manager, as a special treat, to watch The Eminence from this privileged spot. Macready punched the poor man violently on the nose and proceeded to wipe the resulting stream of blood on his hands. At the end of the performance he apologised to the startled stranger and slipped him a £5 note.[19]

Other actors came offstage nursing bruises, tokens of Mac's violence when carried away "in character". If the text suggested the supporting character must be half-strangled, it was likely the hapless character playing it would be feeling his throat for days afterwards. It occasionally seemed miraculous that no corpses were carried from the stage door. His self-absorption in performance could be disconcerting, as Fanny Kemble recalled. She had been warned that he might go berserk when a part dominated him, and had been known to maul his actresses almost within danger of their lives. "He growls and prowls and roams and foams about the stage in every direction", she wrote, "like the tiger in his cage, so I never know which side of me he means to be, and keeps up a perpetual snarling and grumbling so that I never feel sure that he has done and that it is my turn to speak."[20] She added that her only fear in acting Desdemona with him "is dread of his personal violence. I quail at the idea of his laying hold

---

19 *The Everyman Book of Theatrical Anecdotes*, ed. Donald Sinden (1987), p 87
20 *Fanny Kemble's Journals* ed. Catherine Clinton (2000)

of me in those terrible, passionate scenes…As for that smothering in bed, 'Heaven have mercy upon me', as poor Desdemona says."

He was also famous for a device which has become known as "The Macready Pause". Avoiding elision at all costs, he would interpolate a pause in the middle of a sentence, or insert one between two words, keeping them apart artificially. It sounded like this:

Be innocent-a of knowledge, dearest-a chuck,

Till thou applaud-a the deed.

Fanny Kemble suggested that he did this because he was so bad at speaking blank verse that he had to chop it up into prose, but that was more likely a malicious joke. His pauses were a part of his style, as were his lumbering and prowling, the rolling walk with each shoulder thrust forward alternately; they derived from his thoughts.

One of the reviews of his London début in 1816 had dwelt upon his obvious shortcomings. "Mr Macready is one of the plainest and most awkwardly made men that ever trod the stage", wrote the *News*. "His voice is even coarser than his person. And yet – notwithstanding these apparently insurmountable defects, he is undoubtedly an actor…in many points superior to Mr Kean."

The Macready style did not impress Charlotte Brontë, however, on her first visit to London. She astonished a dinner-party given by her host, the publisher George Smith, by declaring her disapproval. "It is the fashion", she wrote, "to rave about his splendid acting. Anything more false and artificial, less genuinely impressive, than his whole style, I could scarcely have imagined….actors comprehend nothing about tragedy or Shakespeare, and it is a failure. I said so, and by saying so produced a blank silence, a mute consternation."[21] It is not, after all, such a shocking opinion from a parsonage on the bleak Yorkshire moors; never having been to the theatre in her life, all stage representation would seem to her to be false, because it is so, of its nature.

An innovation which he introduced and insisted upon continues to this day. He was the first to institute full rehearsal, with the entire cast acting the whole text without an audience. (In1811, when he had appeared with Mrs Siddons, he had done so with only one rehearsal, and with her alone). "No one should ever hazard an unrehearsed effect", he said.[22] To an actor who breezily promised he would be 'all right on the night', Macready said, "Sir, if you cannot do it in the morning, you cannot do it at night." When he came to manage at Drury Lane, he would drill and harangue his cast through long hours until they were exhausted, although he tended to make them do each part as he would have done it himself, with the result that one watched several copies of Macready on stage at the same time. The *Sunday Times* reported that he "takes his recruits, rehearses for and with them, making them all speak in his own peculiar manner, conceive, read, and execute the parts his way."[23] He could even kidnap some of their lines for himself if he deemed the theft would improve his own dominance of the scene. When he played Prospero he incorporated some of Ariel's lines into the part.

Meanwhile, in a kind of dramatic prelude to the high-point of his career, Macready's volatile temper landed him

---

21 Trewin, *op.cit.* p 229
22 J A Hammerton, *The Actor's Art* (1897), p 26
23 Trewin, *op.cit.*, p 201 fn

in a real court before a real sheriff. One of the people he detested most was Alfred Bunn, a man of execrable taste and vulgar reputation who happened to be manager of the Theatre Royal Drury Lane, and for whom he had performed. It was Bunn who, in 1833, had scuppered the chances of ending the monopoly of the two Patent Theatres, which the Select Committee had considered and which the House of Commons had passed, by successfully petitioning the House of Lords to throw it out. His interest in the matter was, of course, all financial; he wanted to protect his rights to put on burlesque and animal circuses without interference, and he did not care a jot for the dignity of the drama. That alone earned him general contempt.

In April 1836, on his way to the theatre, Macready stopped to look at the playbill and saw that Bunn had announced a truncated version of *Richard III* to be performed by him before two other minor silly items. The last Act, which Bunn knew perfectly well was Macready's best, had been cut out. He wondered "what his future would be when the public had come used to him as an item on an evening's variety bill."[24] In the coffee room at the Garrick, he found Tyrone Power and Charles Kemble, both men he did not care for at all, talking of Bunn's behaviour as "scandalous and insulting". Having forced himself to give the performance through teeth most surely gritted, he stalked off the stage and went straight to Bunn's office, still in costume. "You damned scoundrel", he yelled. "How dare you use me in this manner?" Bunn rose from his chair, and Macready reached across and slapped his face with the back of his hand. "There, you villain, take that!" Then he punched the manager, who fell to the floor,

---

24 *ibid.*, p 118

the acclaimed tragedian falling upon him, until Bunn bit his little finger. "You rascal", cried Macready. "Would you bite?" Bunn shouted, "Murder! Murder!" and several people came rushing in to separate them.

As usual, it was to his diary that the actor confessed. "No one can more severely condemn my precipitation than myself", he wrote. "No enemy can censure me more harshly, no friend lament more deeply my forgetfulness of all I ought to have thought upon…Words cannot express the contrition I feel, the shame I endure." At his next appearance at the theatre, he thanked the audience for their support (amid much fluttering of handkerchiefs and cheers) and apologised for his uncouth behaviour, at the same time declaring that it was justified. The court imposed a fine of £150 damages for the assault on Bunn, who, oddly, went on to be elected to the Garrick eleven years later.[25]

It was doubtless with this painful memory still fresh that Macready decided the time had come for him to try his hand at management himself, so that he could fashion the productions, protect the nobility of drama in his way, and challenge the embarrassing nonsense that Bunn was inflicting upon the profession. But first he had to keep an eye on the competition. He invited the up-and-coming young Charles Kean, whose acting he deplored, to join his company at the Garden, but Kean smelt a rat and suspected the real intention was to keep him down. It was, and Kean ever-so-politely declined.

But there was another even more threatening talent signalling from the provinces. A young man called Samuel Phelps was playing to very enthusiastic houses in Exeter

25 *The Journal of William Charles Macready*, pp 61-63, 67-68, and D.N.B.

and Plymouth, taking some of the roles in which Macready had made his name, notably Virginius, and making it known that his ambitions included a London season. He wrote to Benjamin Webster, manager of the Haymarket Theatre, who would himself be elected to the Garrick the following year, offering his services, and stating that he would like to open as Shylock. Terms were agreed. Then Macready got wind that something was up, and wrote to a friend in Plymouth asking him to see a performance of the new actor and report back to him. The account he received was so enticing that Macready was already beginning to worry about competition (the informant happened to be a personal friend of Phelps), and decided to offer him an engagement in his first season at Covent Garden, which had not yet been publicly announced, so that Phelps felt flattered by a confidence. He wrote to say that his representative would be in the audience at his next performance in Southampton.

As Phelps excitedly reported to his wife, the man in the audience that night was no less than Macready himself, who left a note for him and spent an hour with him at his hotel. He made it clear that he could still honour his commitment to Webster at the Haymarket, then join the new company at Covent Garden immediately afterwards. He told his diary that he liked the man's tone and manner.

What neither man could possibly know was that this encounter would herald another bold and important chapter in the history of the London stage, for the reform which Macready would set in motion at Covent Garden would be built upon, and ultimately surpassed in scope and lasting influence, by Phelps at Sadler's Wells. In the meantime, however, the upstart must be kept in his place, especially if he was that good.

Phelps played for six weeks at the Haymarket, with growing success, and without any friends or spies in the audience to foment enthusiasm artificially. His first performance as Shylock was daring, for it lacked all the famous 'points' which audiences had come to expect from Edmund Kean in this part – those moments when the action stopped and the scene froze to hold the actor in the image which they had been waiting for – and seemed all the better for it, though some critics thought the action thereby proceeded at too rapid a pace. He followed with Hamlet, Othello, Richard III and Sir Edward Mortimer in *The Iron Chest*, another Edmund Kean role, and then fifty performances of a new comedy by Sheridan Knowles. Macready watched suspiciously. Phelps' success "depressed my spirits, though perhaps it should not do so."[26] He consoled himself with the thought that he would both benefit by having the new actor in his company at Covent Garden, and be in a position to control him.

Macready's own opening production was a wonderfully pure rendering of *The Winter's Tale*, with himself as Leontes, Helen Faucit as Hermione, and James Anderson as Florizel. At the beginning, the house was silent in anticipation, itself unusual, and by the end tumultuous in appreciation. In the scene where Hermione appears as a statue which then comes to life, Macready was so spellbinding that Miss Faucit was herself frightened. The actor stood motionless, his face a picture of awe.

He touched Hermione's hand with the cry, "Oh, she's warm!", then fell to her feet, then embraced her. Her

---

26 *Macready's Reminiscences*, p 414

amazement caused him to whisper, "Control yourself", while the audience burst into applause. She said later that it was "the finest burst of passionate, speechless emotion I ever saw, or could have conceived." When Bunn at the Drury Lane heard of it, he muttered that he was the one making more money, which proved he was giving the public what it wanted with his cheap entertainments.

Samuel Phelps reported for duty at Covent Garden on 16 October 1837, and negotiated with Macready the parts he was to be assigned. He found the manager beset with anxieties, for, despite critical acclaim and the promise of royal patronage from the new young Queen Victoria, houses were so poor that he seemed destined to lose money. The egregious Mr Bunn had been right about that, at least. In addition, the singers, still a necessary part of the evening's entertainment, refused to co-operate by performing in 'afterpieces'. It was agreed that Phelps' first appearance would be as Jaffier in *Venice Preserved*, with Macready as Pierre. This turned out to be a signal success, Phelps making his mark so positively as to overshadow Macready himself. Rather than being pleased with his new recruit, who, were he to be encouraged, could perhaps bring audiences in, Macready was peevishly jealous, and at the second performance placed another actor as Pierre to avoid being on stage with him again. Worse was to follow. His second role was that of Othello, playing opposite Macready as Iago. If the great tragedian were again shifted off his pedestal by the provincial newcomer, this would be dynamite, and that is precisely what happened. The applause was quite blatantly directed at Phelps, while Macready's Iago, also excellent, drew but lukewarm appreciation. Macready was so furious that he determined to give Phelps no more roles which might allow him to shine, and even to keep him off the stage altogether if necessary. The atmosphere backstage is perfectly realised in the letter Phelps wrote to a friend back in Exeter, where he had enjoyed his biggest triumphs.

"I am sorry to tell you I am not so happy, or even comfortable, as I expected – and ought to be", he wrote. "Macready is using me infamously….so weak a man is he that he cannot bear the idea of sharing the honour of a night with anyone…he has made several attempts to force me into subordinate characters, which I have resisted."[27]

This wretched envy erupted into an alarming moment on the first night of *Macbeth* in November. Phelps was cast as Macduff, and in the swordfight of the last act Macready, in the title role, fell upon the other actor with raw violence, obviously beside himself with childish rage (and, by his own admission, wine). He told his diary that he had been "very vehement [with] unwise, ungentlemanly and dangerous passion."[28] So aware was he that he had utterly lost control that he sent for Phelps the next day and apologised fulsomely. "I was very much to blame", he said, but Phelps, as typically cool and decent as Macready was intemperate and foolish, told him that he took no offence. But the success of Othello obviously still rankled, and it was to spoil the young man's career for some time to come. Macready more or less kept him off the stage, while continuing to pay him for sitting idle. Better that than the risk of his seducing audiences again!

When Phelps mildly suggested that he might be offered more opportunities, Macready was at least frank with him.

27 W M Phelps and John Forbes-Robertson *The Life and Life-Work of Samuel Phelps*, (1886), p 343
28 Shirley S Allen, *Samuel Phelps and the Sadler's Wells Theatre* (1971), p 34

"Do you imagine that", he thundered, "after fighting all these years for the throne, I'm going to abdicate for the purpose of putting you or any other man in my place? Are you aware of the struggle I had to hold my own against Young, Charles Kemble, and Kean? Of the degradation of playing second fiddle as Edmund to the Lear of that amateur boy Booth? No, my dear fellow, watch and wait for your chance. It's sure to come some time, perhaps when you least expect it."[29] That, at least, was straight enough. When Phelps asked, in that case, that he might be released from his contract, Macready would agree only on the condition that he left London entirely; not only would he not be on the same stage with a potential rival, but preferably not even in the same town. The measure of the man's insecurity, when by universal assent he was still at the peak of the profession, is hard to fathom.

Phelps obviously could not agree to this, so he buckled down and grew sad. He was so low in spirit that he accepted a new contract for the next season, 1838-1839, on the same terms. There was nothing else on offer, and he could not help but notice that the roles he was best suited for, and which he had expected might be offered, were assigned to other actors. He sat at home looking at the wardrobe of stage clothes he had bought, wondering whether they would ever find a use.

Then Macready sprang one of those surprises which make him so difficult for historians (and psychologists!) to assess. As a result of years in poorly-paid provincial work with wife and three children to support, Phelps had fallen deeply into debt and went dejectedly to tell his employer about it.

29 John Coleman, *Memoirs of Samuel Phelps* (1886), p 168

"What right had you to get into debt?" Macready yelled.

"I couldn't help it", said Phelps.

"Couldn't help it, sir? No-no-man has a right to live beyond his income."

"Sir", said Phelps, "I came to see if you were disposed to help me. Since you are not, I suppose I must go to gaol"

"Don't talk stuff and-a-a-nonsense", said the great man. "How much do you owe?"

"I don't know, sir."

"A pretty fellow you are to come and talk about money without-a-a-studying figures. Away you go! Come to me at twelve tomorrow morning with a full, true and particular account of every debt you owe in the world. Don't leave out a-a-a-shilling. Let me know the worst, and we'll see what's to be done."

Phelps worked out that he owed £400. He told Macready, who immediately wrote out a cheque for £450 and thrust it into his hands. "At this moment", Phelps recalled, "his face was lighted up with that rare and beautiful smile which at times dignified and almost deified him." As he left the stage-door, a bailiff arrested him for £36, whereupon he led the startled man straight to the bank and settled. Macready had saved him. That this harsh and despotic man should behave with such stunning paradox is bewildering, and endearing too. The smile on his face seemed to suggest that he welcomed the opportunity to reveal the decency which lay buried within him, beyond his own reach, and was *grateful* to Phelps. Nor was this an isolated occurrence. He rescued James Anderson in similar fashion. As one of his biographers remarked, this was "a Macready that Bunn and his tribe would never understand."[30]

The fact that this bounty came at a time when Macready was himself facing financial disaster made it all the more attractive. Audience figures had continued to fall off, whereas Bunn was highly successful at Drury Lane, showing live horses, lambs and lions on stage, and Webster was thriving at the Haymarket by inviting one famous actor after another to 'star' in his productions during the summer season (the first instance of what would be called the 'star system'). Webster was an actor too, but concentrated his efforts on management rather than devising stuff for his own glory. When the pantomime failed at Covent Garden, Macready knew he was in trouble. Friends supported him, and the Queen let it be known that she would attend performances (she had also liked the lions at Drury Lane!).

Recovery came with the presentation of a new play by Bulwer-Lytton called *Richelieu*, which ran for thirty-seven nights, and would remain one of Macready's favourite roles, followed by a new production of *Henry V*, for which fellow Garrick member Clarkson Stanfield painted a spectacular diorama, when the troops painted on the backcloth gradually turned into real people through the smoke, as a huge cast represented both armies at Agincourt.

Samuel Phelps was accorded a small part in *Richelieu*, and gave two performances as Cassius in *Julius Caesar* as well, but when the proprietors of Covent Garden remonstrated about poor receipts, Macready was obliged to give up, and, somewhat subdued, accepted an engagement from Webster to appear at the Haymarket. Webster was also canny enough to include Phelps in the invitation, knowing that such would entice audiences, and

30 *ibid.*, p 172; and Trewin, *op.cit.*, p 158

they appeared together in *Othello*. Macready had asked for James Anderson instead, because he was less of a threat, but Webster would not budge.

The performance was a triumph for Phelps as Iago, while Macready's Othello was again rather tepidly received. Macready, petulantly one might think, although the practice was fairly common, did his best to 'up-stage' his rival, which meant that he would retreat towards the rear of the stage, obliging the other actor, if he was to address his speech to him, to turn his back on the audience and deprive them of his facial expression, a neat trick. On subsequent nights, the roles were reversed, Phelps taking the part of Othello, which brought thunderous applause, as he was decidedly bereft of the 'points' which Macready still insisted on using. One critic wrote, "we are now convinced that the Othello of Mr Phelps is the Othello of Shakespeare."[31] This was too much to bear, and after the audience had called Phelps out in front of the curtain, they called for Macready as well, who refused and walked out of the theatre in a huff.

Another danger loomed when Charles Kean came to the Haymarket for a summer season. He came as a 'star', thriving on the reputation of his late father, and playing only leading roles. For the most part, he also played them badly. He lacked the scholarship and intelligence of Macready, and also the insight to interpret Shakespeare with any success. Charles Kean was far more interested in obtaining a theatrical flourish than in paying attention to the meaning of lines or the delineation of character. One reviewer summed up the general critical view when he referred to "Mr Charles Kean's vigorous and most elaborate

31 Phelps and Forbes-Robertson, *op.cit.*, p 49

misrepresentation of Macbeth", and, on Shylock, "We have now seen Mr Charles Kean in all his Shakespearean parts, and our strengthened conviction is, that he is merely a noisy, yet most tricky commonplace."[32] His ascendancy at the Princess's Theatre would come a decade later, when theatrical effects were virtually the sole purpose of his management which, for that very reason, would make him supremely popular. However, he was never a challenger in the subtle manner that Samuel Phelps was, and Macready ought not to have let himself be made anxious, but his worries were never reasonable. Had he been able to banish Kean from the Haymarket, he would have done so. The law allowed the Haymarket to put on 'legitimate' theatre for the summer months only, while the two 'national' theatres retained the monopoly for the entire rest of the year. Macready had been sturdy in his defence of this right, until, one day very soon, he would change his mind, if one may say so, dramatically.

First, he had to overcome another quarrel, this time with Benjamin Webster, after which he told the manager, very haughtily, that he did not care what Webster thought one way or the other, and this on Webster's own stage at the Haymarket. That closed any further chance of an engagement there. Then he took over Drury Lane for two seasons, neither very successfully. Having selected Browning's manuscript *A Blot on the 'Scutcheon* for the production with which he intended to rescue his failing management, he did not ask, but more or less *instructed*[33] Browning to make important revisions because the actors found the play too funny in its present state. He further

---

32 Allen, *op.cit.*, p 49
33 *ibid.*, p 65

decided that he would not act in it himself, and assigned the leading role of Lord Tresham to Phelps. At the final rehearsal he suggested yet more alterations, including a changed ending which would send the hero to a convent rather than having him die on stage. His motive for this was unalloyed spite. The new ending was not adopted, but it still exists in manuscript, with Browning's comment upon it: "The above, in Macready's handwriting, was the substitution for [what] he found written: this to avoid giving the piece the dignity of a Tragedy, and Mr Phelps the distinction of playing in one!" Poor Mac was utterly brilliant at making enemies.

The fact was, the condition of theatre in the metropolis in 1842 was dire, and the need for fundamental reform urgent. Covent Garden was being run by Mme Vestris, a former French actress now married to Charles James Mathews, at a guaranteed loss. The upper classes no longer hungered for traditional drama and demanded pap. The minor theatres showed cheap opera, melodrama, ballet, translations from the French and *burletta*, a kind of farce with music. In order not to meddle with the monopoly of the two patent theatres, a burletta had to include an orchestra and contain at least five songs in each act, thus nicely evading the licensing laws. It was commonplace for the smaller theatres to put on Shakespeare (which they were strictly forbidden to do) with absurd interpolations of song and dance and call it a 'burletta'. Thus, a performance of *Macbeth* was transformed into a ballet with intermittent recitative, and *Othello* was produced with piano accompaniment, the pianist striking a chord once every five minutes, totally inaudibly. Another original Garrick member, James Planché, specialised in writing burlettas designed to circumscribe the law.

In desperation to cut his substantial losses, Macready sub-let Drury Lane to the Anti-Corn Law League, for which he was reprimanded by the proprietors. Aloof from their chastisement, he invited the League to sublet again during the next season for fourteen nights. This time the proprietors put their collective foot down and declared that Macready was responsible for the minimum rent and he could not, at his own discretion, pass on that burden to others not legally in possession of the lease. Macready could not bear to be thwarted and quickly announced the closing date. He then did something unexpected, and apparently out of character, which was to have profound consequences.

In his last week as manager of a patent theatre, Macready approached the parliamentary draftsman to the government about drawing up a petition for the repeal of the theatrical monopoly. That done, he called at the Home Office to see Sir James Graham, the Home Secretary, and persuade him to present the petition to the House of Commons himself, thereby giving it extra weight (the House had twice rejected similar petitions in the years since the Select Committee report which had recommended reform). So the petition was read to the House of Commons on 1 August, 1843, in Macready's ponderous, and almost self-pitying, prose. The patents had passed in recent years to ignorant and inexperienced people, he said, who had "used their trusts as mere pieces of property to be hired to any adventurer". All kinds of degrading exhibitions had proliferated and abused the trust. He had done his best to maintain standards, at considerable expense to himself, but he had at last to retire defeated. "Your petitioner is brought to this pass", he went on, "that whereas those patent-holders are not able by themselves or their tenant to maintain the national drama in their theatres, yet they are armed by law with power to prevent your Petitioner from exercising his art and calling in any other theatre, and to declare that, unless he live on such terms as they may prescribe to him, he shall not, by his industry and the use of such abilities as he may possess, live at all."[34] This was true enough, and had long been so, but to have this man say it was like watching a general muster opposition to himself by supping with the enemy's infantry.

In the Upper House Lord Glengall voiced indignant disapproval of a petition which contained more "self-sufficiency, self-conceit and vanity" than anything ever presented to the House before. But the momentum was, at last, on the side of reform. The Home Office was sympathetic, and showed Macready the draft of a bill which would be introduced to effect the abolition which his petition had sought. In the ensuing debate the points were repeatedly made that the law as it stood "was calculated to afford irrational amusement at the dearest rate" and that "the Lord Chamberlain's duty was the defense of morals, and that, otherwise, managers should be left free." That fatal English habit of preferring to leave things alone had caused mischief: "It may be that the inert temper of the English people, the mere habit of permitting an old institution to continue, in some degree accounts for the old age of the monopoly in theatrical amusements."[35]

The Theatres Regulation Bill was duly passed by both

---

34 Hansard, quoted in Trewin, *op.cit.*, p 199
35 Watson Nicholson, *The Struggle for a Free Stage in London* (1906), pp 342, 416, 421

Houses of Parliament, and history was made in a wink. The legal position which had held fast for nearly two hundred years, and which had ended by cheapening standards in the theatre to a deplorable degree, was demolished in a matter of weeks.

The bill received Royal Assent on 22 August, 1843, and thereafter classical drama could be performed in any theatre. Suddenly, opportunities for serious actors would be available without compromise, and a new era of theatrical excellence was about to begin.

3
PHELPS

Actors were placed in an entirely different landscape by the removal of the two royal patents, a landscape which, in the immediate sense, was perhaps rather alarming. At least Drury Lane and Covent Garden had offered the promise of fruitful employment for two-thirds of the year, and they were suddenly no longer available in quite the same assured way. All other theatres in the West End could henceforth legally put on poetic drama, but only, of course, if there were managers willing to take the risk of giving the public, not what they wanted, but what they ought to have. It being far cosier to go on as before, no manager appeared ready to take advantage of the new freedom. James Anderson, now a respected tragedian with a devoted public, wrote abjectly to Alfred Bunn asking for employment, and received the cryptic response, "You can't sing". Macready himself sailed for America to undertake a lengthy tour. Charles Kean could appear as a 'star' in cities like Edinburgh without much fuss, but for everyone else it meant banishment to small houses for small fees, a return in fact to the provincial life which was supposed to precede success in London, not follow it.

The situation was particularly difficult for Samuel Phelps. Every appearance he had made in London had been greeted with critical approval and public delight, as everyone noticed that there was in his acting something new, fresh, vigorous, eloquent; but his appearances had not been frequent enough to make him an attractive proposition for provincial managers to bill as a London celebrity. A short engagement before the discerning inhabitants of Bath, however, elicited strong praise for a "matchless" performance as Iago. Writing about the "inimitable manner in which he identified himself with the character", the reviewer went on to suggest that the actor virtually disappeared into the part, in a way which neither Edmund Kean, with his flourish, nor William Macready, with his mannerisms, could have achieved, and Charles Kemble would not have attempted: "indeed, so strongly impressed was this idea upon the mind, that when Othello stabs him, a feeling of delight (if we may so express ourselves) thrilled the bosoms of many present."[1] After a few performances in Glasgow and Liverpool, followed by months with little to do, he returned to London in April 1844, dejected and without prospects.

One day, Thomas Greenwood, who leased a theatre in the far-distant suburbs called Sadler's Wells, called upon him and suggested that they might join forces and manage the theatre together, as co-lessees. It was not, on the face of it, a proposal likely to excite much interest, both because the journey out from central London would deter sophisticated patrons of the theatre, and because Sadler's Wells had an insalubrious reputation as a place which showed acrobats and light music for the rabble. But Greenwood was persuasive; he said he thought they could

---

1 Phelps & Forbes-Robertson, *The Life and Life Work of Samuel Phelps*, (1886) p 60

even transform it into a stage for the serious drama. This was a challenge which Samuel Phelps well might relish.

On the face of it, he was not obviously a man to court attention. His temperance and modesty made him an unlikely actor. He was approachable and friendly, but in no way gushing, and quite devoid of that conviction, close to the breast of some actors, that he was somehow special and belonged to a different breed of men than the rest of us. He had no attitude, no 'side'. Without the walls of the theatre, he would disappear into the crowd, unremarkable and unremarked, a trait of shy reserve which he shared with an actor of a much later generation, Alec Guinness. Despite his resounding successes in Exeter and Plymouth, before the years in Macready's shadow, he did not relish fame or shallow recognition, and would always be the very antithesis of a 'star'. His lifestyle was reserved and simple. While other actors delighted in the press of congratulatory adoration in the dressing-room following a performance, he was made uncomfortable by it, and almost always avoided it by going straight home to a supper prepared by his wife. Indeed, so uxorious was he that he preferred his wife to act as his dresser; she was the one person in the world on whom he relied, and for whom he toiled. Invitations to dinner were always gently and politely refused, even when they came (as they soon would) from Dickens. He was not 'clubbable', and it would be many years before he was persuaded to join the Garrick, which, when he did, he enjoyed precisely because members made no fuss over him. (Had he not eventually joined, he would have found no place in this book, which is unthinkable given the profound influence he was to have on theatrical history).

When he was not performing, his ideal recreation was to stay in a Kentish village inn and spend his days trout-fishing. He became so adept that the rural folk would celebrate his prowess in a quiet, respectful way, having no idea whatever that he was an actor by profession; they never asked, and he never told. On one occasion when a villager brought his family to London to attend the theatre as a treat, he was astonished to recognise the man on stage as the renowned local fisherman. He was fond of children and would kiss babies at the drop of a hat.

So little was he an obvious actor that he suffered all his professional life from extreme attacks of stage-fright, what he called his "excessive nervousness". This disability, itself a form of shyness, would habitually render his opening nights a torment to him and sometimes a disappointment to the audience, for his throat would constrict and his voice weaken. This is probably what his fellow actor James Anderson meant when he called his performance "hard and dry", and suggested that he "ought always to have been fried in lard before he acted."[2] It quickly became known that it was always better to wait and see Phelps in a later performance, with even the reviewers taking note that "Mr Phelps has frequently been inferior on first nights in characters in which subsequently he has won a distinguished reputation."[3]

His modesty was further illustrated by his attractive habit of referring to "we" when talking about his profession, for he did not like the idea of standing out in any way, and would utterly abolish the Macready style of making all roles subordinate to his own. There is good reason

2 James Anderson, *An Actor's Life* (1902), pp 252-253
3 Shirley S Allen, *Samuel Phelps and Sadler's Wells Theatre* (1971), p 153

to suggest that Samuel Phelps would institute the first-known instance of 'ensemble' acting, in which the cast grew together as a unit to produce excellence to which each of them contributed equally. This naturally endeared him to the profession, and began a tradition which is still honoured today by directors like Peter Hall, Trevor Nunn and Nicholas Hyntner. In other words, he detested the 'star system' heartily. He would eschew blatant advertisement and avoid personal contact with critics. Bribery through social accessibility was poison to him.

This studious, unobtrusive, domestic gentleman was about to undertake co-management of a theatre which had everything against it. There can be no doubt that his colleagues thought it folly. One newspaper commented upon the actor's zeal "thus to consecrate a temple to the Drama in the remote waste of Islington."[4] It was to be a brave gamble.

Sadler's Wells had been bound by its location to offer entertainments designed to appeal to the poorer classes, and so its audiences were not emotionally prepared for an evening of serious Shakespeare. During the eighteenth century, wine had been served during the performances, with special shelves provided for bottles in the backs of seats. The amusements on offer included performing dogs and tightrope-walkers, with a very popular Christmas pantomime attended by over two thousand people. In the years leading to the Theatre Regulation Bill there were strange productions known as "nautical dramas", with ships and sailors and battles, for which purpose a huge tank had been constructed under the stage to simulate the open sea. The unsophisticated audiences were notoriously

---

4 *Punch*, 13 July, 1844

rowdy, frequently urging the actors in spoken pieces to get on with it and make way for the visual fun which they were anticipating, so that the cast had to gabble their way through. This was helped by the enormous size of the pit, with its even cheaper packed benches, and relatively few boxes to attract the better-off. Dickens has left a description of Sadler's Wells, which, while it smacks of indulgent exaggeration, is nonetheless too vivid to neglect. The theatre, he wrote, had been "delivered over to as ruffianly an audience as London could shake together. Without, the theatre by night was like the worst of the worst kind of fair in the worst kind of town. Within, it was a bear-garden, resounding with foul language, oaths, cat-call shrieks, yells, blasphemy, obscenity – a truly diabolical clamour. Fights took place anywhere, at any period of the performance…cans of beer were carried through the dense crowd…fish was fried at the entrance-doors. Barricades of oyster-shells encumbered the pavement…"[5] This, then, was the place where Greenwood and Phelps were to be the first to take advantage of the new freedom and attempt to put on respectable productions of Shakespeare. It must have seemed daunting, even forbidding.

Mary Amelia Warner, the actress who had performed with Phelps in Bath a few months before and was second only to Helen Faucit in reputation, was brought into the venture as both leading lady and co-lessee, but in the event it was Greenwood who assumed the initial duties as manager, while Samuel Phelps undertook what we should now call 'artistic direction'. It was he who would be in charge of policy, choice of play, scenery and staging, casting, rehearsal, in fact everything related to

---

5 John Coleman, *Memoirs of Samuel Phelps* (1886), pp 202-203

performance. The three of them were hugely enthusiastic and set about their task with *élan*, not leaving a day to go waste. Phelps recruited his Company from those London actors with whom he had worked, who were all currently unemployed and frankly hungry for the chance to do something. Even better was the promise of working under such a fair and reliable man instead of an egotistic or mercenary manager. They all shared the anxiety about the location and reputation of the theatre, but were united in exhilaration at the task ahead. It was decided to open with a production of *Macbeth*, itself a bold choice given that the potential audience may never have seen it or even heard of it before and their reaction could not be predicted. Within a few days, the set was almost ready and the rehearsals under way.

No announcement was placed in the newspapers and no free tickets were offered to the team of London reviewers. It would be unlikely that any of them would turn up anyway, but the real reason for such a tricky decision lay within Phelps' natural integrity; if they were going to succeed, it would have to be on merit, owing nothing whatever to publicity or persuasion. He did, however, have printed a statement of intent, to be distributed in the neighbourhood of Islington, specifically aimed, therefore, at the anticipated audience. Mrs Warner and Mr Phelps, it stated, planned to turn Sadler's Wells into "what a Theatre ought to be: a place for justly representing the works of our great dramatic poets. This undertaking is commenced at a time when the stages which have been exclusively called 'Patent', are closed, or devoted to very different objects from that of presenting the real drama of England, and when the law has placed all theatres upon an equal footing of security and respectability." For this purpose, they had assembled a "Company of acknowledged talent, playing such characters as they must be called upon to sustain at Drury Lane and Covent Garden, were these houses now devoted to the drama. These attractions are placed in a theatre where all can see and hear, and at a price fairly within the habitual means of all." The surreptitious criticism of the two 'national' theatres no longer being up to their responsibilities was a pretty sure indication that they recognised they were about to embark upon something revolutionary.

They also knew it was highly risky, and so they added a note of elevation, as if to warn the local inhabitants that they should not expect the fun and games they had been used to at this theatre. They sought "above all to exalt the entertainments, and with them the tastes of their audiences…There may be differences of opinion as to the existence of theatres altogether; there can be none as to the truth that if theatres are to exist, they should aim at the highest possible refinement, and produce the most intellectual class of enjoyment which their audiences can receive."[6]

The first night, which also marked the first appearance in London of Samuel Phelps in the role of Macbeth, took place on 27 May, 1844, a date as significant in the annals of London theatre as had been Garrick's *début* on 19 October, 1741. The sense of anticipation was palpable, not least because the theatre was, surprisingly, full to the very edges, the pit crammed and all the boxes taken. There was a feeling that something important was about to happen, something Islington had not seen before, and everyone

---

6 Harvard Theatre Collection, in Allen, *op.cit.*, pp 82-83

wanted to be part of it. That feeling was confirmed when the curtain went up to reveal a wonderful set, suggestive of dark mood and grim portents, which elicited a collective gasp of astonishment. "Then the audience became perfectly still. Instead of the usual rustling and settling down of an experienced group of playgoers, there was the silence of an expectant throng waiting to catch every word spoken on the stage…The expected round of applause was sometimes replaced by utter silence or by an awestruck shudder."[7] Macbeth's speeches were greeted with rapt attention.

By the end, the unsophisticated audience knew they had been delivered of a treat, and the cast were aware that they were on the brink of a great and brilliant undertaking.

As if fired by encouragement, Phelps threw himself into frenetic activity for the rest of the season, performing six nights a week with himself in the leading role, rehearsing other plays for the following weeks, designing sets and productions, and at home quietly with his wife, reading plays which had been performed but rarely and preparing them, with judicious cuts, for performance. He must have had dozens of parts stored in his head at any one time; it was the beginning of that punishing repertory system which would be the gruelling bedrock of all provincial actors in the twentieth century.

A glance at the list of productions given during that first season of 1844, compiled by the historian of Sadler's Wells, makes one dizzy with shock and admiration. There were seven Shakespeare plays (*Macbeth, Othello, Richard III, Hamlet, King John, The Merchant of Venice, Henry VIII*), two by Richard Brinsley Sheridan (*School for Scandal, The*

---

7 Allen, *op.cit.*, p 84

Rivals), two by Massinger (including *A New Way to Pay Old Debts*, in which Edmund Kean had given his bravura performance as Sir Giles Overreach), a Vanbrugh and a Beaumont & Fletcher. In addition, he put on contemporary plays, three by Sheridan Knowles, one by Bulwer-Lytton and Byron's romantic piece *Werner*, a total repertoire of twenty-six shows, often two or three of them given in the same week. All this was achieved, moreover, with a total absence of those onstage jealousies which had so often marred productions at the Patent Houses under egocentric managements. As much attention was given to supporting and cameo parts as to the principal roles, offering an entirely fresh experience of a total homogeneous performance. From now on, at this theatre at least, it would be the play that audiences should come to see, not the actor.

One cannot resist the impression that the Company must have been a happy and contented one. They certainly eschewed any attempt to 'milk' the lines for effect, or upstage one another, or inject an unwritten pause in the hope of provoking cheers and applause. Phelps rehearsed them in such a way as to instil a devotion to the text above all else, even going so far as to make it clear that he himself was merely one actor among many, who happened to play the title role. His modesty was not only attractive, it was of huge benefit to the play. An example is afforded by the production of *Richard III*, wherein he not only pared down the role of King Richard, getting rid of all Colley Cibber's additions which had padded it out and made it unhelpfully dominant, he re-inserted the part of Queen Margaret, which Cibber had excised entirely, making her as important to the plot and the performance as Richard himself. We shall see later how Phelps rescued Shakespeare from generations of useless accretions and wilful degradation. Even in the first year it was apparent that Sadler's Wells was the only theatre in London producing serious work.

As a result, discerning playgoers from central London began to make the journey out to Islington to see what the fuss was about, thus ensuring that the boxes were well attended. But a dribble of posh people from the metropolis could not alone have accounted for the phenomenal success of Sadler's Wells. For the truly astounding fact was that Phelps had, perhaps unwittingly, found that the untutored inhabitants of Islington were actually starving for some real theatre, and nobody had noticed. In giving evidence before the Select Committee in 1832, Charles Kemble had boldly declared, "I maintain that, if the audience will only behave themselves properly in an English theatre as they do in a French theatre, they would not hear one word exaggerated; the fault is in the audience instead of the theatre."[8] At Sadler's Wells the haughty Kemble would now find that the audience behaved themselves in a manner beyond anything that he could have imagined. This would be one of Samuel Phelps' greatest achievements. He was an educator, and he found a people eager to be educated.

There were times when disappointed customers had to be turned away at the doors. Those who gained entry sat in thrall to what they saw on stage, attentive, silent, hanging on every word. They were as if possessed, which is the effect that the magic of real theatre should strive to attain. They were not the fashionable folk who deigned to bestow "the muffled applause of scented gloves"[9], but the relatively under-educated working class and local tradespeople who

8 *Report of the Select Committee*, p 55
9 Allen, *op.cit.*, p 156

were transported with delight to discover a real theatrical experience on their doorstep. They behaved as if Sadler's Wells *belonged* to them, which, from a community point of view, it did; it was *their* theatre.

One reviewer was so taken aback by the reverential silence of the audience that he wrote, "It is our firm belief, from the hushed stillness that reigns at times through the house, that one-half the spectators are dreaming without knowing it, and that they only wake up when the curtain drops, and are surprised to find they have a play-bill in their hand. The belief is strengthened by the fact of the unusual sparingness of the applause. All motion, all action, seems to be involuntarily suspended. Occasionally a loud laugh bursts out, but it is quickly succeeded by a deep stillness, as of midnight sleep."[10]

The notion that the locals owned the theatre was made especially clear in a letter Phelps received from Garrick member and Macready ally John Forster, who noted the peculiar atmosphere of proprietorial pride which obtained in the theatre, whereby regular patrons would tell newcomers that they were expected to keep quiet during the performance. "I have not, for a considerable time, had so much pleasure in an English theatre", he wrote. "[The audience] seem to have formed themselves into a police for security of their own enjoyment, and nothing can be more marked than their intelligent appreciation."[11] The reviewer for *The Examiner* wrote, "They do not applaud rant at Sadler's Wells."[12]

The *cognoscenti* of London did not conceal their

---

10 *ibid.*, pp 137-138
11 *The Life and Life Work of Samuel Phelps* (1886), p 372
12 Allen, *op.cit.*, p 139

astonishment that such a class of people in such a tawdry neighbourhood should be able to understand, let alone appreciate, the Shakespearean canon, but the fact was, they did so with greater discernment than the monied classes who had been used to declamation and rodomontade in central London. It was as if Shakespeare had rediscovered, through Samuel Phelps, his natural audience, the people he wrote for, and, given proper and honest attention to his text by responsible actors, the playwright was able once more to speak directly to them. It was a tremendous lesson to learn, for it demonstrated that one did not have to have a university education in order to hear what Shakespeare said; on the contrary, too much learning might get in the way and inhibit the poetic truth. It is a lesson we may still heed today. Hence the paradoxical remark by a commentator who declared that this was "beyond comparison the most intellectual pit of any theatre in London." Playgoers were seen to discuss the performance during intervals. The contrast with a typical Sadler's Wells audience of only a year earlier was stark indeed.

Undoubtedly, one of the principal attractions was the fresh, clean style of Phelps' acting, uncommonly free from hyperbole. He banished the old habit of making 'points', that is employing some artificial trick to freeze the action and elicit applause. By allowing his speech to flow normally from one sentence to the next, pulling one idea out of the preceding one, he depicted the whole of a character and not just bits of it enlarged for dramatic effect, as one would in life without thinking about it. In addition, and arising from this, he was able to excite in the audience a degree of identification which made them feel the sufferings and anxieties of the character portrayed, as if they experienced them from the inside. This quality of drawing the spectator into the emotion of a part, rather than displaying it for their admiration, was known as 'pathos', and had never found a finer advocate than Samuel Phelps. He disappeared; the person being interpreted took his place. A critic observed, "In each character in which we have had the opportunity of seeing him, he has appeared a different man; he loses his identity, in fact, in the character he for the time portrays."

At times he was so submerged that he seemed not to be acting at all, the feeling expressed so genuine as to be beyond impersonation. The *Daily Telegraph* said of his performance as Othello that he "merely yields himself as it were to the torrent of emotion flowing through his heart, and is borne along without any effort on its impetuous current." Moreover, all this was achieved with "the apparent absence of histrionic art", making it real, not assumed.[13] Macready had also been psychologically true, but he wanted you to know it. He was impressive, because he calculated how to impress. Phelps made you know what it was like to be the man, with the result that you felt more wounded than impressed, and might indeed need a rest afterwards.

His very first performance at the theatre displayed a Macbeth who was visibly suffering with emotional intensity but trying to keep it under control, and the audience obviously believed him. In the dagger soliloquy he stared at some point before his eyes and allowed the audience to see his imagination slowly working as he withdrew in horror at the thoughts coursing through his mind. He *created* the reality of the dagger, a far more awe-inspiring vision for the audience to endure than some grand posture

13 *ibid.*, pp 29, 167, 175

of astonished fear. As King John a few months later, a reviewer wrote (they had started to come up from the West End by then), "He has more real genius in him than any actor of our time, and it is now making itself manifest. He was kept down by the overbearing power of Macready; but not disadvantageously, for all the while he was gathering strength and acquiring a mastery of his high art, the fruits of which are now ripening. A small theatre is the true test of an actor's genius. Tricks won't do there, all must be genuine."[14]

When it came to *The Tempest*, the fantasy on stage so completely held the audience entranced that it required all the reason of Prospero's final speech to break the spell which had been cast. And this was the third innovation which Phelps brought to his art. He was blessed, like Gielgud in the twentieth century, with a voice of real music, which he treated with great respect. He knew well that clarity of expression and phrasing were essential to the proper delivery of blank verse which carried in its very distribution of sounds, emphases, alliterations, and juxtapositions the truth of the meaning Shakespeare had designed it to convey. The poetry was in the words as they stood, and where they stood, not in some approximation. Phelps honoured this notion and gave the verse its inherent dignity, with sound elocution and intelligence. In comparison, Macready's stuttering progress through a speech, great tragedian though he was, seemed destructive of the underlying poetry. In this, too, Phelps was an educator.

As Hamlet he showed the prince a spiritual and philosophic young man "who was shaken to the depths

---

14 *ibid.*, p 90

of his being by the knowledge imparted by the Ghost…
possessed by a sorrow so deep that he could find no
adequate response and therefore turned to humour."[15] Even
for those in the audience who were familiar with the play,
Phelps's portrayal was a revelation. A Mr Whitney wrote, "I
have seen several stage Hamlets, but never Shakespeare's
till now. So fresh, so new, so clear is your portraiture that
I could not avoid troubling you with the expression of my
pleasure and my obligation. I am ignorant of Mr Charles
Kemble's Hamlet; but nobody since his time has made
us feel, as you do, Hamlet's grief, his filial love – in all its
depth and fullness – and the exquisite refinement and
spirituality of his character. These are so finely expressed
that the agony of his situation and the utter repugnance of
its requirements to his nature are intensely felt throughout
the play. Moreover, the real worshippers of Shakespeare
owe you a world of thanks for giving them a performance
free from stage quackeries and conventional tricks. It is
inexpressibly refreshing to see the forms and dictates of
simple nature so faithfully adhered to. Nothing can surpass
the beauty and affecting power of the chamber scene with
the Queen – so new in style, yet so simple and truthful, but
so tremendous in effect. Never have I witnessed that scene
before without a wretched violation of all truth, propriety,
and force, in order that the Queen shall throw herself into
the arms of Hamlet (who is obviously preparing himself for
the event) for the purpose of making a stage tableau."[16] The
letter goes on a bit, as fan letters do, but it is useful to see
confirmed in it the very qualities I have been suggesting –
honesty, freshness, truth, the ability to make the audience

15 *ibid.*, p 168
16 *The Life and Life Work of Samuel Phelps*, pp 399-400

feel what Hamlet is going through, and the refusal to make a pretty picture for applause.

After a performance of *Othello* the critic of the *Morning Advertiser* declared, "This mixture of elocutionary power and deep feeling Mr Phelps is probably the only man on our stage who can properly render; and it is the perfection of his art."[17] And as Leontes in *The Winter's Tale*, he managed to suggest the character's instability and pathologically suspicious nature long before the devastating eruption of jealousy, which enabled the audience to recognise symptoms in their acquaintance in daily life, and so permit Shakespeare's subtle insights to be revealed.

He rarely tackled the romantic leads such as Romeo, but he was a highly accomplished interpreter of Shakespeare's most gloriously comic characters, such as Bottom, and Malvolio. Henry Morley, in the *Examiner*, picked up on the subtlety of the acting at the moment in *Midsummer Night's Dream* when Bottom emerges from the spell in which he has assumed the form of an ass: "Quite masterly was the delivery by Mr Phelps of the speech of Bottom on awakening. He was still a man subdued, but subdued by the sudden plunge into a state of unfathomable wonder. His dream clings about him, he cannot sever the real from the unreal, and still we are made to feel that his reality itself is but a fiction. The preoccupation continues to be manifest during his next scene with the players, and his parting, 'No more words; away; go away', was in the tone of a man who had lived with spirits and was not yet perfectly returned into the flesh."[18]

The conception of Malvolio was likewise psychologically plausible and devoid of stage 'business' designed for comic

17 4 November, 1861
18 Allen, *op.cit.*, p 184

effect. "He made Malvolio the embodiment of colossal conceit. Carrying himself with a frozen calm of self-esteem, he walked with a heaviness that implied a consciousness of his own grandeur, and there was condescension in every gesture. His face was gravely serious through sheer emptiness of expression, and his eyelids were lowered in disdain."[19] He did not try to be funny, because, of course, Malvolio had no idea that he was funny; as the character took himself seriously, so did his interpreter, with delightfully hilarious results. Indeed, it took some time for the audience to realise that the actor, transformed in shape and costume, was Phelps himself. Within his first three seasons at Sadler's Wells, he established himself as the most versatile man of the stage since Garrick.

Perhaps most important of all, he was at all times subservient to the text. He shared with Macready that reverence for the genius of Shakespeare which had for so long been stifled by triviality, but he surpassed him in humility; he was never an actor 'showing off'.

Meanwhile, Macready himself had returned from a year-long tour in America to bask in domestic life for a while, the opportunities in the West End being somewhat sparse. The two families of Dickens and Macready grew ever closer, to the extent that he came to feel more affection for Dickens than for any other man he knew, even including Forster and Talfourd. His biographer has called this "a friendship unstained by quarrel", which, for this incorrigibly disputatious man, was rare indeed.[20] When the Dickenses went abroad, they left their four children in the care of Mr and Mrs Macready, and the actor told his

19 *ibid.*, p 182
20 Trewin, *op.cit.*, p 248

diary, "Dear Dickens called to shake hands with me. My heart was quite full; it is much to me to lose the presence of a friend who really loves me. He said there was no one whom he felt such pain in saying good-bye to."[21] He sounds almost surprised that he should be able to inspire such affection, but it proved fast and secure, lasting to the end of Dickens' life.

After some desultory appearances in short engagements, including one at the brand-new and opulent Princess's Theatre in Oxford Street, and while Samuel Phelps was continuing his triumphant seasons at Sadler's Wells, Macready accepted an invitation to play Hamlet in Edinburgh. This was to prove to have disastrous consequences which would lead to a terrible rivalry and ultimately even to public riots. The rivalry was with the handsome American actor Edwin Forrest, who watched Hamlet from a box and demonstrated his disapproval. But the story and its ugly aftermath needs a preamble.

Forrest was the darling of the American theatre, a rugged and strong performer with a powerful, deep voice, muscular appearance, and charismatic appeal. He was not, however, an actor with any refinement, and his popularity reflected the American contempt for the intellectual approach to play-acting, as to anything else. The dramatic critic William Winter referred to him, vividly, as "a vast animal, bewildered by a grain of genius." One imagines him a little like a modern Hollywood film-star, striding the stage with gruff authority and boldly representing the American taste for straight-talking and plain-dealing, translated into his performances. Indeed, his favourite role was the Roman soldier-hero Spartacus, as far removed

---

21 *Journal of William Charles Macready*, p 178

from Macready's punctilious intelligent interpretations as it is possible to imagine. Nevertheless, Edwin Forrest had appeared in London in 1836, his fame preceding him, and 'Mac' had treated him as a colleague.

After visiting the Garrick Club, he called on the American and wrote that he liked him much, "a noble appearance, and a manly, mild, and interesting demeanour. I welcomed him – wished him success, and invited him to my house."[22] All might have been well, had not the newspapers whipped up the pretence of a serious rivalry. When Forrest played Othello at Drury Lane, some reviewers thought his style vulgar, while others praised him beyond measure and suggested he was superior to Macready, who, hearing this, prevailed upon his close friend Forster to go easy when writing his notice in the *Examiner* lest bitterness might breed. It did not work, and when the notice appeared, Macready said it gave him "very great pain. I thought it ill-natured and not just – omitting all mention of his merit, with the enumeration of his faults. I would have done much to have prevented it."[23] He told Forster as much.

Three weeks later, eighteen members hosted a dinner at the Garrick Club in Forrest's honour (Charles Kemble was there, but not, thankfully, John Forster), and Macready did his best to be sociable. "I greeted Forrest, and told him I was anxious to be among his hosts." When Macready's health was toasted by Talfourd, a rather inelegant gesture in the circumstances, Macready got up and said that "the attention was unexpected; that I came to pay, not to receive, a compliment; and could assure my highly-talented friend that no one extended the hand of welcome to him more

22 *ibid.*, p 78
23 *ibid.*, p 81

fervently or sincerely than myself."[24] But the damage was done. News of their hero's treatment at the hands of the snooty London critics reached Forrest's fans in New York, and the resentment festered for a long time.

That the Garrick Club and its members were exempt from this antipathy was evidenced by the presentation of an exquisite portrait of Forrest to the club by its American artist Thomas Sully in 1840; it hangs there still.

Edwin Forrest returned in 1845, and it was then that he attended the performance of *Hamlet* in Edinburgh. Macready did his regulation 'business' of flourishing his handkerchief above his head, at which point there issued from the box a resounding, long hiss. Macready went pale, waving the handkerchief all the more, while the audience turned upon the box angrily, some yelling "Turn him out". The supporting actor John Coleman came on stage, looked up at the box, and recognised the miscreant as Forrest, who turned and slowly moved out of sight. The scandal of this insult reverberated throughout Edinburgh and was even mentioned in a police report of what had happened that evening. Macready was beside himself with fury. "I do not think that such an action has its parallel in all theatrical history", he scribbled, evidently enjoying the exaggeration. "The low-minded ruffian! The man would commit a murder, *if he dare*."[25] Worse was to follow, when Forrest both stated, and wrote to the newspaper in support of the statement, that, since he gave applause to actors, he claimed an equal right to hiss them when he felt like it.

It was with the memory of this event strong on both sides of the Atlantic, that Macready sailed to New York on 9 September, 1848.

---

24 *ibid.*, p 83
25 *ibid.*, p 234

The timing was not auspicious. America was gripped by nationalist fever aroused against the British and their condescending manner towards the fledgling democracy, as revealed in the writings of both Mrs Trollope and Dickens, both of whom found fault and gave voice to it in polished, merciless prose. For this reason, Dickens forbore going to see his friend off at the quayside, lest he be contaminated by association when the news reached New York. Nevertheless, Macready might have remembered that, when the 'hissing' scandal had been at its height, James Anderson had played in Philadelphia and been subjected to vicious harassment. A hand-bill had been circulated, headed "Friends of Forrest, to the Rescue", urging Americans not to allow "your favourite tragedian to be insulted by a British audience and not resent the outrage. Sons of 'Seventy-six, will you see one of your brothers hooted at and mobbed by the English aristocracy, because he was selected by his patriotic countrymen to deliver an oration on the Fourth of July? If there be a spark of patriotism left in your bosoms, avenge this insult to our National Actor!" Readers were exhorted to drive Anderson from the stage. They very nearly did, and the manager wanted to close the theatre, but Anderson insisted on battling on bravely. His performance as Hamlet was greeted with groans, whistles, tin-trumpets, apples, oranges, rotten eggs and broken chairs. The din lasted one and a half hours, during which Anderson and his colleagues proceeded with the play with no hope of a single word being heard. Eventually, the police were called and several people arrested.[26] Macready should have pondered this, perhaps.

---

26 James R Anderson, *An Actor's Life* (1902), pp 130-131

The first sign of trouble came, also in Philadelphia, where he was to appear as Macbeth. (A few days earlier, he had passed Forrest in the street and affected not to notice him, an unwise move). At his appearance, there were hissings from a section of the audience, and at the curtain-call, some booing. Macready addressed them, saying that he had been warned of organised disturbance, and firmly denying that he had shown any hostility towards Mr Forrest in England. Forrest responded with a letter to the *Philadelphia Public Ledger* in which he candidly called Macready a liar. He wrote of the Englishman's "narrow, envious mind and selfish fears" and boldly stated that he had got Forster to do his "dirty work" for him by attacking him endlessly in print, even before he had appeared on any stage in England. He went on, "Mr Macready has no feeling of kindness for any actor who is likely by his talent to stand in his way. There is nothing in him but self-self-self; and his own countrymen, the English actors, know this well....Mr Macready has a very lively imagination, and often draws upon it for his facts." He then said that some people in New York had been intent upon punishing him for his treatment of Forrest in London, but that he had warned them to desist. "My advice was, do nothing; let the superannuated driveller alone; to oppose him would be but to make him of some importance."[27] It would be difficult to invent a more injurious piece of writing, and one must assume that Forrest knew he was likely to incite some trouble; perhaps he wanted to.

In New York, Macready went to the Astor Place Opera House to give a performance as Macbeth. The audience was in a foul mood. Divided into factions, those for Forrest

27 Trewin, *op.cit.*, pp 218-219

and those for Macready, they made so much noise that they could hear nothing of what Macready was saying when he stepped forward to warn that he would cancel the performance rather than put up with this. A rotten egg flew passed his ear and a man shouted, "Down with the English hog!" The play began, at a pelt. Coins were thrown at the actor, followed by fruit, bits of wood, and a nasty smelly gum which stuck to his costume. The second and third acts continued under identical circumstances, the whole theatre a heaving mass of loud and volatile people. Chairs rained down on the stage and into the orchestra. The musicians fled. Still Macready went on, did his duty to the final word, and walked home to his hotel in apparent calm; he noticed a huge crowd outside the theatre.

Forty-seven prominent New York figures, including Washington Irving and Herman Melville, signed a petition urging the actor not to cancel future performances, and the City Recorder visited him at the hotel to assure him that the theatre would be guarded by police. He decided therefore to repeat *Macbeth* three days later. On his walk to the theatre he noticed police vans discharging officers, who were placed in great numbers around the theatre, and once inside, saw they also lined the walls; there were hardly any women in the audience. At his first appearance, "wretched creatures…shook their fists violently at me, and called out to me in savage fury." The first few scenes of the play took place against a pandemonium of jeers and cheers from rival parts of the house, until the police closed in and roughly ejected the rioters from the pit, as the audience cheered. But that was only the beginning. The sound of smashing windows interrupted the performance as a volley of stones was hurled from the street outside, where the pavement was conveniently under repair and plenty of loose paving-stones were available. Some of them landed inside the theatre, to the excitement of rioters in the audience. It was not only an outrageous scene, but by now a fiercely dangerous one as well. An actor on stage whispered in frightened tone to Macready that he should call it a day and scuttle off. The very idea incensed his proud nature and roused him to indignation. "I turned on him very sharply and said that I had consented to do this thing, to place myself here, and whatever the consequences I must go through with it, it must be done; that I could not cut out. The audience had paid for so much, and the law compelled me to give it; they would have cause for riot if it were not all properly done." One of the stones struck the chandelier, and some of the audience made way for the exits. When Macready went to his dressing-room to change, water was raining down the walls, as stones had broken the pipes.

He went on for the last act notwithstanding the racket, "and in the very spirit of resistance I flung my whole soul into every word I uttered." At the end he went before the curtain to express his gratitude to those who were supporting him, which was brave indeed, for the situation was becoming nasty. Several people came to the dressing-room looking decidedly anxious, as word had reached them that the mob outside had grown in size to menacing proportions and the military had been called in for reinforcement. In fact, there were two hundred soldiers, cavalry and infantry, facing a crowd of twenty thousand in dark, unlit streets. Orders were given to fire above their heads and against walls, but some mis-heard and fired instead into the thick of the mob and many were shot dead. Young men hurled themselves at the soldiers, who fired yet again; a full-blown riot was now under way. Macready and some friends made to leave by the stage-door, but the doorman, fearing their lives were in danger, Macready's in particular, would not let them pass. They went back to the stage, climbed down into the orchestra, walked through the empty pit and, disguised in unfamiliar clothing (Mac wearing a cap instead of his usual hat), walked out into 8th Street unnoticed. They did not go to the hotel, as a mob was urging entry to seek him out and would have torn him to pieces had they found him; there were yells to the effect that they intended to kill him. Instead, he took refuge in the private house of one of their company (Robert Emmett) and stayed downstairs by the fire until four in the morning, unable to rest. A carriage was called and, again surreptitiously, they left New York for good, and by seven in the morning were safely taking breakfast in New Rochelle, some twenty miles distant. He then stayed in Boston, more or less *incognito*, before sailing for home.[28]

Seventeen people were killed that night, in what came to be known as the Astor Place Riot, for the cause of supporting the fame of one popular native actor against another intemperate foreign one. It was in fact a class and nationalistic riot at base, having nothing to do with the theatre, but it stained the reputation of the profession for years. It also served to remind people that, at the very time that Samuel Phelps was changing the nature of audiences at Sadler's Wells, the theatre was still liable to attract an audience that would not be tamed.

As the half-century approached, the leading actors of

---

28 *Journal of William Charles Macready*, pp 261-268, and D.N.B.

the day, all Garrick men either then or later, were each on the pivot of a major moment in their careers and in the development of the London stage. Macready was about to retire, Charles Kean was about to launch his tenure at the Princess's Theatre and transform the way in which staging and scenery were regarded, elevating them to an art form in itself, and Phelps was working his way through the whole of Shakespeare in the original texts. Each had huge influence and each would be honoured by subsequent generations of actors. And there was a fourth.

In the audience at Sadler's Wells one day, watching *Hamlet*, was a boy from Cornwall, nearly twelve years old, who had begged his reluctant mother to let him see a play, and had finally squeezed permission from her on condition that it should be by Shakespeare. He sat transfixed by the passion and excitement and magic before him, and would later declare that Phelps was "the greatest actor I ever saw, or ever shall see."[29] That one singular experience changed his life. The boy's name was John Henry Brodribb, and we would come to know him as Henry Irving.

---

29 Michael Holroyd, *A Strange Eventful History* (2009), pp 94-95

4

SHAKESPEARE

Although it took a little time before full advantage was to be taken, the removal of the monopoly on drama from the Patent Theatres caused a huge shift to be made in the way that Shakespeare was presented on stage. It is no exaggeration to say that Shakespeare was rediscovered in the middle of the nineteenth century after generations of sorry mutilation and neglect. The two strands of this rebirth were in the hands of divergent talents working in parallel direction - by Samuel Phelps on textual reform, and by Charles Kean on scenic accuracy. And it was the textual purifications undertaken by Phelps that were to have the most enduring legacy.

Dr Johnson had famously declared that "There is not, perhaps, any play of Shakespeare which could be represented on a modern stage as originally written." Why? Because he "never has six lines together without a fault", in consequence of which "many of Shakespeare's plays are the worse for being acted."[1] To us today this appears to be an asinine judgement from the great man, for Shakespeare wrote specifically and directly for the stage, intending all his plays to be acted with immediacy. He did not write so that his work could be studied in libraries. But from the Restoration onwards the general view was that Shakespeare

1 Boswell's *Life of Johnson*, Vol I, pp 363, 365

had to be improved by making 'acting editions' of his plays, as if there could be any other kind. The consequence of this wretched habit was that the original texts were never performed in their entirety.

What audiences had been accustomed to see on the stages of the Patent Theatres was at the least risible, and mostly deplorable. Two-thirds of the 'acting edition' of *Richard III* was written not by Shakespeare at all, but by Colley Cibber (one of his lines remains even now, as actors cannot bear to lose it: "Off with his head! So much for Buckingham."). *King Lear* was performed in a vile adaptation by the poet laureate Nahum Tate, to which he even put his name as author in 1681, and in which Queen Cordelia marries Edgar at the end, and Lear retrieves his kingdom. Here is part of Lear's closing speech according to the acting edition:

> *But Edgar, I defer thy joys too long:*
> *Thou servdst distress'd Cordelia; take her crowned*
> *Th'imperial grace fresh blooming on her brow..*
> *...No Gloucester, thou hast business yet for life.*
> *Thou, Kent and I, retired to some close cell,*
> *Will gently pass our short reserves of time*
> *In calm reflexions on our fortunes past,*
> *Cheer'd with relation of the prosperous reign*
> *Of this celestial pair*

who went on to live happily ever after.[2]

---

2 John Philip Kemble's prompt copy, as used by Charles Kemble, is in the Garrick Library

Even the sainted David Garrick could not resist tampering with tragedy, writing his own jolly ending to *Romeo and Juliet* and having Juliet wake up on the tomb with the words, "Bless me! How cold it is!" Colley Cibber's son (impervious to irony) chastised Garrick thus: "Were Shakespeare's ghost to rise, would he not pour indignation on this mender of poetry which wants no repairs, who thus mangles, mutilates, and transforms his plays?"[3] *The Taming of the Shrew* was reduced to the Katherine and Petruchio scenes performed as a farce in an 'afterpiece'. Dryden and Davenant transplanted the storm in *The Tempest* to the second act and plonked Prospero's speech at the end of it, where it could be more effective, calling the resulting mess an 'opera'. *Midsummer Night's Dream* was retitled *Fairies* by Garrick and given as a musical with Italian singers imported, and the Pyramus and Thisbe dialogue was later rewritten as a mock opera, while dancers had pranced to Mendelssohn's music, interpolated into the play since 1826.The most egregious example of the destruction which Shakespeare's text had suffered was in Colley Cibber's version of *Richard III*. The character of Queen Margaret had been excised wholesale, not a trace remaining. A scene depicting the murder of the princes in the tower had been added. More dialogue had been written for the character of Anne, to add romantic interest and make King Richard more of a suitable lover. Most of the scenes in which Richard does not appear at all, had been scrapped, with the result that the actor playing the lead was on stage for nearly the entirety of the play. Indeed, it was clear that Cibber's purpose had been to sacrifice

---

3 quoted in John William Cole, *Life and Theatrical Times of Charles Kean* (1860). Vol I, p 109

the subtleties and psychological insights of Shakespeare's moral drama to render it a mere vehicle for an effectively lung-proud actor; that, one supposes, was what was meant by an 'acting edition'.

Astonishingly, that version of the play was still being lauded as late as 1838, when Charles Kean took the lead. The original text was said to be "less fitted in its integrity [entirety] for representation on the stage than almost any other generally acted play of the great poet", while Cibber's "modification…has been pronounced one of the most admirable and skilful instances of dramatic adaptation ever known." The review of this production elicited from the *Times* some exalted praise: "Many plays of our great dramatist have, from time to time, been altered by various hands; but Cibber's alteration of this piece is undoubtedly the best effort of the kind that has yet been made. He has lopped off superfluities, which, however beautiful in the closet, were not calculated to produce a powerful effect on the stage; and he has condensed within a reasonable compass, more of interest, of striking situation, and of stirring action, than is to be found in almost any other drama."[4] And, one might add, less of Shakespeare's poetry than in any other adaptation.

It would therefore be with *Richard III* that Samuel Phelps would initiate his comprehensive revolution at Sadler's Wells; this would be his first production, and whereas all previous tragedians had also striven to stamp their signature on this flamboyant role, he would be the first to place his mark upon the play rather than the part.

To be just, Macready had already begun the business of rescuing Shakespeare from this morass, at least partially,

---

4 Cole, *op.cit.*, Vol I, p 283; Vol II, p 101

before Phelps made it his *idée maîtresse*. He had restored Queen Margaret (banished for a century and a half), as well as Clarence's wonderfully evocative dream and the dramatic moment when Hastings is summarily condemned and cast to his doom, but these were piecemeal fiddlings with a cherished theatrical monument, and the public would not tolerate more. It was not a success. The *Times* called it "merely another arrangement, and certainly inferior in dramatic effect to that of Cibber." Fear and vanity also colluded to dilute Macready's reforming zeal, for his instincts as an actor, hungry to dominate centre-stage, would not allow him to throw away too much of such a juicy (though counterfeit) role.

When it came to re-adapting *Macbeth* under the management of Stephen Price at Drury Lane, Macready suggested dispensing with the traditional music to make way for more of the text, and Price retorted that he could not do that, "but, if you like, I'll cut out the part of Macbeth." Price had the measure of his man; as one of Macready's biographers put it, "We have to imagine the icy growl, the grinding of an Alpine avalanche, with which this would have been received."[5] And when he prevailed upon Sheridan Knowles to assist him in mutilating Beaumont & Fletcher's *The Maid's Tragedy* into an 'actable' version which they entitled *The Bridal*, he was totally blind to the inference that he was guilty of the same bastardisation of great works as he had accused Tate and Cibber of being when they each clobbered Shakespeare so villainously.

Likewise, Macready's partial restoration of *King Lear*, in which he gave a resounding and famous interpretation of the king, put the role of the Fool back in the text, but not

---

5 J C Trewin, *Mr Macready* (1955), p 810

all of it, as the actor distrusted Shakespeare's stagecraft and judgement and could not countenance the distraction from Lear himself. He still maintained the traditional ending of Act I, with the thorough-going flourish of the curse on Goneril (poor Shakespeare had made the mistake of placing it in the middle of Scene Four) to mark a proper climax for the actor. This meant he could still act the rest of the play as a gradual access of wisdom rather than a descent into degradation. Nevertheless, his faithful friend John Forster publicly declared that Macready had rescued Shakespeare at a stroke and buried Cibber's version, that he had "banished that disgrace from the stage forever."[6] He had done nothing of the sort.

In announcing his own season at Covent Garden in 1838, Macready wrote that "no exertion will be spared in presenting the National Drama, whether as a branch of literature or as a department of art, with every advantage. The revival of the standard plays of Shakespeare in the genuine text of the Poet will be persevered in with increased activity, and without regard to expense in attaining the utmost fidelity of historic illustration." For some years he was credited with having done just that, but the truth was otherwise. In his second purpose, that of the scenic effect, one would wait for Charles Kean to show the way, while in the first, that of the genuine text, it was Phelps in Islington who would complete what Macready had started.

What not even he could have expected was that the people of Islington would be not just willing, but eager to follow him. In a way, it was they who led the revolution, by demonstrating their receptiveness to unadulterated poetic drama in all its complexity at a time when the middle-class

6 The *Examiner*, 4 February, 1838

play-going public assumed they alone were the arbiters of taste with the required intelligence to appreciate high art. On the contrary, it was the sophisticates of the West End who were taught how to enjoy true Shakespeare by the novitiates of the suburbs. Phelps' vision would be triumphantly rewarded without his having to make any but the most trivial of compromises. In the end, of course, Shakespeare himself was the victor.

The *Richard III* which opened Phelps' management at Sadler's Wells was not what we would nowadays term an 'uncut' version, for there were still conventions which he was obliged to take into account. The duration of the action had to be contained within three hours, which meant the sacrifice of some minor characters, and the trivial adjustments he made were in order to comply with the Lord Chamberlain's decrees concerning decency. The words 'God', 'prostitute' (even as a verb), 'womb', 'bastard', 'bawd' were all forbidden on stage, as were any expressions which could be construed as blasphemous. Apart from this, Phelps did not interfere with Shakespeare's words, syntax, poetry or characterisation. The portrait of the king, flawed and vile but destined from childhood to commit infamy, was there intact, almost for the first time since it had been written. He was no longer a monster given to rant, but a man so damaged by accident of birth and thwarted ambition as to destroy himself and others in revenge against Fate. The people of Islington recognised human truth before their eyes.

By any judgement, *King Lear* is a difficult and demanding play, but Phelps did not shrink from presenting almost the whole of the original drama and discarding every 'improvement' which Nahum Tate had imposed to make the story more palatable and approachable. He showed the harrowing suffering of the old man in all its intensity (both in his direction and in his own performance) and revealed the huge poetic awfulness of this majestic text at last. Very little was torn from the page, apart from the blinding of Gloucester, which was too cruel to be shown in 1845 and would have unnerved the Lord Chamberlain. It was understood that Gloucester would have his eyes gouged out, there was no doubt about that, but it would happen later, offstage, as if in accordance with the decorous classical rules of French theatre. Thus the audience was spared the scene of horror we take for granted today, but they still had the closest presentation of what Shakespeare had intended since the Elizabethan era. Nobody had dared go so far before, and even Samuel Phelps, after ten years of protests from critics (but not from audiences) about the brutality of the scene, would eventually tone it down further. At the first night, however, the reviewer of the *Athenaeum* was in celebratory mood. "We announce this restoration with pleasure", he wrote. "for, to speak the truth, it is the only one which has been made in perfect good faith, and with a full reliance on the poet."[7] The telling remark as to 'good faith' was a just acknowledgement of Phelps' aims and intentions.

Similarly, the critics noticed that his production of *Romeo and Juliet*, having discarded Garrick's foolish happy ending and much else besides, offered "an entire perfect version of the text, for the first time." The approbation must have cheered him, for he then undertook to give a pure version of *Macbeth* which would remove the most

---

7 8 November, 1845; and see Shirley S Allen, *Samuel Phelps and Sadler's Wells Theatre* (1971), pp 216-217

popular and traditional element of previous productions, namely the singing witches. A good deal of Shakespeare's text had been habitually discarded in order to make way for a ludicrous display by the Weird Sisters, who sang and danced with words absent from the original and tunes added later. Not even the influence of the Romantic movement, with its avowed admiration for the Bard, dared to suggest removing these aberrations. Phelps did. He discarded the 'acting version' entirely and returned to Shakespeare. Everyone, including the educated critics, lamented the disappearance of the singing witches, as also the inclusion of the scene between Lady Macduff and her son, who is murdered on stage after declaring that "there are liars and swearers enough to beat the honest men and hang up them"[8]; this was deemed too unjust and cruel for a Victorian audience, but Phelps boldly kept it in. However, he discovered that he had gone too far by following Shakespeare's stage direction that, at the very end, Macbeth's head should be brought in on a pole. A critic pointed out that his veneration for the original text might have impelled him to cut off the actor's head and impale it, had he not been playing the part of Macbeth himself. In this, as with the blinding of Gloucester, Phelps eventually yielded, and in later performances omitted both the murder of Macduff's son and the head on a stick.[9]

Antony and Cleopatra was virtually unknown on the stage before the Sadler's Wells production, having been wholly neglected by previous generations, except for the occasional patchwork with bits added by Dryden, which had never been popular. For a change, then, Phelps "had a

8 Act IV, scene 2
9 Allen, *op. cit.*, p 219

free hand as if he were dealing with a new work. There was no acting text, no tradition of previous interpretations by famous actors, and no precedent in staging."[10] He cut only superfluous lines, inserted by the playwright by way of explanation, and left untouched all the sumptuous poetry and psychological depth of characterisation. It was a total novelty, a revelation. As such, it was too much for some, lacking as it was any edifying element usually thought essential in Victorian production. The *Theatrical Journal* pointed out that there was "little or nothing to elevate and purify in this play. It appeals to the lowest passions, and in spite of its poetry, is sometimes disgusting."[11]

For similar reasons, *Henry IV Part II* had been rarely shown, largely because the scenes with Doll Tearsheet were too risky. Phelps used an almost pure text (not quite) which included these scenes, and they proved to be so hilarious that "the voice of propriety was lost in gales of laughter."

By this time, it was clear that Phelps was engaged upon an undertaking far in excess of anything attempted by his predecessors. He was delivering Shakespeare to Shakespeare's audience. Gradually, the obscenities and cruelties and baroque extravagances of the Elizabethan theatre came to be accepted as part of the genuine article, for which the audience should be grateful rather than grudging. One reviewer said that Sadler's Wells had become "a sort of museum for the exhibition of dramatic curiosities, and we have no more right to be astounded at finding some Elizabethan crudity within its precincts than

---

10 *ibid.*
11 1 November, 1849

at finding a Buddhist idol in a missionary collection."[12]

With *Midsummer Night's Dream* Phelps scored an unreserved hit. Discarding all the songs and dances, he presented the text joyful and unadorned, relying upon the text to fire the imagination of the audience without recourse to cheap tricks, and creating an evening of utter magic. The rustics' fun with Pyramus and Thisbe was performed in dialogue, an innovation beyond the memory of anyone present, and the result was delightful. The play has been a perennial favourite ever since.

It would be tedious to march through the canon listing all Phelps' achievements, and indeed in some cases he did resort to 'acting versions', possibly owing to the heavy workload with which he burdened himself. But the achievement in the round was without precedent. In the eighteen years of his management at Sadler's Wells, he mounted productions of thirty-one Shakespeare plays, established an appetite for the original language and style which has not abated since, and demonstrated that Shakespeare was not too difficult a genius to be let loose upon the discerning public.

As if in celebration of all this activity (but in fact, by mere coincidence), the club's President, The 6th Duke of Devonshire, presented us with a fine terracotta bust of Shakespeare by Roubiliac dating from 1742. It was, he said in a letter announcing his intention to make the gift, by the way of a gentle apology for not having been able to visit the club regularly. The club chairman, Lord Tenterden, immediately following the meeting of the General Committee at which the letter was read, wrote fulsomely to the Duke on 15 December, 1855, that the bust "will

---

12 Harvard Theatre Collection, quoted in Allen

indeed be most highly esteem'd, not only as a memorial of Shakespeare and as the ornament of our rooms, but also as a testimony of the classical taste of our President and of the zealous feelings entertain'd by him for the welfare of our Society." [13] The recompense outweighed the fault in spectacular manner, and the Roubiliac bust has been a source of pride ever since.

A few miles away, and at the same time, another revival of Shakespearean production of a quite different order was taking place at the new Princess's Theatre in Oxford Street. This, too, would leave a legacy far into the future, one that sought to give a feast for the eye rather than nourishment for the intellect. Such were the lavish displays invented by Charles Kean. They would be famous in their own day, and the subject of much dispute for years to come.

Phelps and Kean were of course known to one another, though not as fast friends. Personally as well as professionally, they were as divergent as it was perhaps possible to be. Acting together in Sheffield many years before, they had already been compared, always to the detriment of Kean. Being the son of the fabled Edmund Kean, young Charles had been lobbed into leading parts as an inexperienced boy in his early twenties. The local newspaper damned him with the prediction that he would never be more than "an excellent second-rate performer", which surely rankled when the same journalist preferred the interpretations of Phelps, who had no name whatever. While Kean was the star, the older Phelps was assigned supporting roles in which he displayed his talent to signal effect.

Macready in particular took exception to the young man's presumption, grumbling that "the conceit. the

---

13 Devonshire Mss, Chatsworth, 2nd Series, 106.4C

effrontery, of this puppy is really astonishing." The fact that the awful Mr Bunn thought Kean was rather good, and thanked God he had at last found somebody capable of doing justice to Shakespeare (an opinion one suspects he put forward precisely to annoy Macready, for Bunn could not have cared whether anyone was good or not, as long as the audience paid to see him), made the wound fester the more. He was furious when somebody spoke of himself and Charles Kean in the same breath as "actors".[14]

In 1840 Charles Kean played a summer season at the Haymarket, again as the leading actor, and Phelps, now established in London, once again as second fiddle playing the Ghost in *Hamlet*, Macduff in *Macbeth* and Henry VI in *Richard III*. There is no evidence that he ever complained, for he was not a troublemaker by nature, but privately he knew well enough that he was a much finer artist than Kean, who was far too ready to sacrifice the beauty of the verse to the temptation of a bit of stage 'business', and had no insight into character. Ever since his premature *début* as Hamlet two years before, he had been scorned in print. A critic had written then, "Charles Kean is simply absurd in the part – violates every rule of decency, and is intensely ridiculous." Now they were saying that he was sloppy, grotesque, "vigorous and elaborate" (epithets not intended to be complimentary). Still he was demanding salaries double the normal rate, and he got them. The name was heavy, even if the talent was slight.

By the time he took over the lavish Princess's Theatre in 1850, he had developed his style in a downward direction. He was always best suited to melodrama,

---

14 Trewin, *op.cit.*, pp 138, 144, 177

with its gestures and preordained signals (inheriting all his father's tricks and nothing of his genius). In Boucicault's adaptation of Alexandre Dumas' *The Corsican Brothers*, for example, he had a moment of drama, taking the blood-stained handkerchief from his lips to display the wound that would kill him, and audiences waited for this moment with rising anticipation. His voice was not at its best in the delivery of passion, so he toned it down and made it more casual. This did not make matters any better, especially in Shakespeare, for he gave the impression that he did not believe what he was saying, a fatal defect in acting on any stage.

It may be that he was aware of this, and that he knew his talents would be put to more fruitful use as a stage-manager, or it may just be by accident, but the fact is that Charles Kean's ten-year rule at the Princess's was devoted above all to creating a spectacular effect. He wanted his audiences to know that something had hit them, and never to be able to eradicate from their minds the memory of what he gave them. Whereas Phelps tended to keep his scenery quiet, and not allow it to overwhelm the action, Kean did the opposite, and made the scenery the principal reason for going to see his productions. The staging of a play at the Princess's grew ever more elaborate, ambitious and technical with each new season, to the extent that so much time was taken in preparing and changing scenes, that huge amounts of text had to be cut to accommodate the required timing. For instance, his production of *The Tempest* opened with a shipwreck so dramatic and realistic that it took twenty minutes to clear the stage to make way for the action. For Kean, the words were far less significant to an evening at the theatre than the spectacle, and he made it his business to present better spectacles than anyone had ever done before him, or would ever do again. In this he succeeded.

Some evidence of his staging has been preserved in photographs in the archives of the Garrick Club. The sets for *Midsummer Night's Dream*, designed by Thomas Grieve, are of a gleaming and fantastical beauty. For the scenes in the wood, when the four lovers are wandering in search of one another, Grieves created not a single panorama stretching across the back of the stage, with one very long canvas unfurled from one vertical end-roller to the other to present a moving picture, but a 'diorama' consisting of two rolling views, one in front of the other, with intervals in the closer one to revel the other open behind. This was moving all the time, creating an effect not unlike modern cinema. Kean also included a complete ballet of Amazonian soldiers, and an avenue of arches made with flowers and held by fairy dancers. Lastly, the magic was completed by more fairies who appeared to fly in from the wings. For *King John* there was a startling back-cloth of a windmill scene in blustery weather, painted by Frederick Lloyds, and for *A Winter's Tale* the interior of a sumptuous palace, with Doric columns, garden courtyard and heavily decorated ceiling. In *The Corsican Brothers* Kean used a daring innovation, the double transparency gauze at the back of the stage, which served with clever lighting to allow one brother to see the action of another brother, showing two scenes at the same time. In the following act, the gauze is used for a different effect, allowing the dying brother, bleeding in the snow, to see his twin thinking of him back in the castle. The ingenious trap devised for this play entered theatrical lore as the 'Corsican trap'. Finally,

Kean's production of *The Merchant of Venice* achieved the astonishing feat of creating the lagoon city on the stage of the Princess's, complete with *palazzi*, canals, boats, bridges which were serviceable and upon which the action took place, and even a huge crowd scene for the carnival.[15] The watercolours Kean commissioned to preserve an eternal record of these scenes are now in the Theatre Collection of the Victoria & Albert Museum.

There was exhibited a meticulous, one might almost say manic, attention to detail in the preparation of scene and costumes alike. The 'French tent' in *King Lear* had to be precisely accurate, in accordance with the drawings presented by experts, the materials for the bed totally authentic. The wands carried by court officials in *A Winter's Tale* (in which an eight year-old Ellen Terry made her stage *début*) had to be correct in colour and shape for the period. In his programme notes Kean declared his intentions very clearly, "to embellish his magnificent conceptions with all the accessorial aid of pictorial and mechanical appliances; to resuscitate history whenever the opportunity presented itself, even to the most minute details, so that every scene should be a text to lecture on; and to base all that he presented to the spectator on unimpeachable authorities." To this end, he consulted scholars and read many volumes, urgent in his desire to get everything right. For *Macbeth* he made sure that the architecture of the sets reflected the excellent iron-work which was dominant in Anglo-Saxon and Scottish buildings between the seventh and twelfth centuries and that the buildings were coloured as they had been in reality. "On this subject I have availed myself of the valuable knowledge of George Godwin Esq., F.S.A., of

15 Richard Southern, *The Victorian Theatre* (1970), pp 40-47

the Royal Institute of Architects", he proudly announced on the 'fly-leaf', for "nothing would be introduced except under the sanction of historical authority." The programme notes for *Richard III* listed twelve authorities that had been consulted, with regard to costume, effigies, and ornament.[16] The one authority he forbore to include, however, was Shakespeare, for the play he put on was the version by Colley Cibber.

The result of all this work was to enliven the London stage with astonishing visual vivacity. At Sadler's Wells the scenery was subdued in comparison, informed by an effort on Phelps' part to allow the set to suggest atmosphere rather than attempt verisimilitude, as when the ghost of Hamlet's father took form gradually out of the gloom, making the darkness on stage almost part of the action. Kean gloried in display. His care for accurate detail was no doubt honest and true, and it earned him a lasting place in the history of the English theatre. But it was not universally appreciated by critics. His former colleague and friend Douglas Jerrold (also an original member of the Garrick) was both playwright and journalist. In the latter capacity he wrote of Kean's work with dismissive contempt, "Play-going at the Princess's is *sight-seeing*, and nothing more; and a visit is invariably accompanied by the *ennui* that accompanies sight-seeing." That Jerrold's opinion was possibly shaped by personal animosity is indicated in a letter to Kean wherein he accused him of being "a person vain, capricious, unstable in his agreements, with a festering anxiety to consider every man his mortal enemy, who is not prepared to acknowledge him the eighth wonder

---

16 Cole, *op.cit.*, Vol II, pp 48, 52, 102, 203

of the habitable world."[17] While the cause of this enmity was Kean's failure to put on a play by Jerrold which he had commissioned three years earlier and then neglected, the sarcastic reference to an eighth wonder did hit the mark in a way, for these fabulous productions had become an end in themselves, no matter what they were meant to illustrate. As one reviewer nastily but justly remarked, "in Garrick's day we had a Macbeth without the costume, and now we have the costume without the Macbeth." But one of his greatest admirers was the young Queen Victoria, a circumstance which did him no harm whatever.

Wherever the Queen bestowed her favour, the aristocracy followed. She confessed to being entranced by the spectacles at the Princess's Theatre, even to swooning, and was often present. Fashionable folk therefore concluded that this theatre was beyond compare, and they flocked. Furthermore, from 1848 onwards Kean was put in charge, as Master of the Revels, of a series of dramatic performances to be given by Royal Command at Windsor Castle, by implication sealing the reputation of Kean, not Phelps, as the foremost representative of the drama in Victorian England. (The appointment also provoked one of Macready's last squabbles, when he suggested an acquaintance of his for a small part in *Julius Caesar* at Windsor, and Kean told him in polite terms to mind his own business). Phelps did not complain about royal patronage being diverted away from him (the Queen did not visit Sadler's Wells even once), but he did suffer from it indirectly, for it meant that ambitious actors were ever on the alert for opportunities to appear before the monarch and so advance their careers, and having spent

17 ibid., pp 76, 86

every season looking for new talent and training young actors to his style, he would lose them just as rapidly to his more glamorous rival.[18]

It was being put about in the press that Kean had engineered his position in royal favour by standing in the way of all possible rivals. The *Lloyds Weekly Newspaper* accused him directly of having thrown "immense blocks of ice" to block their passage. "He has used this privilege for the glorification of himself as an actor and a manager, until the Queen and the Court have been brought to believe that there was but one English actor, and but one English theatre; that actor being Mr Charles Kean, and that theatre being the Princess's!!" The author of this blatant sneer was, again, Douglas Jerrold. One wonders how the two men could bear to be in the same club together. But he was not alone. While people from 'society' continued to relish such translations from shallow French melodrama as *The Corsican Brothers*, critics were more and more moving to the realisation that Phelps was delivering something of real quality. The old conflict between commercial success and good taste was turned on its head, for Sadler's Wells was regularly packed, and the Princess's regularly lost money, being unable to sell enough seats (except when the Queen was there) to cover the gigantic costs. "Were Phelps in royal favour as Kean is", said the *Theatrical Journal*, "we should soon find such horrid *omelettes* entirely driven from the stage."[19]

Phelps was finally commanded to perform at Windsor in 1853 (Kean was in Paris hunting authenticity for his next production), on which occasion the whole company

---

18 Allen, *op.cit.*, p 121; Trewin, *op.cit.*, p 228
19 21 September,1853

was transported from Sadler's Wells to give a performance of *Henry V*. He followed this with a celebrated production (in what was snootily referred to by the *Times* as "the Pentonville district"[20]) of *Henry IV* in which he played both King Henry and Justice Shallow with such brilliance that he transcended the mere feat of virtuosity to show "that plasticity of imagination which…raises the office of the actor into the highest department of literature and the arts."[21] He also, by the by, showed what he thought of the star system which ruled elsewhere by sacking a very famous actress for refusing to play the part of Gertrude in *Hamlet* because the brevity of the part would demean her. She is supposed to have asked him whether John Philip Kemble had ever been expected to appear in a pantomime. Phelps would have no truck with such an attitude. She left.[22]

One day Kean went a little too far in his assumption of right at Windsor Castle. The Court wished to put on a special performance as part of the festival being mounted to celebrate the marriage of the Princess Royal to the Crown Prince of Prussia. Kean was approached. He had recently been replaced as Master of the Revels and was consequently in a mood, so he declined. Too grand to descend to a row, the court officials calmly removed the honour to Samuel Phelps, whose company gave a performance of *Macbeth* not at their own theatre but at Her Majesty's. The *Times* objected that a Shakespearean drama without Mr Kean would be like the Lord Mayor's Show without the Lord Mayor (which, though the editorial did not realise it, was a very apt metaphor), but the *Islington Gazette* retorted in

---

20 20 January, 1858
21 *Morning Advertiser*, 18 March, 1853
22 Allen, *op.cit.*, p 131

defence of its local hero that the only proper reason Kean was not there was the "very simple one that he cannot act Macbeth, and could not easily transport to Her Majesty's the stage properties which at the Princess's he shows in lieu of it."[23]

It must have gone deeply against Phelps' instinct to present the old adulterated version, with the chorus of singing witches, which he must presumably have been commanded to do by royal authority, and in accordance with royal taste; the posh audience did not mind, as they were busy stealing glances at the Queen and adjusting their finery lest she in return glance at them.

An amusing insight into the characters of the two men was demonstrated when they each, separately, appeared at a public event to raise money for retired and needy actors. Kean's appeal was launched in a theatre, where he presided on stage over a provisional committee enjoined to accept the offer of five acres of land in Berkshire upon which would be built an asylum consisting of "charitable houses for the reception of aged and worn-out brothers and sisters of the stage...decayed and indigent actors". He went on in orotund and pompous prose for about an hour, in front of cheering fans, but it has not been possible to discover whether any such houses were ever built.

Phelps agreed to act as chairman at an annual Theatrical Fund Dinner, one of his rare appearances off the boards anywhere, and spoke simply and eloquently of the nobility and high calling of the actor's art. Charles Dickens, also present, proposed a toast to Phelps, who was not used to receiving honours and never sought them. Dickens spoke of his "sensible subservience of the scene-painter and the

---

23 30 January, 1858

mechanist to the real meaning of the play." In his response, Phelps told how his young daughter, having attended a local private school in Islington (where the family had lived since 1845) for six months, was suddenly summoned by the headmistress one day and expelled. Mrs Phelps went to enquire why. The teacher said, "I have under my roof three young ladies, sisters – daughters, Mrs Phelps, of a gentleman who is an immediate neighbour of yours. He has been to me, and threatened to remove his three daughters from under my roof if I persist in receiving little Miss Phelps as a pupil, for he will not allow his children to be educated under the same roof with an actor's. Gentlemen, the moral of this story is, that either in honouring my name as you have done, you have evidently committed a great error, or the gentleman in question acted the part of a great fool."[24] Thus with good humour and palpable humility (one imagines he did not relish the idea of being praised at all, and deflected his embarrassment by turning the attention away to his wife and daughter), he was able gently to remind his fellow actors, who were present in great numbers, that the profession still had some way to go before it would be accepted as entirely respectable.

That day would come within the century, sooner than anyone present could have imagined. In the meantime, the next decade would see a significant shifting of personalities, on and off the stage of life, which would herald profound changes in the nature of the London theatre, as well as the reputation of its actors. First, there was the farewell to the great lion of the past generation. Macready announced his retirement in 1851, and with characteristic grandeur, went out with trumpets blaring. Not before,

24 Cole, *op.cit.*, Vol II, p 293; Allen, *op.cit.*, p 149

naturally, having a tiff with James Anderson, who was by then manager of Drury Lane, where the final performance would take place. It was to be *Macbeth*. In a friendly gesture, Anderson cast himself and two other actors as the Singing Witches; had he hoped to raise a smile on the great man's face he hoped in vain. Macready called it an impertinence and ordered the names to be deleted from the playbill. Anderson was crushed, embarrassed, but Mac would not be Mac without a squabble to mark his pride, even at the end. Still, he sent a stage prop he had worn as Richelieu to Samuel Phelps, which was nice.

Not often in the history of the theatre, much given as it is to grand emotional moments, had there been a leave-taking quite as stupendous as Macready's. Ageing now, Maria Warner took the role of Lady M., and generous-hearted Sam Phelps appeared as Macduff. As soon as Mac appeared, the whole theatre rose to its feet, stamping, cheering, waving handkerchiefs and hats, and calling out his name – "Macready! Macready!" His children, whom he had imperiously banished from his appearances for years, were there, visibly affected; they could not have known what a response their father could evoke for, still ashamed by his job, he had not told them. He 'milked' it, of course, taking a splendidly long time for Macbeth to die and drawing thunder from the pit and boxes alike. This was acting of the old school; this was what they wanted. He left and went to his dressing-room to change. Then he came again before the audience, in front of the curtain, dressed like a gentleman, and, once the cheering had subsided, gave a speech to make tears flow.

"Ladies and gentlemen", he began, "my last theatrical part is played." The address looks stiff and stilted on the page, even unfeeling, and it would be an injustice to him to print it all; it actually came from the heart, but Macready's heart was heavily protected and difficult to discover. He said that he had resolved to retire while he was still able to perform, rather than linger and watch himself wither, and he added, "With sentiments of the deepest gratitude I take my leave, bidding you, ladies and gentlemen, in my past professional capacity, with regret, a last farewell." It was the speech of "an honest man".[25] He bowed repeatedly to the roaring crowd, then left the theatre for the last time.

He was yet unable to rid himself of the gnawing notion that he had devoted his life to an ignoble profession, albeit with a noble aim. Twenty years before, he had told the Select Committee that "persons who could find any other occupation would not take to one in which they are depending entirely upon the humour of the public."[26] That public had demonstrated in what regard they held him, but before going to bed that night, he wrote in his diary, "Thank God!"

Three years later, in 1854, Charles Kemble died, relic of a still earlier generation, quietly ebbing in the Garrick Club with his huge ear-trumpet, where he was pointed out to new members with delight. At about the same time, the adolescent, driven young man from Devon, who had found his calling when, at the age of twelve, he had seen Phelps play Hamlet, went back several times and was introduced to Phelps, who advised him against becoming an actor. The boy said that nothing would deter him, upon which Phelps offered him an immediate engagement at £2 a week. This,

---

25 Trewin, *op,cit.*, p 237
26 *Report of the Select Committee* , p 135

astonishingly, he refused, on the grounds that his talent was still raw and would need to be honed in the hard grind of the provinces. This is what Henry Irving then did, playing 700 parts in 10 gruelling years of obscurity. When finally he conquered London, the two men would actually appear together in the same productions.

That was some time after Phelps had relinquished his historic management of Sadler's Wells, however. Unlike Macready, he retired totally without fanfare, without even an announcement. In 1862 he was told that his wife was dying of cancer, and there was no possibility that he would continue without her. Devoted as he was to his craft, she was nevertheless the central emotional core of his life, the person to whom he went home after every performance, never lingering with admirers or colleagues, his closest friend for thirty-four years. On his last night, he caused a timid announcement to be placed on the playbill to that effect. "Here is Mr Phelps retiring from Sadler's Wells in such a modest quiet way that people knew nothing about it until the thing was done…Mr Phelps slips out of sight with neither flummery nor fuss, and so modestly takes leave of us that we have scarce the opportunity to say how much we liked him."[27] For eighteen years he had set an example at Sadler's Wells from which we are still today feeling the ripples at the National Theatre and the Royal Shakespeare Company.

He then spent six years as leading man at Drury Lane, and when his wife died in 1867 he withdrew with his fishing-rod to Kent, and moved to a smaller house in London with his surviving children. The following year his professional

---

27 *Punch*, 29 November, 1862, in Allen, *op.cit.*, p 162

antagonist Charles Kean died, and in 1871 Irving appeared for the first time in *The Bells* at the Lyceum Theatre, marking a tumultuous moment in theatrical history. Two years after that, the new phenomenon was black-balled at the Garrick Club (possibly due to the influence of James Anderson), only to be elected triumphantly a few months later by the entire membership. Phelps, too, joined the club in 1874, proposed by John Coleman and heavily supported, where, belatedly, he discovered the pleasures of quiet intimate colloquy with his fellows, and enjoyed the companionship with obvious delight. He was said to be "a lovable man", yet he would never have joined while his wife lived.

Macready spent over twenty years in retirement at Sherborne, Dorset, dying a venerable old man in 1873, clutching a volume of Shakespeare; as he pointed at it, he said, "a poem in every sentence, music in every line."[28] Phelps was still appearing in London and the provinces in his seventies, playing Cardinal Wolsey, Richelieu and Peter Teazle. Like Edmund Kean before him and Henry Irving after, he would die virtually on stage. He fell ill during a farewell performance at Drury Lane and never recovered. His last role was as Wolsey. In the same performance was Norman Forbes, brother of a young actor and friend whom Phelps had trained, to whom he taught elocution and the fine art of delivering poetry with musical phrasing and perfect tone. This was Johnston Forbes-Robertson, who had been an artist in oils before taking to the stage, and who painted a full-length portrait of Phelps in the robes of Wolsey. He later donated this painting to the club, where it still hangs.

And so the threads of theatrical legacy tie together

---

28 Frank Benson, *Memoirs*, p 159

generations which are mathematically separated by unbridgeable years. The voice of Phelps could be heard by those who saw Forbes-Robertson on stage at the beginning of the last century, and that purity of diction, so perfect as to evoke involuntary excitement, would pass on to John Gielgud, whom many of us alive today could listen to for hours, no matter what he said.

But first there was the marvel, the enigma, of Henry Irving to blast through stage history like a frenzied, dazzling meteor.

5

IRVING

The era of Henry Irving unquestionably achieved startling progress in the evolution of two of the themes of this study, namely the social reputation enjoyed by actors, and the consequent respectful behaviour of audiences towards them. But on the third matter, concerning the removal of corrupted Shakespearean texts, it was arguably a step backwards, or at the least it marked a reluctance to continue the march towards re-establishing the original plays in their entirety. On the face of it, Irving was the least likely man to have any influence in any direction, for he appeared to lack virtually all the ingredients necessary to make a good actor. Except one: self-belief. His colleague, Baliol Holloway, when asked if Irving had been a tall man, replied, "He was what he *wanted* to be."

Any account of Irving's career must needs come to grips with his astonishingly long list of defects. For a start, there was the dreadful voice which was, according to Henry James, "wholly unavailable for purposes of declamation. To say that he speaks badly is to go too far; to my sense he simply does not speak at all – in any way that, in an actor, can be called speaking…Shakespeare's finest lines pass from his lips without his paying the scantest tribute to their quality. Of what the French call *diction* – the art of delivery – he has apparently not a suspicion."[1] William Archer admitted that there had never been an actor of such importance "whose talent, nay whose mere competence has been so much contested". His voice was so poor that he could only overcome it by throwing it forward into a cavernous nose, so producing a strikingly resonant effect.[2] Drama students have ever since been trying to imitate it, avoid it, make fun of it, but none has been able to make of it the majestic instrument that Irving secured for himself. For it was the result of a fierce and unrelenting struggle with a stammer he had developed in his adolescent years in response to his mother's and aunt's attempts to steer him into a course he did not relish (the church) and which thereafter crippled his speech. He had chosen the stage in part because it was the only way he could control the humiliating stammer.[3] That effort of will would shape his entire career.

The effect of this concealed but always lurking problem was that he garbled his speech on stage with grunts and drawls, hesitations and mispronunciations. 'Rich' came out as 'ritz, 'sight' as 'seyt', 'hand' as 'hond' or 'hend', 'God' as 'Gud', 'go' as 'gaw'. "Sterility' was stretched to 'stair-ril-la-ta-a.' He often seemed to chew at words, or fight with them. Henry James, again, warned that his eccentricities of speech were "so strange, so numerous, so personal to himself, his vices of pronunciation, of modulation, of elocution so highly developed, the tricks he plays with the

---

1 Quoted in William Archer, *Henry Irving: A critical study*.
2 Richard Bebb, *Tragedians of the City*, talk broadcast on BBC, 12 April, 1972, and
   published in the *Journal of Recorded Sound*
3 Michael Holroyd, *A Strange Eventful History* (2009), p 97

divine mother-tongue so audacious and fantastic, that the spectator who desires to be in sympathy with him finds himself confronted with a bristling hedge of difficulties."[4]

In addition to the odd manner of talking, Irving had a weird way of walking. His gait was ugly, his knees bent awkwardly and his back hunched, and thus he "moved about the stage with depressed head, and protruding shoulders, making with his legs sidelong and backward skirmishes."[5] William Archer vividly complained that his attention was "absorbed in making the phonetic changes necessary to transmute Mr Irving's speech into English, or wondering where his limbs were going to carry him next." Early in his provincial training, a journalist had advised him "to take the first steamer back to his comfortable home and to abandon all hope of becoming an actor"[6], and one delightful if unkind story holds that when he saw an old lady in tears at a performance he told her afterwards that he had been moved to see her so upset. "Indeed I was", she replied, I've a young son myself play-acting somewhere in the north, and it broke me up to think that he might be no better at it than you."[7]

Notwithstanding all of this, he held the stage like nobody before or since, and hypnotized the audience into total surrender. He subjugated them. His profile eventually became so famous that children used to parade beside the railway line to catch a glimpse of it as his train passed. Next to Queen Victoria he shared with Gordon of Khartoum the distinction of being the most revered English person alive.

---

4 *ibid.*, p 165
5 Frances Donaldson, *The Actor-Managers* (1970), p 51
6 Edward Gordon Craig, *Henry Irving* (1930)
7 Ned Sherrin, *Theatrical Anecdotes* (1991), p 126

How on earth did he achieve this pre-eminence against all the odds?

Not to be frightened of the obvious, he did it through acting; indeed, he may be the only example of a great actor who rose to stardom precisely through great acting. Usually, one is a great actor first, then a star for different, tangential or additional reasons. Irving had nothing additional. He was nothing but The Actor. He was not especially funny, he was not beautiful (Henry James said his face was "sedentary", which was a bit severe), not really so interesting as a man. He was not intellectual. His conversation was unenlightening, his friendships not profound, with the single exception of J. L. Toole to whom he was close and with whom he shared a taste for practical jokes. But on stage he was magnificent, and it was on stage that he was a star, imposing his view of the world he was representing by sheer imaginative concentration. "Irving was not only able to impart more meaning to his words than they expressed in themselves", wrote a contemporary, "but was addicted even to making them subservient to his own ideas, and making the public accept his conception in the face of a text which was in flat contradiction to it."[8] In other words, he *improved* everything merely by his dignified presence and thought, cancelling his idiosyncrasies of posture and gesture by obliterating them from view and replacing them with what he wanted the audience to see; "never was a man more gracefully awkward."[9] Of all the actors of the past, Irving is the one most difficult to grasp, to see, to experience at a distance. But whatever it was he did, it bestowed a kind of veneration upon him which

---

8 Bertram Joseph, *The Tragic Actor* (1959), p 367
9 Donaldson, *op.cit.*, p 53

did not glitter so much as glow with tremendous depth. At a dinner in honour of Ellen Terry over thirty years later, Winston Churchill referred to Irving's "mysterious and sinister grace" which got it about right.[10]

He maintained that it was not possible to teach a man how to act. In a lecture given at Harvard University, Massachusetts, in 1885, he said, "you may learn down which trap the ghost of Hamlet's father vanished; but the soul of interpretation is lost, and it is the soul which the actor has to recreate for himself."[11] He had many years of practise, for the shy, stuttering, self-conscious John Brodribb had been banished from reality as he created the entirely new personage of Henry Irving every day. This required positive hard work and the conquest of mind over body – there was no point in waiting for inspiration, which was like "trusting to a shipwreck for your first lesson in swimming." To a young actor possibly too pleased with himself, he gave this sober advice: "I will give you a year to learn that speech so that you will make your audience imagine for the moment that you have not got it by heart." That implies dry, plastic technique, as was evident in his staging, in *Hamlet* for example, the opening royal procession of Claudius and Gertrude with Polonius in attendance, to prepare the scene, then, fanfares stilled and lights dimmed, they left to reveal Irving at the back of the stage, alone in a pale glow, pensive and perplexed. But the inference is misleading. Most actors can manage stage and character through long experience, but Irving went much further; his physical self, not just his speech and manner, were part of the performance. His legendary

---

10 At the Hotel Cecil on 17 June, 1906
11 J A Hammerton, *The Actor's Art* (1897), p 70

leading lady, Ellen Terry, described how he "lost" himself when he played Matthias in *The Bells*: "Every time he heard the sound of the bells, the throbbing of his heart must have nearly killed him. He used always to turn quite white – there was no trick about it. It was imagination acting physically upon the body."[12]

That was the secret of his power. Audiences went to watch him suffer, which is why he created an awful sense of apprehension and dread in the theatre; it was almost supernatural, as if they wondered whether he would actually survive. In *The Bells*, his tortured soul was such that the audience looked on in horrified sympathy as the man's spirit collapsed. Gordon Craig said he was "fearful to watch", and Laurence Olivier would describe him as "dangerously good." It was not uncommon for women to faint with too much emotional strain. That this is no exaggeration is attested within living memory by Athene Seyler, an actress who celebrated her 100th birthday in the club and died as recently as 1993. She saw Irving when she was a small girl, and said that "when he came to his death scene, I actually fainted in my seat."[13]

Irving's own shades of personal, mysterious anguish informed his acting, which was what Sarah Bernhardt noticed when she said, "Je ne vous dis pas que c'est un très grand acteur, mais c'est le plus grand artiste qu'il y ait au monde."[14] Even more eloquent is this anonymous tribute: "Had I not seen him…and only heard his demerits discussed by his detractors, I still think I should have been curious to see the man with the much-abused legs, who

---

12 Ellen Terry, *The Story of My Life* (1908), p 338
13 Athene Seyler and Stephen Haggard, *The Craft of Comedy* (1943), p 172
14 Sir George Arthur, *From Phelps to Gielgud* (1936) p 75

could not pronounce English properly, and from the door of whose theatre a crowd was turned away each night because there was not standing-room."[15]

In the light of all this, it is at last possible to read Craig's much-quoted account of the applause which followed an Irving performance without a smile of sardonic disbelief. "A terrific sweep of applause is not 'bringing the house down'", he wrote. "Bringing the house down is when everybody simultaneously calls out, and applauds simultaneously and electrically. A vast number of people can ponderously express approval, but that is not what I mean. You have been to the Russian Ballet perhaps on one of its great nights, or you have heard Chaliapine's reception at Covent Garden. Well, that is not what I mean either. Those are ovations, but mild ovations. The thing I mean had three times the capacity of that."[16] He seemed not to pay much regard to applause, but to endure it, bowing only slightly, not at all theatrically. This has been variously interpreted as disdain, contempt, indifference or the echo of bitter memories of those early years when audiences had chastised him with booing and screaming. I tend to think, on the other hand, that it was an expression of his own wonderment, in awe at a talent he knew he had, but did not know why or where it came from. He respected it, and bowed to it, rather than to those who merely witnessed it.

This is why reviewers who responded to his peculiarities as if they defined him entirely missed the point. Even George Bernard Shaw, who derided his acting on countless occasions, recognised that he was in a category all by himself, that "he could give importance and a noble melancholy to

---

15 Richard Southern, *The Victorian Theatre* (1970), p 98
16 Edward Gordon Craig, *Henry Irving* (1930)

any sort of drivel that was put into his mouth." As Frances Donaldson has written, "The crime that those who write critically for money are always in danger of committing is not to fail in the detection of faults but to fail to recognise genius when it appears unheralded."[17]

That genius burst upon a startled theatre on 25 November, 1871, with the play forever thenceforth associated with his name, Leopold Lewis' melodrama *The Bells*. After years of penury and drudge (when he had been close to starvation), Henry Irving scored a significant success in Manchester, reciting the story of a conscience-stricken schoolmaster in 'The Dream of Eugene Aram' in front of the curtain, and holding the audience spellbound "in motionless silence"[18]. In the audience that night was an American theatre manager, Hezekiah Bateman, who had taken a lease on the Lyceum Theatre in London in order to display the talent of his actress daughter Isabel. He immediately offered Irving the position of leading man at that theatre. With uncanny foresight, Irving accepted on condition that he be allowed to play the lead in *The Bells*, adapted from the French but not especially well-known. In Paris the part had been played by the great Coquelin. Bateman gave his promise then forgot it, but Irving held him to it. The story of an impoverished innkeeper who murders a stranger for his money, then rises to a respectable position in his small society, the drama centred upon the man's guilt, returning to haunt and destroy him in a dream. It was a perfect vehicle for Irving's special ability to convey horror and disquiet, and he held the audience in agonised suspense as he disintegrated before their eyes, a very pleasing

---

17 Donaldson, *op.cit.*, p 52
18 Holroyd, *op.cit.*, p 103

sensation to the moral-bound Victorian psyche; they were in shock at the end, as though they had been present at a confession. "What Irving achieved in the late winter of 1871 was to raise a mediocre historical drama to the status of a dramatic masterpiece."[19] He seemed somehow in this performance to command total attention, to expect the audience to concentrate with him and go through a tunnel from which they might or might not emerge secure. He sucked their energies by focusing his own with such intensity as to draw them to him, then discarded their caterpillar carcass when once they had shared his exotic experience. He dominated them.

Gordon Craig's famous description of the moment when Matthias hears somebody mention the murder all those years ago, powerfully evokes the actor's mesmerising quality. "Irving was buckling his second shoe, seated, and leaning over it with his two long hands stretched down over the buckles. We suddenly saw these fingers stop their work; the crown of the head suddenly seemed to glitter and become frozen – and then, at the pace of the slowest and most terrified snail, the two hands, still motionless and dead, were seen to be coming up the side of the leg…the whole torso of the man, also seeming frozen, was gradually, and by an almost imperceptible movement, seen to be drawing up and back, as it would straighten a little and to lean a little against the back of the chair on which he was seated." The description continues in some detail, but it is the grip of attention which is most fiercely clear.

There then occurred the most famous insult in theatrical lore. Irving's young wife Florence, who had a small son and was pregnant with another, was deeply jealous of the

19 *ibid.* , p 104

pubic adulation which she witnessed on that first night and felt stung by it. She had no understanding of or patience with the hunger of a driven actor, and could not wait to get back home to normality, away from these absurd pretensions. She had first to endure a celebratory supper and to hear her husband praised to the skies for something she could not take seriously. On the way home, at Hyde Park Corner, she said to him, "Are you going on making a fool of yourself like this all your life?" Irving, for whom the theatre mattered infinitely more than home, wife or children, immediately descended from the carriage and walked off into the night, never to return. He did not meet with or speak to her again for the rest of his life, doing his duty by making her a generous allowance, but never forgiving the assault on his pride. She, uncomprehending, for the next twenty-four years drew a heavy line in black ink around the date in her diary when they had married, 15 July, "as if for a death".[20]

Irving was immediately the talk of London, and his ascendancy would suffer no abatement for the rest of his career. *The Bells* remained in his repertoire for the rest of his life, even when he was possibly too old to withstand the emotional demands of the part. His success saved Bateman, who had been on his way to bankruptcy, and placed the Lyceum Theatre at the core of London's theatrical history. Just as Drury Lane and Covent Garden had been regarded as 'national' theatres before 1843, and Sadler's Wells became the *de facto* 'national' theatre between 1844 and 1862, now the Lyceum assumed its reputation as the premier theatre in the metropolis, due entirely to Irving's presence. When he suggested that he might replace Isabel Bateman with

---

20 *ibid.*, p 148

the fresh young actress Ellen Terry to play opposite him, he encountered no resistance but, on the contrary, the newly-widowed Mrs Bateman passed over the lease of the theatre to him entirely amicably, and the long partnership of Irving and Terry began.

Ellen Terry, a protégée of the playwright and Garrick member Charles Reade, had been recommended to Irving by the most unlikely ambassador, Lady Pollock. Wife of the jurist Sir Frederick Pollock (another Garrick member since 1844), she was an 'unlikely' champion because she had been a close friend of Macready, whose flame she might have been expected to protect. She would even write a slim personal memoir of the man, *Macready As I Knew Him*, and her husband edited his *Reminiscences*. Nevertheless, Lady Pollock saw that Irving's fate was ordained, and he very soon came to trust her. She, meanwhile, was his most ardent admirer. "Your future may be such as will make you one of the highest reputations in Europe", she wrote, "for you have the rare quality of resolution in conquering a fault and of unceasing energy in cultivating beauty. You have won from your deep voice harmonies such as few believed it to possess."[21] That was certainly true, and he must have been hugely gratified to hear her say it.

The other judgement that counts with vast resonance all the way down to the present day is that of his colleagues. The entire acting profession held him in the highest regard, without exception, and for that to happen only a few years after the intense rivalries which had characterised the mid-century was almost revolutionary. The company that he assembled around him at the Lyceum did not shrink with dread at his coming, were not kept in submission

---

21 *ibid.*, pp 113-114

by terror, but looked upon him with a certain kind of astonished love. It was as if he hypnotised them as well as the audience, and the power of this spell is of enduring quality. At the Garrick Club he has been mythologised.

(The most striking example of this mythology is the century-old certainty that few members dare usurp Irving's chair at the head of the Long Table lest his ghost softly chide. Everyone reveres this solemn tradition, which has even made its way into print several times. The truth, alas, makes nonsense of it, for both the Long Table and the chair as its head did not arrive at the club until some time after Irving's death. So he never sat in 'Irving's chair'. The table and chairs were ordered at the end of 1905 as an 'experiment' with an estimated total cost of £88. Irving's ghost, however, knows that the will conquers veracity, and he is still exerting his power from a very distant stage, for the story refuses to die.)[22]

Even more remarkably, he was granted total loyalty despite an intense, but professional, egotism. He would manage rehearsals by starting with a read-through, himself alone reading and taking all the parts. Supporting actors were therefore expected to do the part as he would have done it himself, and to remember that their function was subordinate. He saw the play as a wheel with all the spokes pointing to himself at the centre, and that for the integrity of the drama, not for personal gratification. Nobody minded, because everyone realised the intent and trusted him without question. His discipline was total. Ellen Terry told her son Gordon Craig always to address him in the theatre as "Mr Irving", never "Henry". Craig would later write that the Lyceum days were exciting days, that Irving

---

22 Michael Davies, *The Garrick*, 15 August 2005

would feel keenly hurt if he suspected any of his cast of taking their destiny too lightly, for to him the theatre was a sacred trust. It feels as if he created a family atmosphere in which everyone – actors, carpenters, scene-painters, stage doormen – was engaged in a joint venture (and adventure) from which they would all derive pride and satisfaction.

Even this was a triumphant piece of play-acting on his part, for in truth he was tormented with nervous tension and anxiety before every entrance on stage. He would stand in the wings long before he was due, manifestly troubled and getting worse. It was an ineffaceable trait of his personality to be closed in by melancholia, which rendered him so private a man that he would neither seek nor accept help from anyone; indeed, he would have shrunk with distaste at the very idea. Black moods would descend and grip him in long silences. He was neurotically sensitive and secretly very vulnerable. Probably the only person he really trusted was Ellen Terry, his "Nell", and she alone dared to discuss personal matters with him. It was she who persuaded him not to lurk in the wings like a wary fox waiting to be hunted, but to return to his dressing-room and wait for the call-boy to come. He "never wholly trusted his friends", she wrote, "and never admitted them to his intimacy, although they thought he did."[23]

He was convivial in his reticent, guarded way, and liked occasionally to entertain after the performance in the Beefsteak Room, the former lumber-room up a winding staircase above the stage at the Lyceum, where men and women came by his invitation only. The room was named in memory of the Sublime Society of Beef Steaks, a dining-club which had been formed by John Rich in 1725 and had

---

23 Ellen Terry, *op.cit.*, and in Holroyd, p 122

convened in an irregular fashion ever since (the modern Beefsteak Club, in its present building since 1896, bears the name in recognition of this heritage). But his real comfort was the Garrick, which had moved into its new home in 1864 when the tiny cobbled streets had been swept away and the Committee had commissioned the Metropolitan Clerk of Works, Frederick Marrable, to design a building for us. The splendid Italianate palace which he built (his first) is unchanged, save in small particulars, since then. Like most members from that day to this, Henry Irving *felt* (there is no other verb which will suffice) the welcome and comfort of this place, its easy comradeship and friendliness. It was the one place where he could relax (in his fashion) and talk with unforced interest about matters other than acting. For a man so touchy, so aloof, so visibly austere, the club was solace. Although he could not confide, he could at least share in the atmosphere of the place. If Ellen Terry was right, that he could not trust anyone, he could at least trust in the calm decency of his club.

Nevertheless, the aura of authority which he had contrived in self-protection to assume, made him a creature apart. He would arrive late, at about 11:45 p.m., sometimes alone. A member recalled the effect of his entrance in the Coffee Room with these words: "He would stroll quite unselfconsciously to the desk to order his haddock or kidneys, but I can feel it now as I did then. Literally a hush fell on the room, and every eye at the table, be it young or old, would follow that man from the door to the desk. No other figure of the theatre of that epoch or perhaps of any other would command that."[24] Some have suggested

---

24 Geoffrey Wansell, *The Garrick Club* (2004), p 59, and George Pleydell Bancroft, *Stage and Bar* (1939), p.58

that there was a hidden strain of mischief in him, that he privately enjoyed the fun of inspiring such awe, but I rather fancy it was too important to him, that it mattered too much, for it to be treated as a matter for amusement, however genial. He had worked hard to earn respect for his person, and he would not demean it in frivolity.

Another clue to Irving's private character is afforded by his somewhat surprising degree of generosity, surprising only because it is a quality not generally associated with egocentricity. Everyone at the Lyceum, from call-boys and ushers upwards, was paid well above the usual wage, while he himself drew a modest £60 a week. He was alert to the needs of anyone who fell upon hard times, and would hand out sovereigns to strangers with carefree largesse accompanied by a slight smile. He kept a list of forty retired actors to whom he gave weekly allowances, and would often organise a 'benefit' performance whose proceeds would go largely to a particular member of the company. The point surely was that he was egotistic as far as his art and calling were concerned, and altruistic when dealing with the individual; they are not contradictory impulses, for they move in different directions.

If he was capable of being hurt, it was always at the hands of reviewers and literary men who questioned his abilities. Criticism wounded him severely, especially when it came from people whose intelligence he respected (and probably assumed was more refined than his own). This went especially deep when it touched upon his productions of Shakespearean drama at the Lyceum, then as now a risky, contentious issue. While critics might point out his faults of diction or pose, they were being personal and could be disregarded, but when they derided his handling of the revered canon, they went to the very core of his professional integrity. Bernard Shaw was especially spiteful, saying that he acted "in flat contradiction of the lines, and positively acted Shakespeare off the stage" and recommending that he should be tied up in a sack with the works of Shakespeare and dropped into the nearest volcano in the hope he might finally understand some of them.[25] In more recent times, John Gielgud declared that Irving did a disservice to the poet by "putting his acting between the lines" rather than through them.[26]

In view of the fact that he was inspired to become an actor when, at the age of twelve, he had seen Samuel Phelps on stage, it is odd that he did not follow Phelps' example in purity and economy of style, but chose instead to tamper with the texts, as Macready had done, and make a spectacle of them, as Charles Kean had. His legacy is thereby debatable.

Having made his reputation in melodrama, he sought to consolidate it with the great poetic tragedies and set about revising the so-called 'actable' plays of Shakespeare, of which he determined there were about a dozen. Inevitably, he had to tackle *Hamlet* first and he set about preparing the text for production. It now seems shocking that to do so he cut about 40% of the play, 1,216 lines to be precise, and reduced the twenty scenes Shakespeare had written to thirteen. Fortinbras was chucked out altogether, and the parts of Rosencrantz and Guildenstern were severely curtailed. When playing opposite Isabel Bateman, he had even reduced some of Hamlet's passion for Ophelia, which he restored when Ellen Terry took over the part. As for the

25 The *Saturday Review*, 26 September, 1896
26 Lewis Funke and John Booth, *Actors Talk About Acting* (1961), p 7

prince himself, he was depicted as a thoughtful, pensive young man, a gentleman-scholar not a ranting lunatic, who was "not frightened by the ghost of his father, but exalted; for under his pleasant manner he was working out a devious strategy for revenge. He threw aside his assumed madness in the potent scene with his mother as he assaulted her conscience and appealed for her penitence – revelatory moments to which he brought a terrible earnestness."[27] All this was quite new, and the psychological reality of it held the audience in thrall. If it entailed altering the text, then so be it, for he "valued Shakespeare less as a dramatic poet than as an actor who knew how to provide opportunities for other actors, virtuoso actors, over all time." As Ellen Terry pointed out, "Henry Irving did not go to the audience. He made them come to him."

The only doubts are with hindsight. At the time there was universal, undiluted acclaim for the novelty of Irving's approach to the part. His grandson would write, "Gone were Hamlet's funereal plumes and trappings of woe and the air of pompous melancholy…his bearing and manner were those of a young aristocrat in whom grace and self-assurance were modestly combined. There was nothing to distract the attention from the pale face framed in his own raven curls."[28]   At the end of the first Irving/Terry performance, the audience seemed overwhelmed, as if they had been shown a wholly new play. The only person not convinced was Ellen, who left the theatre as soon as her part was finished and lingered on the Embankment before going home, as she thought she had acted badly. So she was not there to hear the rapturous cheering which

---

27 Holroyd, *op.cit.*, p 110
28 Laurence Irving, *Henry Irving: The Actor and His World* (1951)

greeted Irving as he stepped before the curtain to say that he had worked "all his life for the result that the Lyceum had witnessed that night."

Hamlet ran for two hundred consecutive nights, a run never before achieved in a play by Shakespeare. History was made. The loyal Lady Pollock saw it twenty-one times.

Next came *The Merchant of Venice*, and, once more, a revolutionary interpretation. The standard representation of Shylock as a malignant, sinister, craven villain was discarded in favour of an entirely recognisable human being, a man of some dignity and bearing, respected in Venice and aware of his superiority to the vulgar Christians who scorned him, yet not deigning to respond in kind. Irving's portrayal was of a wounded and humiliated man standing up for decency. To this end, the text had to be slightly adapted, giving more lines to Shylock and less to others, both to place the role at the centre of the play and to appeal to Victorian morality. The result was "the triumph of personal magnetism over plot-line."[29] Still, far fewer cuts were made than had been the case in *Hamlet*.

His reading of the role of Othello was by all accounts pretty bad. He screamed and shouted, was at times incoherent and making little sense of the lines, at others so rapid in delivery that people could not catch what he was saying. He knew it was a failure, tore off his costume in disgust at the end of the run (forty-nine nights) and never played it again. There seems to be no clear explanation of why this part should have defeated him, but it has always been a notorious danger; more than half a century later, Laurence Olivier would come to grief with it at the Old Vic.

---

29 John Gross, *Shylock: Four Hundred Years in the Life of a Legend* (1992)

Irving simplified *Romeo and Juliet* by removing scenes which were extraneous to the main story and concentrated attention on the two main players. Romeo had been the first part he ever played on stage, at the age of eighteen, in a performance for which he had paid for the right to appear (a not unusual convention). Now that he was forty-four, the undertaking carried some risk, and his estranged wife Florence, who continued to attend first nights as the legal spouse, wrote in her diary that he was "awfully funny". Her opinion never bothered him, but presumably he was unaware of this cruel, dismissive sneer.

Malvolio in *Twelfth Night* was yet another role which he transformed to suit his style and talent, making him innocently comic, not malevolent as the name implied. He appeared to want the audience's sympathy. If so, he miscalculated badly, for they were not satisfied with his interpretation at all, and thanked him with a torrent of boos, an experience to which he was no longer accustomed and to which he responded with an angry address before the curtain. When he came to tackle the Herculean part of Lear, as all tragedians eventually must, he studied hard and long, but in performance he missed the pathetic nobility of the man, adding so many grunts and groans and laboursome vocal devices that the audience grew restless and the critics were, well, critical. It was remarkable indeed that this actor's reputation stood so high that it could survive any amount of setbacks or disappointments; Irving seemed impregnable. Everyone agreed, however, that he was right to eliminate the blinding of Gloucester, a scene no Victorian audience would have tolerated. He gave as his reason that "to use things vile and squalid and mean is a debasement of Art", thus encapsulating the Victorian standard very neatly. One would have to wait until the twentieth century to see the horror of Shakespeare's vision finally realised.

As he matured, it was in the grand historical dramas by contemporary playwrights that he excelled and wherein he found roles to suit his hunger for dominance. *The Corsican Brothers* and *The Lady of Lyons* were both in his repertoire, and he prevailed upon fellow club-member Bulwer-Lytton to re-write *Richelieu* for him, so that he could emulate or surpass the memory of Macready's interpretation. This did not seem remotely presumptuous either to him or to the playwright, for it was accepted that history itself should be re-designed if necessary to adapt to Irving's wishes. The theatre of the late nineteenth century still belonged to actors, for whom writers were providers of material. This was never more clear than in the plays which Tennyson wrote for him, especially *Queen Mary* and *Becket*. In the former he played the part of King Phillip II of Spain, which Ellen Terry thought was the best portrayal he ever gave, an assertion of "the power of the actor to create as well as to interpret, for Tennyson does not suggest half of what Henry Irving did." But in everyone else's judgement, Becket was to be the part that immortalised him.

Tennyson delivered the play to Irving in 1879, but it would not be performed until fourteen years later. Irving declared that it was good, but needed extensive reshaping to prepare it for the stage, to which the Poet Laureate happily consented. Then delays and American tours and other productions interfered and the script was set aside. The play was published in 1884, but it was not until eight years later that Irving raised the matter again, and asked Tennyson if he could continue with the changes. Tennyson, already dying, said he trusted Irving to do whatever he liked with it. He died in October 1892, and the play went on at the Lyceum four months later.

In this, Irving rose to the summit of his powers like a man finally grasping the destiny which had been waiting since the promise of *The Bells* had announced it. All his mannerisms and peculiarities evaporated, leaving behind a true and clean portrayal of the priest as he really was, come to life, palpable, credible, real. Never was the proverbial "suspension of disbelief" more appropriate, and the audience summoned the actor in front of the curtain, not at the end, but at every interval. He admitted that no part had brought him so close to his public, or affected him so deeply. Queen Victoria commanded a recital performance in the Waterloo Chamber at Windsor, and afterwards told him that Tennyson would have been very pleased.

Under Henry Irving, the productions at the Lyceum had become major events, and not only because of the actor at the centre of each of them, but also for the sumptuous spectacle they delivered. Irving personally superintended every detail of the sets, the lighting and the music, as well as the direction. He was not just an actor-manager, but an impresario, virtually ruling a kingdom. The time and money devoted to these productions were lavish, with attention to historical verisimilitude which recalled aspects of the obsessional creations which Charles Kean had mounted at the Princess's. Hawes Craven was in charge of scene-painting, and he and Irving selected the greatest artists of the day to design sets, including Edward Burne-Jones and Alma-Tadema. The awe-inspiring final scene of *Romeo and Juliet* in the tomb-vault, designed by William Telbin, was of surpassing beauty as well as evoking a chillingly eerie atmosphere. For his adaptation of Goethe's *Faust* (a travesty according to Shaw, a banal exhibition according to Henry James), Irving called upon the very latest technical advances to summon apparitions from nowhere, force electric sparks to fly across the stage, conjure forth coloured lights and smoke, and altogether create theatrical magic. When W.S. Gilbert was asked if he had seen the production, he replied, "I go to pantomime only at Christmas."

William Archer, who had earlier derided Irving's mixture of phoney scholarship and flashy effects, was eventually bound to allow that he "has the art of inspiring to the verge of genius his scenic artists and machinists...There rises to the mind a whole gallery of scenic pictures, each as worthy of minute study as any canvas of the most learned archaeological painter."[30] His reach extended to the music as well, transforming a small troupe of players into an orchestra of thirty-five musicians, and commissioning composers of such renown as Arthur Sullivan to provide incidental music. Almost £50,000 was spent on music while Irving controlled the Lyceum, which would be about £3 million today.

That Irving's taste was old-fashioned, not visionary, is confirmed by his wilful neglect of Ibsen and Shaw, whose plays he refused to countenance in his theatre; he did not understand them, and saw no quality in their intimate and subtle, rather than grandiloquent drama. But what is truly surprising is his rejection of a play by his own very close friend and business-manager Bram Stoker. One might have thought *Dracula* had all the ingredients he would desire, but still he could not discern them. Stoker was bitterly

---

30 William Archer, *Henry Irving, Actor and Manager* (1883)

disappointed. Nor had he any interest in going to see performances by other actors, and once, when prevailed upon to watch his own son in a play, he delivered the awful snub of not bothering to go backstage afterwards to see him. Actors dread that sign of disapproval more than any heckling, because it is personal.

Such behaviour is all the more surprising when one considers Irving's high regard for the status of the theatre in civilised society, a status he had done more than anyone to elevate. By the 1890s, people who would not have permitted themselves to be seen in a theatre a generation earlier, including peers of the realm, judges, bishops and cabinet ministers, regularly patronised the Lyceum and treated Irving as an equal. The fact is, he professed enormous respect for the acting profession as a whole, and less for actors in particular. Addressing the Royal Institution in 1895, he spoke on behalf of the profession, and not for himself, when he said, "official recognition of anything worthy is a good, or at least a useful thing. It is a part, and an important part, of the economy of the State: if it is not, of what use are titles and distinctions, names, badges, offices, in fact all the titular and sumptuary ways of distinction?" Bernard Shaw craftily detected what lay beneath all this in a typically frank paraphrase. "What Mr Irving means us to answer is this question: The artist who composed the music for King Arthur [a pageant recently shown at the Lyceum] is Sir Arthur Sullivan; the artist who composed the poem which made King Arthur known to this generation died Lord Tennyson; the artist who designed the suit of armour worn by King Arthur is Sir Edward Burne-Jones; why should the artist who plays King

Arthur be only Mister Henry Irving?"[31] Shaw further said, with supreme and laudable honesty, that one owed Irving "an unhesitating assumption that his jealousy is for the dignity of his art and not of himself."

What was here being suggested was entirely without precedent. Although it had been known that Macready secretly hankered after a knighthood and that Charles Kean had curried favour at Court in the vain hope of such a reward, neither would have dared to publicly propose such a thing, and it would surely have been refused anyway, with some lofty disdain, too. Twelve years earlier the matter had been unofficially raised by Gladstone on behalf of Irving, only to be vetoed by members of his Cabinet because the actor had left his wife and formed a close connection with Ellen Terry, herself the mother of two illegitimate children (Lady Salisbury pointed out that "she was *never* immoral, only rather illegal."). But now the time was ripe.

Lord Rosebery, the new Prime Minister, sent a letter to Irving to inform him that the Queen proposed to confer upon him the dignity of a knighthood. News travelled fast, and crowds assembled at the Lyceum to hear a congratulatory address signed by four thousand members of the acting profession, written by Arthur Pinero (a Garrick member) and read aloud from the stage by Squire Bancroft (another Garrick member). In accepting, Irving gravely, but with a choke, said that "in olden times our Britons showed their appreciation of a comrade by lifting him on their shoulders, and I cannot but feel, and feel it with an unspeakable pride, that you, my brothers in our art, have lifted me on your shields. There is no more honour to come to the life of a man so raised."

---

31 Donaldson, *op.cit.*, p 93

Irving went to Windsor Castle on 18 July, 1895. Max Beerbohm happened to be crossing the street at Marble Arch when he spotted the brougham carrying Irving to the railway station. "His hat was tilted at more than its usual angle, and his long cigar seemed longer than ever; and on his face was a look of such ruminant, sly fun as I have never seen equalled."[32] The Queen herself seemed to appreciate the delicious piquancy of the occasion when she departed from traditional practise to tell him, "It gives me great pleasure, sir." It soon became clear that the first theatrical knight would not use his honour as if it were a personal right; he might in society be Sir Henry, but on the stage he was first and always an actor, therefore plain Henry Irving. It was an example to be followed by all subsequent knights of the theatre, whose titles do not appear on billboards.

Two of the actors who appeared with him on stage would inherit different aspects of his legacy. Johnston Forbes-Robertson and William Terriss were both in the Lyceum production of *Henry VIII*, and Terriss played a major role in *Becket* as well as giving a fine youthful interpretation of Romeo and touring with Irving's company in America. Terriss remained at the Lyceum for five years, before moving to the Adelphi, where he played in a vastly popular series of melodramas, mirroring the earliest Irving style. He was probably the first "matinee idol" with his sharply handsome face and manly demeanour, was "beloved by all who knew him" and "conveyed to his audience a feeling of joyousness which was quite infectious".[33] He became the victim of an absurd tragedy in 1897.

As he arrived at the stage-door of the Adelphi he was

---

32 Max Beerbohm, *Around Theatres* (1953)
33 Johnston Forbes-Robertson, *A Player Under Three Reigns*, pp 116-117

attacked and stabbed to death by a deranged fellow-actor, Richard Prince, who had been fired for heavy drinking and lurked around the West End pubs thereafter. Terriss had recommended him as deserving aid from the Actors' Benevolent Fund, and Prince had turned up at their offices demanding money. On being informed that his case would be considered at a council meeting the following day, he sunk into an incredulous rage and waited for William Terriss to arrive at the stage-door. Prince was subsequently tried at the Old Bailey, declared insane and sent to Broadmoor.[34]

That same year, Forbes-Robertson made his first appearance as Hamlet, marking another milestone in theatrical history, for this Hamlet was universally accounted to be flawless. Never before had the poetry and music of Shakespeare's words been so beautifully conveyed, and not before John Gielgud's interpretation would the exquisite voice of this actor find an equal. It is significant that Forbes-Robertson had worked with Phelps before his five years with Irving, and it was Phelps who left the more enduring influence upon him by virtue of his having regarded Forbes-Robertson as his pupil.

William Terriss never did become a member of the Garrick, but Forbes-Robertson was elected in 1888 and remained a popular member for just short of fifty years.

With the turn of the century, Irving's formidable strength was failing, after years of strenuous activity and intense concentration in full pubic view. His heart weakened and he suffered from minor fatigue, then major collapse. In 1905 he summoned the power to appear as Becket at Drury Lane, despite obvious difficulty. Word went around

---

34 Philip Lowrie, *Actors' Benevolent Fund: A Short History* (2002), p 7

London that Sir Henry Irving was in the process of dying in front of his public, slowly, surely, sadly, night after night. Feeble and quiet in the wings, as soon as he gained centre-stage the old magic returned and the blood coursed through his veins to buoy him up and carry him through. Truly, the theatre was his home, more so than the place where he slept or the club where he dined with friends. The audience knew it, too, and they cheered and shouted their love at him with standing ovations every night. They could scarcely believe what they were witnessing, and willed it not to happen.

Afterwards, he went to Bradford, where he gave a final performance of *The Bells* in which, his grandson would report, it was "an agony to watch him". He sent the stage-sets back to London the following day in sober and rueful acknowledgement that he would not need them ever again. Then he played his favourite role of Becket, which appeared to go well until the final words, which rang out with uncanny firmness as Becket died: "into Thy Hands, oh Lord, into Thy Hands!" He stumbled, clearly exhausted, and collapsed into the arms of Gerald Lawrence (Garrick Member). Helped into a cab, he arrived at the Midland Hotel, where he immediately called for a chair as he entered. It was a small wooden chair without arms. He slumped on to it, then lost consciousness and slid to the floor. He was dead just minutes after leaving the stage for the last time.

The population of Bradford turned out to salute his coffin as it went through the streets to the railway-station, men raising their hats in silence. In London, the noble columns at the portico of the Lyceum Theatre were draped in black, and everywhere flags hung at half-mast, as if for royalty.

Ellen Terry was appearing at the Gaiety, Manchester, in a play called *Alice Sit-by-the-Fire*, in the closing scene of which she had to say, "I had a beautiful husband once, black as the raven was his hair…" She faltered, choked, was overcome and broke down utterly. The curtain descended, and the audience filed out in silence, feeling they had intruded upon a private sorrow.[35]

Irving received the ultimate accolade of being interred in Westminster Abbey. The funeral cortège passed through crowded streets to muffled drums, a performance too poignant to bear for many who were there. All the ushers in the Abbey were fellow-actors. The coffin (symbolic rather than real for it contained his ashes, not his corpse) was borne by fourteen pall-bearers, including Forbes-Robertson, Squire Bancroft, John Hare, Charles Wyndham, George Alexander and Beerbohm Tree, and it was accompanied by a cross sent by Queen Alexandra. Two French actors came from the Comédie Française in Paris and knelt beside the coffin as flowers were strewn. In an unprecedented gesture still mentioned today as part of London's unique character, the city's cab-drivers tied black ribbons to their whips.

More than all these tributes, from the highest to the lowest, there was one which would have broken even Henry Irving's aloof, lonely reticence and caused him to weep. The news of his death had been given on a telegram to Beerbohm Tree at the Garrick Club where he was dining. His sober look passed by osmosis from person to person and from room to room, whereupon everyone, wordless, left his meal on the table and walked out of the club in

---

35 James Agate, *Ego I* (1935-1948), p 146

solemn silence. Without Henry Irving, the building was indeed better left empty.

The chair on which he died is now on the second landing of the great staircase.

6

ACTOR - MANAGERS

Irving was such a colossus that he cast a shadow to all but obliterate everyone else, so that it comes as a surprise in the present chapter to discover that the other great actor-managers of his ilk did not follow in his wake, but were his contemporaries. Squire Bancroft, John Hare, Herbert Beerbohm Tree, Frank Benson, George Alexander, Charles Wyndham, were all working at the same time as Irving, were all reaping the rewards of the liberation of 1843, with different emphases and opposing styles, and would all leave a mark on theatrical history the ripples of which are still felt. And, of course, they were all Garrick Club members.

It is fair to say that none of them was stamped with the same melodramatic flair which made Irving unique, but some of them shared that exigent egocentricity which exuded from actor-managers like steam, while others established a milder, gentler influence which changed the habits of play-going. That colourful combination of austerity, vulgarity, flamboyance, fear and a makeshift kind of glamour somewhat subsided, to erupt once more a generation later with the intemperate genius of Donald Wolfit, but the need to control and dictate remained. They were no longer despots, for the most part, but retained that right to make all the decisions as to choice of repertoire, assignment of roles and staging, to themselves. They were essentially impresarios. And yet they were also subservient to the theatre as art although, with the sybaritic indulgences of the Edwardian era, they were less ready to embrace an existence of privation in obedience to it. In his play *The Dresser*, Ronald Harwood has "Sir" tell an ambitious young actress who begs him for a job, "You must be prepared to sacrifice what most people call life."

The actor-managers of the previous era had condemned themselves and their wives to a existence of touring the provincial circuits, living in miserable "digs" with breakfast and supper prepared by the landlady, packing every week, travelling around the country in draughty trains, rarely having a chance to go home (if home there was), making do and surviving. There was precious little of luxury in such a life, and much of hard drudge. When the notice went up in a provincial theatre to announce the arrangements for the company to move on to the next date on Sunday, it would soon become necessary to stipulate "no brown-paper bags on train-call" in order to encourage actors to invest in a suitcase. The actor-manager took the leading role in every play, and his wife as often as not took the female lead. Other parts were handed out to actors who specialised in their own 'stock' character, such as *The Heavy*, *The Female Heavy*, *The Old Man*, *The Juvenile Lead*, *The Light Comedian*, *The Low Comedian*, *The Ingénue*, and even smaller parts as *The Walking Gentleman*, and *The General Utility*. The schedule was punishing, the emotional effort exhausting. But if it were not for the actor-manager, the audiences of little theatres dotted throughout the land would never have experienced the magic of a theatrical performance. He was a hero of sorts.

The new breed, however, which rose to prominence after the noble pioneering work of Phelps and in tandem with the soaring spark of Irving, ushered in a wholly novel way of describing a theatrical experience. And none was more revolutionary than Squire Bancroft, the utter antithesis of Irving in every particular.

Squire (originally Sidney) Bancroft was the son of the impoverished widow of an unremarkable gentleman. As a child, his toys were theatres, and as a young man he went as often as he could to see whatever was playing. He was still young when his mother died, upon which he decided to be an actor himself. Starting in Birmingham with the obligatory melodramas, he played in one season alongside Phelps, who had just given up his long management at Sadler's Wells, then went on to Dublin and Devonport. Charles Kean saw him in Dublin and personally sought him out for praise. His destiny was sealed the following year when in Liverpool he met the burlesque company from London which included Marie Wilton, who had been on the stage since the age of four and had been much admired as a child actress by Charles Dickens, and a personable young man called John Hare. The three of them would shortly join forces. Bancroft would marry Miss Wilton, and give Mr Hare the parts which would make his name.

Marie Wilton had very recently taken the bold step of becoming a manager herself. Borrowing £1000 capital, she had taken a lease on the Queen's Theatre in Tottenham Street, off the Tottenham Court Road, which had fallen into such disrepute that it was commonly known as "the

Dusthole". It looked like the rashest possible decision, doomed to certain failure on such a spot with such an audience. But this was a brave young woman with a good sense of 'public relations'. She took possession of the theatre one month in advance, then scooped out the seats and replaced them with brand-new ones as well as redecorating the entire place. She turned the Dusthole into a place of comfort and desirability, and renamed it the Prince of Wales. Two years later Bancroft became her leading actor and co-lessee (replacing the playwright H.J. Byron), and they married in 1867. Together they continued with the clever "sprucing-up" of the theatre, putting in carpets and calm, warm colours, and turning it into a cosy, small place where middle-class families could go for an evening's entertainment without embarrassment. "Thus they laid the foundations for the change in status of the theatre which was to take place over the next twenty years."[1]

The next innovation lay in the Bancroft's choice of repertoire, which was based almost entirely for the first few years upon the comedies of Tom Robertson, whose sister would become the actress Madge Kendal. Robertson's plays were not so much lightweight as weightless, and other managers had declined to mount them at all; Henry James would loftily describe them as "infantile". But the point was they were a delightful novelty, full of froth rather than fury, easy to digest, easy to perform in an intimate style without bombast, and a sure vehicle for the talents of light comedy actors, of whom none was better than Hare, soon to be renowned for his assumption of a variety of eccentric "character" parts. Robertson specifically fought

1 Frances Donaldson, *The Actor-Managers* (1970), p 33

to deliver the stage from those rigid "stock" characters which had had to be represented by actors in a pre-orchestrated manner with the correct grimace and the proper growl; he gave instructions to banish them. "No tragedy, no tears, no pocket-handkerchief" is an example of his sensible stage-directions. The characters he created were not two-dimensional, either 'good' or 'evil', but often ambiguous in a way that the intellectual Henry James would not recognise. We owe to the much-mocked Tom Robertson the cleaner, more credible stage manner which we nowadays take for granted, and to the Bancrofts the determination to promote it.

There was always the risk that the public might welcome the new style only to tire of it quickly, but the Bancrofts took the view that danger was better than dullness, an illustration of that freedom of action which is the reward for the actor-manager's assumption of total responsibility. As Hesketh Pearson remarked, "In art, the daring of an individual is preferable to the discretion of a committee."[2]

They put on six of Robertson's plays: - *Society, Ours* (about the Crimean War), *Caste* (about class difference), *Play* (about gambling), *School,* and *M.P.,* now all totally forgotten. Yet they were reliable, well-made, and very popular, and the Bancrofts had the foresight to withdraw them even when they were doing well, so as to excite the appetite for their revival a few months later.

Apart from décor and seating and repertoire, the Bancrofts introduced the matinée performance, which has been almost *de rigueur* at every theatre ever since, and a stark but simple realism in stage furnishings. The rugs on the floor were real rugs, the oak panelling was real

2 Hesketh Pearson, *The Last Actor-Managers* (1950), p vi

oak, the crockery was real china, and the bread and butter consumed on the set was bread and butter. This attention to intimate detail gave body to plots which were thin to say the least and reassurance to audiences that such stories could really happen. When they came to mount *The Merchant of Venice* they applied the same principles, travelling to Venice with their scene-painters to capture the right colours and accurate style with the result, as Squire Bancroft himself said, that "it all looked so unlike a theatre and so much more like old Italian pictures than anything that had previously been shown upon the stage." Those in the audience with especially good eyesight might make out the gold leaf on the interior of arches above Venetian windows.

This was in 1875, some twenty years since Charles Kean's sumptuous staging of the same play, and in their smaller theatre the magnificence did not quite succeed. The part of Portia in this production was played by Ellen Terry, *before* her long partnership with Irving, and she always maintained that it was this part in this production which changed her life and drew forth her commitment; it was also at her suggestion that her lover and father of her children E. W. Godwin was engaged to design the sets, so meticulously rendered.

In their production of *The School for Scandal*, on the other hand, this approach to stage property was entirely appropriate for an interior comedy. They went to Knole to get ideas for the furniture, draperies and pictures for Lady Sneerwell's drawing-room, they hung a real chandelier in Sir Peter Teazle's house and placed a real Turkish carpet in Chares Surface's room. The books on the shelves were bound in genuine Russian leather, Lady Teazle wore satin and diamonds and was escorted by a page who was genuinely black (and stayed as a guest of the Bancrofts during the run). The sense of comfort made the comedy even more delicious and believable. What might have been merely fussy was, in theatrical effect, a stroke of genius.

It was above all in their attitude towards actors as highly qualified people that the Bancrofts made their most cherished innovation, assuring another great leap in the long progress from despised members of the lower ranks to respected, and finally revered, men and women in the highest *échelons* of society. That leap was to raise them from players to professionals, and this through the simple medium of affording them a decent income. Until Bancroft's time, actors were paid disgustingly low wages, and were often reduced to starvation; both Phelps and Irving had in their early struggles to snatch crumbs where they could find them and repair clothes which had long been worn out. There was the further disgrace of the 'benefit' system, by which the profits of one performance on a particular night was given for the 'benefit' of one actor, who could choose which play he wished to use for this purpose. The system was hit-and-miss, because the 'benefit' performance for a Macready or an Edmund Kean would bring in a larger audience and bigger profits than that for an unknown supporting actor, but it was widespread and abused, excusing managements from providing a living wage. Bancroft abolished this egregious custom, and then went one better.

It had been perfectly normal for the actors to line up outside the manager's office on a Saturday morning, alongside the cleaners and the call-boys, to collect their wages. Bancroft saw this as intolerably humiliating, and his first reform on becoming an actor-manager, before all the others, was to have the actors' salaries delivered to them by messenger in their dressing-rooms. Moreover, it was a good salary, up to three times the usual rate. The consequence of this was that his fellow-actors felt proud of their work and formed a happy and loyal band. He then gave them the unheard-of luxury of wardrobes in their dressing-rooms.

John Hare, who had played in all the Robertson comedies and was Sir Peter Teazle in *The School for Scandal*, eventually left the Prince of Wales and formed his own company at the Court. It says much for the good humour and sweet nature of both the Bancrofts that this was not seen as a rupture, but rather an encouragement, despite Hare taking with him the style and experience of his years at the Prince of Wales. They knew that there was room for both and did not fear rivalry; times had indeed changed. Hare later went on to become leading actor at the St James's (which he managed in partnership with the Kendals) and at the new Garrick Theatre, and to create the title-role in Pinero's *The Gay Lord Quex*.

Meanwhile Squire Bancroft acquired the lease of the Haymarket Theatre and embarked upon his last and most robust reform. He demolished the interior of the theatre and rebuilt it entirely, making it luxurious and glamorous, with comfortable soft seats. He also got rid of the pit and removed the cheaper tickets to the top of the auditorium, then placed the orchestra under the stage. The stage was set inside a gigantic gilded frame, like a glorious picture, adding a feeling of glow to the spectacle. This is essentially the theatre which is known and appreciated so widely today. Within it, he put on revivals of his Robertson successes, as well as Sheridan and Bulwer-Lytton, and achieved such success that he made a sizeable fortune, a unique achievement at the time. And all this without being greedy, grand, or difficult. Six years later, in 1885, he retired, while Irving was in mid-flow of his fame at the Lyceum. Bancroft, Hare and Irving were all fellow-members of the club by this time, but it is odd to reflect that Hare had been the first of the three to be elected, in 1868, and Bancroft the second, in 1869, both of them before London had even heard of Henry Irving; retrospective renown does play tricks with our perception of relative worth.

After his retirement he once appeared on stage with Irving at the Lyceum in a play called *The Dead Heart*. "What a big name you might have made for yourself had you never come across those Robertson plays", said Irving to him on that occasion. "What a pity, for your own sake; for no actor can be remembered long who does not appear in the classical drama."[3] That was the theatre as seen through Irving's eyes; he was blind to the new kind of theatre as seen through Bancroft's signal achievements.

The Bancrofts were seen at first nights in London for thirty years afterwards, she a little Victorian pigeon, he a mighty leonine figure in top-hat and cane and cascading white hair. Though known as manager more than actor, Squire Bancroft never stopped acting off-stage for the rest of his life. He was knighted in 1897, two years after Irving, as was John Hare in 1907.

Another actor-manager thriving at more or less the same time, with another style altogether, was Herbert Beerbohm Tree. His particular attraction was most deftly pinned by Richard Huggett when comparing him to Irving. "The

---

3 quoted in Donaldson, pp 30-31

difference between the acting of Irving and that of Tree",
he wrote, "was the difference between hypnotism and
enchantment."[4] Indeed, there is some evidence that Irving
watched the rise of Tree's popularity with apprehension,
aware that the enchantment could threaten his own
ascendancy.

Beerbohm Tree's power to bewitch arose from two
parallel sources; first, his ability to create magic in the
theatre with an excess of ornament and beauty which
took audiences back to their childhood, or perhaps took
them with him back to *his* childhood dreams; second, the
obvious exuberant fun and delight which he derived from
acting, performing, being on stage, or merely passing by
the theatre and smelling the whiff of excitement which
emanated from the stage-door. His joy was infectious, his
rhapsodic devotion to his theatre handsomely shared with
his audiences.

The most magnificently indulgent of his productions
came in the latter part of his career when he mounted
several of Shakespeare's plays at Her Majesty's Theatre as
if they were glorious kaleidoscopic pictures for him to play
with, and each one became a major event in itself. The
opening scene of *The Tempest* featured a real ship rocking
on a violent sea of waves which splashed over the deck
and made some spectators feel sea-sick. A scene in *The
Winter's Tale* included a waterfall, a willow-tree, a stream,
reeds, a convincing country cottage which seemed to have
been transplanted from Warwickshire. As King Richard II
Tree rode across the stage on horseback, an occurrence to
which Shakespeare merely alludes in reported speech in
the mouth of the Duke of York. The wood of *A Midsummer*

---

4 Richard Huggett, *The Truth About Pygmalion* (1969), p 60

Night's Dream had real rabbits scampering across the stage, presumably immune to rehearsal. He loved the spectacle of great crowd scenes, even when they included animals; during the run of *Joseph and His Brethren*, the street outside the stage-door was packed with asses, camels, donkeys, goats, oxen, sheep, all to conjure up the spirit of a real Palestine. In Stephen Phillips' *Nero*, Tree drove a chariot pulled by two milk-white steeds, and the burning of Rome was so realistic, with houses and temples swaying, then crashing to the ground, and flames shooting up to engulf the lot, that anxious people in the stalls looked for the nearest exit, just in case. The production of *Julius Caesar*, in which Tree played Antony, was the most sumptuous ever seen, with scenery and costumes by Alma-Tadema.

As for the effects he wrought with stage-machinery, the best account is given by Hesketh Pearson, who witnessed many of them. "Just before his entrance in *Macbeth*", he wrote, "there was a long roll of thunder, a roar of wind and a rattle of hail; the darkness was suddenly pierced by blinding flashes of lightning, in which one could see rocks falling and a stout oak-tree, rent to the roots, toppling to the earth; following this the elements howled invisibly for a space; then came an ear-splitting peal of thunder, a final shriek of the blast, and against the dazzling background of a lightning-riven sky stood the figure of Macbeth. Then Shakespeare got a look-in. Emerging from the theatre after one of these stage-quaking exhibitions into a real thunderstorm, one had to admit that Nature put up a pretty feeble imitation of what several barrels of stones and a few sheets of tin could do in Her Majesty's."[5] To those who grumbled that such display was meretricious (and there

---

5 Pearson, *op.cit.*, p 13

were some), Beerbohm Tree said that people who did not like theatrical illusion need not go to the theatre. "The bookworm always has his book."[6]

Tree understood that essential component of the theatrical experience which is make-believe, and his enthusiastic embrace of it was exhilarating to behold. He was in himself a demonstration of that hackneyed attribute to be "in love with" the theatre. In his case it was true. He revelled in it, threw himself into it with flair and fun, and made everyone else wonder at the delicious pleasure it afforded him. Nor did he seek to hide it, excuse it, or explain it. It was his extraordinary charm to be what the French call *"bien dans sa peau."* He would not have wanted to be anyone else, and would not spare a second to envy or emulate Irving. Once when an acquaintance greeted him getting out of a cab with "How are you, Mr Tree?" he shook the man's hand, looked around him, and said, "I? Oh, I'm radiant." The man later said that such a remark from any other man would have sounded ridiculous, but with Tree it was merely accurate. "He looked radiant, it was obvious that he felt radiant, and he told the simple truth in saying that he *was* radiant."[7]

It accords totally with this apparently whimsical, absent-minded happiness that Tree never bothered to rehearse himself or his cast with any thoroughness. In fact, rehearsals were chaotic, and likely to terminate without decisions because, even if Tree made them, he would forget them immediately. Were one of the cast to make a sarcastic suggestion for improvement in staging, he would jump upon it as a terrific idea, for he entirely lacked the

6 quoted in Donaldson, p 162
7 Max Beerbohm, quoted in Donaldson, p 145

taste to distinguish invention from absurdity. The cast would often turn up for opening night not quite sure of what was going to happen, for Tree was quite capable of throwing in a bit of 'business' on the spur of the moment, then forgetting he had done so. There is a story that he once demonstrated outside the stage-door how he swept the crown from his head as King John in his death-scene by taking his hat off there and then and discarding it. In the next instant, he spied it in the gutter and exclaimed, "Whose hat is that?"[8] His daughter Viola said gleefully that he was "a never-failing excitement, a surprise, an event", and one can sense what she means.

In keeping with his cavalier attitude towards rehearsal, Tree maintained that he had no technique, and did not want to have any, for he would hate to give the same performance again and again as if by rote. "When a performance is fixed, it ceases to live", he claimed, and is variously reported to have said that technique "destroys the inspiration so dreadfully" or "enslaves the imagination." That's the cardinal word, for Beerbohm Tree's performances were magnificent structures of his imagination. In this he was an actor of the Romantic tradition, big, grandiose, not rule-bound. His insights into the characters he portrayed informed the way in which he interpreted them, and this could be subtly different with each performance, as he hurled himself into the role anew, as if for the first time. On the positive side, this enabled his performances to retain freshness and vigour, to tap the immediate emotional reality of the part *at that moment* rather than in preparation, which made him a wholly different performer from Irving, who meticulously practised every move until

---

8 Forbes-Robertson, *op. cit.*, p 230

he got it right, then did it the same way on each occasion. When Tree got it right, it was momentous; when he got it wrong, it might seem silly. But it was always spontaneous. On the negative side, it meant that attention to the actual words to be spoken was less than total, and he would resort to scribbling prompts on bits of paper which were hidden all over the stage – on the backs of chairs, under lamps, beside doors, behind curtains. This kept him on his toes. If he ever referred to a production as "an obstinate success", it usually meant he was getting fed up with it.

Refusing to impose an interpretation upon the character from the outside, Tree would find the character from within, allowing his imagination to work upon the props and costumes until he *felt* he was who he was supposed to be. He liked nothing better than dressing up, for that was his route into the character he was to impersonate. *Klade machen leute*, wrote Heinrich Böll many years later – "clothes maketh the man." This was never more true than with Beerbohm Tree, who transformed himself with costume and make-up gradually to become somebody else, by instinctual identification, rather than by practise. He may well have surprised himself each time, and be delighted by the result. George Arthur wrote that "he could alter the shape of his head as easily as he could rearrange his features."[9] When he announced that he would play the title role in a now-forgotten play called *Beethoven*, his colleagues were apprehensive, for Tree was a tall, looming man, with presence, and Beethoven had been short, shaggy and stocky. Yet when he first appeared in costume at the dress-rehearsal, the company gasped in surprise, for he had managed to turn himself into a different shape. Time

---

9 Sir George Arthur, *From Phelps to Gielgud* (1936), p 134

and again one reads that audiences were amazed at these metamorphoses. And yet, in a way, they were all still Tree having fun; "even when he was hopelessly miscast Tree's acting was so clever, so inventive, so varied, so intensely interesting, that for unalloyed entertainment one would rather see him in a bad play than anyone else in a good one."[10]

In further confirmation of both his love for the theatre and his lack of selfishness, Tree surrounded himself with the best actors he could find, quite happy to be acted off the stage by them if they were good, and never concerned about keeping himself in the spotlight. He was generous to work with, even if his inventions and sudden changes made the rest of the cast nervous.

Herbert Beerbohm Tree's first experience of management was at the Comedy Theatre only a few years after his début as an actor. He had come from unlikely beginnings, the son of a grain merchant, and his half-brother was Max Beerbohm, equally flamboyant though more cerebral than intuitive. It was said that Herbert took the surname Tree after being told that the acting profession was no good as a career unless you could get to the top of it. This is precisely what he proceeded to do, with much acumen. He moved to the Haymarket, taking over management there two years after the Bancrofts left, where his place in theatrical history was assured by some notable productions, including the première presentation of Wilde's *A Woman of No Importance*, in which he played Lord Illingworth as if he were Oscar Wilde himself, and then a lively version of *The Merry Wives of Windsor* in which he played Falstaff with gusto. It was very quickly to become one of his best

---

10 Pearson, *op.cit.*, p 15

parts, despite Shaw's withering judgement that he might as well have tried playing Juliet. Critics commented that the portrayal was really of Tree in Falstaff's clothes, but they did not allow for the fact that, with his idiosyncratic style, he would develop it with each performance and eventually become more Falstaff than Falstaff.

He also added the obligatory Hamlet to his list, and came perhaps to regret it. He was hardly the kind of actor to play a ruminative philosopher prince, and his quicksilver imagination drove him into a piece of 'business' which was not only extraneous to the play but absurd to the characterisation. After Hamlet's scene with Ophelia in which he insults her so deeply as to promote her madness, he stole back on stage, unseen by her, to kiss a tress of her hair. It was ridiculous and no doubt made up on the spur of the moment by his irrepressible inventiveness. W.S. Gilbert famously said that he never saw anything so funny in his life, though he allowed that it was, somehow, "not vulgar".

However, Beerbohm Tree was also a man of courage. He could have sought refuge in easy and safe plays as many others had, adaptations of French farce being the most secure, but instead he turned to that dark, brooding dramatist from Norway whom nobody else would touch, Ibsen. He was the first to dare put on *An Enemy of the People*, himself taking the taxing role of Dr Stockman, the man of soaring naïve honesty isolated in a society of liars, and gave a performance of great dignity and truth. This part illustrated Tree's strengths and weaknesses alike, for he understood the character in his usual manner of gradually assuming his skin and feeling the man's hurt and frustration from the inside, but he also cluttered the action with some quite unnecessary extra business to liven it up; fortunately, most of this was discarded in later performances, leaving the kernel clean and vivid. At first, he ventured only a matinée, but this being well received, he gave many evening performances afterwards, earning the respect of intelligent playgoers who had been denied this harsh Nordic vision of corruption in public life.

In 1895 the whole company from the Haymarket went on tour in America. While he was in Philadelphia there was playing at another theatre a dramatised version of George du Maurier's novel *Trilby*, and reports of its theme and success intrigued him. He later managed to see the play for himself in New York, and in a demonstration of his flair for spotting theatrical gold, he left his box at the end of the second act and immediately bought the English rights from the man who had written the adaptation, Paul Potter. That same year he staged the play in London and established at a stroke what would become a legendary addition to the dramatic lexicon. (1895 was already something of a landmark year for the London theatre, with the first night of *The Importance of Being Earnest* at the St James's, and Irving's historic knighthood).

Trilby is the story of a young lady who is blessed with the natural voice of a great singer, but who cannot sing a single note in tune. Under the tutelage of Svengali, who fortunately is a hypnotist as well as a musician, she is taught how to use her gifts professionally and becomes a world-famous soprano, her talent acclaimed by all. But she is Svengali's creature, and that kind of supernatural influence has entered the language with his name. The girl was played by the eighteen year-old Dorothea Baird, and Svengali by Beerbohm Tree. It was the part he was born to play, for it made full use of his uncanny ability to alter his appearance. Hesketh Pearson wrote about it with wonder. "While Irving used to spend an hour or more to make himself look like another edition of Irving," he said, "Tree transformed himself completely in ten minutes. Yet, though the Svengali disguise was remarkable, the performance was an epitome of Treeisms: the quick slinking walk, the flashing eyes, the hand on hip, the fluttering fingers, the foreign gestures, the slightly guttural accents: in this part even his faults were turned into virtues, and the total mesmeric effect, as if Trilby's singing entirely resulted from Svengali's power, was a triumph of suggestion."[11]

The resounding success of *Trilby* made Tree's fortune, and enabled him to fulfil a yearning ambition. Opposite the Haymarket Theatre had been a derelict old opera house only recently demolished. The fact that the original theatre on this site had been designed by Vanbrugh appealed to Tree's romantic nature, and he had long wanted to acquire the site and build his own theatre. Now he was able to do just that. The house he built was elegant and beautiful, with the atmosphere of magical expectation which Tree carried in his own heart, and he named it Her Majesty's. It is there that he created those marvellous Shakespearean productions with which we opened this account, and it made him supremely happy. I suspect that it was here that he described himself as "radiant". Frances Donaldson says this theatre "became not merely the scene of his creative triumphs, the spur of his ambition, but his solace from pain, his refuge from society, and at times his home."[12] Donaldson also quotes the touching account his daughter

11 Hesketh Pearson, *Beerbohm Tree: His Life and Laughter* (1956)
12 Donaldson, *op.cit.*, p 160

Viola gave of her wedding-day. Sitting gowned and veiled in the carriage on her way to church with her father, he turned to her suddenly in Regent Street and said, "Will you drive me down to the theatre first, dear?" "And so at the stage-door I, the bride, sat watching his beloved figure – flamboyant coat-tails, hat, stick and all – vanish through the swing doors, only to return a few minutes later having found out that all was well. I was so glad afterwards, as it would not have seemed natural for me to be driving with him and not to stop there." One senses that he simply wanted to touch the walls.

At Her Majesty's Tree created his second immortal role as Professor Higgins in Shaw's *Pygmalion* with the wilful and irresistible Mrs Patrick Campbell as Eliza Doolittle. Typically, he tried to improve the part by adding bits of his own invention – a limp and a Scottish accent for example – exasperating Shaw who told him roundly to stick to the character he had created and leave it unmolested. It also afforded a priceless example of Tree's absent-mindedness. There was a scene in which Eliza, in a tantrum, throws his slippers at Higgins. When Mrs Pat duly did as the script demanded, and hit Tree squarely on the jaw, he was dumb-founded and looked genuinely hurt, as if she had intended some spite (she could, after all, drive her fellow-actors screaming from the theatre on occasion). Tree had absolutely forgotten that they had done this in rehearsal, and so on stage his mind was fresh, empty of expectations.

He went too far when, some time into the run, he altered the ending to enable him to fall in love with Eliza before the curtain falls, and was mystified when the playwright did not seem pleased. "My ending makes money, you ought to be grateful", he said, to which Shaw retorted, "Your ending makes nonsense, you ought to be shot."[13]

Perhaps the most heart-warming evening Tree ever achieved at Her Majesty's was a new production of *The Merry Wives of Windsor*, which he had previously mounted at the Haymarket. This time he enticed Ellen Terry and Madge Kendal to appear with him, as Mistress Page and Mistress Ford respectively, which was quite a *coup* as the two actresses had a hearty dislike for one another. The idea was suggested as a joke by the actor Oscar Asche, who had just joined the company and would one day make history at this theatre with his own fantasy *Chu-Chin-Chow*, playing without interruption for five years. If so, Tree saw that the casting would be triumphant, and Ellen Terry, by then fifty-five, gave what her son Gordon Craig said was the best work of her career. Hesketh Pearson wrote that the three of them romped through the play like children, and it was evident that they were having the time of their lives. The sheer exuberance of the production cheered the audience as seldom before, and one can see it captured in John Collier's huge and wonderful painting of the last scene (my own favourite picture in the club).

One can also see in photographs that Tree's portrayal of Fagin in an adaptation of *Oliver Twist* caught the shifty wickedness of the character to perfection, in another opportunity for impossible transformation. It also showed how, despite his disdain for technique interfering with the soul of acting, he sometimes knew how to make an audience hold its breath. After Bill Sikes had murdered Nancy off-stage, the house was stiff with disquiet. Fagin walked slowly on to an empty, quiet stage, carrying a

---

13 Huggett, *op.cit.*, p 162

candle, which was virtually the only light on his face. On reaching the centre, he stood there for several seconds, then suddenly, and in absolute silence, blew the candle out and enveloped everything in dark hush. The sense of finality and pity was so shocking that the audience gasped, and one's heart can miss a beat merely by telling the story a century later. Tree would put that incident down to theatrical intuition or imagination. But in order to be effective the idea had to rely on the actor's considerable technical experience in timing, in building tension, in suggesting mood, finally in commanding an audience and making them feel what he wanted them to feel.

His one big misjudgement was to turn down Barrie's *Peter Pan*, on the grounds that he did not fancy himself in the part of Captain Hook. When asked why he had rejected it, he said, "God knows, and I have promised to tell no one else", a neat way of avoiding the question, and a typically amusing quip. He could not resist the temptation to release his abundant energy in stories and eloquent nonsense, and nearly all of them die on the page. There are, however, stories told about him, rather than by him, which sound unlikely. That he should entertain the young and handsome actor Esmé Percy to supper in his private rooms at the theatre after a performance, and be told by Lady Tree, "Enjoy your dinner, Mr Percy. The port is on the chimney-piece, and remember, it's still adultery", does not convince; he was unfaithful, but not in that direction. Another tale has him appearing before the curtain in the interval on a double-bill, when he had finished his part, and Mrs Patrick Campbell was due to do hers, and wishing the audience a safe journey home. This does not sit well with his benign disposition; on the other hand, it is quite possible that he simply forgot there was another play on the bill.

There is an evergreen tale about "billing" which is ascribed to him. Leading actors are mentioned above the title, with supporting actors below, and a special honour is sometimes given to one of these by placing him or her last in the list, in larger type, and prefixing the name with "and". It is a device reserved for guest artists or rising celebrities. The young actor William Armstrong, who had come to Her Majesty's from Frank Benson's company at Stratford-upon-Avon and would years later be a shining light in Liverpool, had scored a hit in a small part and was a favourite with audiences. With Tree at front of house, he pointed to the billboard and said, "You see, sir, my name is at the very bottom." "Yes", said Tree. "Well, sir, um", faltered the young man, "do you think perhaps it could be elevated a little, or could it read, so-and-so, so-and-so, AND William Armstrong?" Tree paused. "Yes", he said, "but why 'and'. Why not BUT?"[14] Personally, I like to think he was teasing.

He was on the whole so encouraging to younger actors that, almost on a sudden whim, he bought two houses in Gower Street, furnished them, and established within them the Academy of Dramatic Art (now RADA), offered his theatre to students for performances, and gave them jobs whenever he could. But he appointed other people to run the place commercially, as he was hopelessly green on questions of finance. When he was told that he had urgently to save money at Her Majesty's, he suggested supplying the Green Room with the *Daily Telegraph* instead of *The Times*. Again, one suspects he may have been having

---

14 *The Everyman Book of Theatrical Anecdotes* ed. Donald Sinden (1987), p 141

his little joke, yet he did believe in living in the proper style. It was further proposed by his business manager that he might not want to lunch every day in the rather costly Carlton Hotel, whereupon he marched the man across the street to a shop, bought him a bun and a glass of milk, and invited him to see what it was like to exist in penury; the suggestion was not repeated.

It was during the Great War that Asche took charge of Tree's beloved theatre with the shallow *Chu-Chin-Chow*, while Tree himself went first to Hollywood, then to New York to mount his Shakespearean productions. In a tiny twist to theatrical history, the part of the Artful Dodger in *Oliver Twist* was played by an expatriate Londoner called Charlie Chaplin.

Herbert Beerbohm Tree had been a member of the Garrick since 1884. It remained only for the knighthood to be bestowed, which came quite properly in 1909 for services to the drama. In view of his having followed Phelps at Sadler's Wells and Irving at the Lyceum in establishing what was in effect an unofficial National Theatre, all three of them in contrasting styles and with sometimes conflicting purpose, it was an honour the country shared in celebrating with him. At the same investiture, fellow Garrick member Arthur Pinero was to receive his knighthood. Tree whispered to Sir George Arthur, "Pinero is very nervous and wants to know if he can have gas." There was no occasion so solemn that it could deflect Tree from a good joke.

* * *

While Tree seduced audiences with his frank enjoyment of the theatre, inviting them to share it with him, there were many among his contemporaries who developed a new style of such studied languor that the audience felt that they could easily have jumped up on stage to join them. These were the heirs of Tom Robertson's new, cosy, approachable dramas and the 'common touch' with which the Bancrofts had acted them. Men like Charles Hawtrey, Allan Aynesworth, Gerald du Maurier, Charles Wyndham, demonstrated such ease and conviction in what they did on stage because they did not appear to step very far out of themselves. They were quintessentially English gentlemen, performing as quintessentially English gentlemen, with mild irony, wit, composure, good manners, style, excellent diction and intuitive decency. They were the sort of actors who drove Bernard Shaw mad, and gave the public uncomplicated delight. John Gielgud would cunningly mock their style when he played the butler in a Hollywood film called *Arthur* (1982) for which he won an Oscar. These actors looked as if they had wandered into their own sitting-room and might as well be paid for doing it as for anything else. The nonchalance was, however, deceptive. They were artists of consummate control. The fact that they seemed unperturbed was because their artistry demanded they be unperturbed. Perhaps English reticence needs to be conquered, and acting is one of the best ways to conquer it, even if it means turning it into an art-form of itself. They were all Garrick members and nearly all actor-managers.

Hawtrey is a fine instance of the type. He was unsurpassed in his portrayal of the man-about-town, a model of grace and effortless charm, who was so popular that his roles came to be known as 'Hawtrey parts' for forty years. He had perfect poise and conviction, and always made sure to wear a moustache since the day when he had shaven it off and caused the play to fail. Aplomb and *sang-froid* were ingrained in his nature, as was shown by his telephoning directly to the Chancellor of the Exchequer to complain about his taxes. Nevertheless, the artistry was detectable to anyone familiar with stage-craft. George Arthur wrote, "He never moved a finger (and his hands were as eloquent as his lips) without meaning, and conveying, something; the infinite pains which he took over a particular phrase often went far to illuminate a whole play. When he seemed laziest he might be working his hardest, when he seemed crassly stupid he was using all his wits to give the effect of a slow brain; when he was apparently strolling through his part, every nerve might really be strung and his body bathed in perspiration."[15] He will shortly have some tangential significance in this narrative, with regard to Oscar Wilde.

Of them all, the outstanding exemplar, whose contribution made the theatre a valued hobby of aristocrats, bestowing upon it far greater social status than ever before, was George Alexander. With a deliberate policy of commissioning new playwrights, he elevated light comedy from the shabby nonsense it had been fifty years before to the glittering summits of wit and satire. For twenty-seven years he managed the St James's Theatre as if it were an adjunct of the Court. Hesketh Pearson wrote that "the more expensive seats were occupied by Society with a capital 'S', the less expensive ones by those who longed to be in Society, the least expensive by those who wished to see what Society looked like." He went on

---

15 Arthur, *op.cit.*, p 214

to claim that George Alexander catered for the dramatic taste of the aristocracy "much as the Savoy Hotel catered for their gastronomic taste; the dramas, like the dishes, were pleasant to the palate and left nothing disagreeable in the mind or the mouth. In a typical St James's play the humorous characters were delightfully playful, the serious characters charmingly sentimental, and the plot savoured of scandal without being objectionably truthful."[16] These observations are very nicely turned, but faintly unfair when one remembers that in *The Second Mrs Tanqueray* he gave London an unnerving shock, and in *The Importance of Being Earnest* the finest comedy of manners ever written.

Alexander had worked with Irving at the Lyceum, and made his mark when, on tour in Boston, he had to take over from the Great Man at short notice when he was indisposed. Altogether he spent six years in Irving's employ, an experience which would have a positive effect upon his own style of management. "When I was at the Lyceum", he said, "after five or six hours of rehearsal by Irving I would go home almost crying. I would tell my wife that I was afraid I had made a dreadful mistake in going on the stage. And I made up my mind that if ever I had a company of my own, I would let them down pretty easy."[17] That opportunity arose in 1890 when he took over the gorgeous St James's Theatre, against the strong advice of Irving himself, who told him he could return to the Lyceum after six months. One of the first actors he engaged was Irving's own son Harry (H.B. Irving). He invested in new upholstery on the seats and installed electric light.

Most importantly, Alexander invited English playwrights

16 Pearson, *op.cit.*, p230
17 quoted in Donaldson, *op.cit.*, pp 108-109

to submit their work for consideration, and persuaded some people to become playwrights just so that his theatre could show their work. This was a clear break from the established habit of only putting on translations from the French. Over the coming twenty-seven years he would produce sixty-two full-length plays, of which only half a dozen were translations. Moreover, he appeared in most of them.

Almost within weeks of starting at the St James's, he approached Oscar Wilde for a play on a modern subject and paid him £50 in advance, the manuscript to be ready by 1 January, 1891. Nothing arrived, and Wilde offered to return the advance, which Alexander very shrewdly refused. He would wait.

When it was delivered, Wilde read the whole thing to Alexander in private. It was called *Lady Windermere's Fan* and it played neatly with the ideals of self-sacrifice and social morality. Lady Windermere is the daughter of Mrs Erlynne, although she does not know it. To save her daughter's reputation, Mrs Erlynne must assume the blame for an indiscretion, without ever revealing her real identity to Lady Windermere; she does this by falsely claiming ownership of a fan which had been left on a chair, as evidence of Lady Windermere's presence in the room. The reading over, Wilde said, "Did you like it?" George Alexander replied, "Like is not the word, it is simply wonderful." "What will you give me for it?" Alexander offered the huge sum of £1000, which Wilde took as confirmation of the commercial value of his work, and declined. "I have so much confidence in your excellent judgement, my dear Alec, that I cannot but refuse your generous offer. I will take a percentage."[18] He was right, of course.

The play went into rehearsal in February 1892, Wilde attending so regularly that he got in the way. Alexander made suggestions for minor changes, and one major one. As written, the secret of Mrs Erlynne's identity was not revealed until the last act. Alexander proposed that, though Lady Windermere must be kept in the dark, the audience should know the truth earlier, in order to share the tension. Wilde acquiesced, for Alexander was playing Lord Windermere, and knew what actors could and could not do with a text. On smaller points of dialogue the author refused to budge, having chiselled his words like diamonds. Alexander was such a gentleman that the disagreements were resolved diplomatically, though Wilde professed to be in agonies over them; actually, the playwright was more 'theatrical' than the actor over this affair.

The play was a triumph, and is now legendary. Indeed, legend has so infected the story of that first night that everyone assumes Wilde appeared before the curtain at the end to declare, in Alexander's telling of the tale, "Ladies and gentlemen: I have enjoyed this evening *immensely*. The actors have given us a *charming* rendering of a *delightful* play, and your appreciation has been *most* intelligent. I congratulate you on the *great* success of your performance, which persuades me that you think *almost* as highly of the play as I do myself." This is how theatrical stories are born, with relish, an actor's timing, and some choice editing. What Oscar Wide actually said was, "I think that you have enjoyed the performance as much as I have, and I am pleased to believe that you like the piece almost

18 Richard Ellmann, *Oscar Wilde* (1987), p 315

as much as I do myself." He also played gracious tribute to the actor-manager: "My acknowledgements are due in the first instance to Mr Alexander, who has placed my play upon the stage with the admirable completeness that has characterized all the productions at the St James's Theatre during the time it has been under his management." And he smoked a cigarette throughout.[19]

Some people took offence at Wilde's condescending tone (not the last time that he would be undone by his own clever wit), while others harboured more malicious resentments, among them Charles Hawtrey. He and another actor called Charles Brookfield cobbled together a short burlesque travesty of Wilde's play which they entitled *The Poet and the Puppets*, and Hawtrey poked fun at Wilde personally by dressing up in vulgar disguise as the playwright.[20] A little professional jealousy lurked behind this unkind spoof, and perhaps something more.

The following year Alexander put on Pinero's new play *The Second Mrs Tanqueray*, another bold plunge into devious Victorian morality. The central character, Paula, is a woman 'with a past' (i.e. she had been a prostitute of sorts) who has made a good marriage into high society and is determined to maintain her place there. The dilemma upon which the plot turns arises when her husband, Aubrey, discovers that she had once been the mistress of the man whom his daughter now wants to marry. Alexander would obviously take the part of Aubrey; decent, formidably correct and seasoned in the skill of concealing emotion, the role was tailored to suit him. But the casting of the leading lady, whose suicide in the last act would be the climax of the piece, was a major problem.

19 *ibid.*, p 346
20 *ibid.*, pp 349-350

Alexander sent his wife Florence on a tour of London theatres in search of somebody to play Paula Tanqueray. She went with a friend, Graham Robertson, and after some discouraging days they came upon an unknown actress in a small part in a vapid melodrama called *The Black Domino*. Years later Robertson recalled the occasion he first clapped eyes on Mrs Patrick Campbell: "She did not look wicked – a startling innovation. She was almost painfully thin, with great eyes and slow, haunting utterance; she was not exactly beautiful, but strangely interesting and arresting. She played weakly, walking listlessly through the part, but in one scene she had to leave the stage laughing; the laugh was wonderful, low and sweet, yet utterly mocking and heartless. Florence Alexander and I both realised that there before our eyes was the ideal Paula Tanqueray. If she would only move, speak, look, above all laugh like that, the part would play itself."[21]

George Alexander felt from the first rehearsals that trouble might be ahead. Used to doing everything according to the rules of politeness and professionalism, he was alarmed that Mrs Pat might turn out to be wild and thrilling, like a skittish mare. He was right. That is exactly what she was, and the contrast between their styles – he earnest and restrained, she mercurial and emotional – would give the play its tension and resonance. *The Second Mrs Tanqueray* took London by storm and rendered immortal the name of Mrs Patrick Campbell. But it also threatened to tip George Alexander into unaccustomed hysteria. Her behaviour, off-stage and on, was wilful and child-like in its indifference to others. On one occasion she

21 John Dawick, *Pinero: A Theatrical Life* (1993), p 184

amused herself by flicking chocolates against the backcloth during a tense moment in the drama, interrupting the dialogue with a series of audible plonks. Alexander was furious. He went up to her, eyes blazing, colour rising, and before he could articulate, she said, "I see you are angry. Your wife would not like me to speak with you when you are angry. She says it upsets your digestion." Thereafter he refused to have anything to do with her off-stage, the better to avoid her sarcastic barbs. She said that "acting with him was rather like acting with a walking-stick"[22], and described one encounter between them as follows: "Mr Alexander had to look into my face and tell me that I was beautiful and that he adored me, or some such words. And one night he said it with such a look in his eyes, as though he would willingly have wrung my neck, that I burst out laughing. When the curtain fell, his stage-manager came with pompous dignity to the door of my dressing-room and said, 'Mr Alexander's compliments and will you please not laugh at him on the stage.' I replied, 'My compliments to Mr Alexander, and please tell him that I never laugh at him until I get home." For his part, he admitted that he never in his life felt so relieved as when the curtain came down on the last performance.[23]

The depth of his distaste for her is measured by the unhappy fact that Shaw wrote *Pygmalion* originally for Alexander, with a wonderful part in it for Mrs Pat (whom he called "perilously bewitching"), but the twenty year-old memories were still raw. "That play is a cert", he told Shaw, "a dead cert. Now listen to me. I will get you any actress you like to name for the flower girl. I will pay any

22 Alan Dent, *Mrs Patrick Campbell* (1961), p 179
23 Donaldson, *op. cit.*, p 113

salary she asks. You can settle your own terms. But go on for another play with Mrs Campbell I will *not*. I'd rather die."[24] And so the play went to Beerbohm Tree with Mrs Pat as part of the package.

The truth was, Mrs Pat's capricious, teasing nature unsettled him. He was a graceful, decorous man, a gentleman, so well-dressed that other men studied his clothes before ordering their own, so well-behaved that he did not raise his voice, did not lose his temper, did not say anything that might wound. Mrs Pat punctured all that suavity, and he resented her for it, resented the weakness which she uncovered.

Following the historic success of *Tanqueray*, Alexander enjoyed another huge triumph in *The Prisoner of Zenda*, for which the queues stretched into St James's Street; his portrait in costume for this part now dominates the club bar. But the year before he had surpassed anything that could be deemed a mere success with his scintillating production of a masterpiece. This was *The Importance of Being Earnest* in 1895.

Wilde offered the play to Alexander with some deference, saying that it might not suit his romantic style, and that Charles Wyndham or Charles Hawtrey would fit better. Indeed, he had offered it to Hawtrey first, despite the offence of his parody two years earlier, but his theatre refused to advance any money. One can readily understand why he would imagine Hawtrey in the play, for the two leads of John Worthing and Algernon Moncreiffe would need to be portrayed with deadly seriousness if they were to be convincing, by men-about-town in fact. John Gielgud pointed out that the two men must conduct themselves

---

24 Pearson, *op.cit.*, pp 25-26

with "irreproachable exactitude…hitching their trousers before they sit down, stripping off their gloves, shooting their cuffs. Their hats are worn at exactly the right angle, their canes carried with an air of studied negligence."[25] They must above all not act as if they know they are in a comedy. Subtitled 'a trivial comedy for serious people', it had perforce to be acted with stylized precision and stiff dignity, so that only the audience laughed, while the people on stage before them regarded their social posturings as necessary and important. What Wilde was doing was to invite the audience to look at itself through the epigrammatic jewellery of his dialogue. One can imagine the Victorian audience shifting with delicate approval at Lady Bracknell's remark, "Never speak disrespectfully of Society, Algernon. Only people who can't get into it do that."

"None of Wilde's plays cost him less effort than the best of them", wrote his biographer.[26] He dashed it off it in the space of days, not months, every word perfect in its place. When George Alexander suggested that one scene might be omitted, he declared, "This scene which you feel is superfluous cost me terrible exhausting labour and heart-rending nerve-wracking strain. You may not believe me, but I assure you on my honour that it must have taken fully five minutes to write."[27] The scene stayed.

Those who saw the original production averred that George Alexander and Allan Aynesworth were never equalled in those parts by any other actors. Aynesworth, whose portrait also hangs in the bar, had started his career

25 John Gielgud, *Stage Directions* (1963), p 80
26 Ellmann, *op.cit.*, p 398
27 Pearson, *op. cit.*, p 118

with the Bancrofts at the Comedy Theatre and played only minor roles until Alexander cast him as Algy. He was elected to the Garrick in the wake of this performance. Aynesworth lived to the age of ninety-five, within the memory of some members alive today, and was always held with fond regard in the club. He used to say that in fifty years on the stage he had never known a triumph as resounding as that which greeted *The Importance* in 1895.

Sadly, it was also the year of Oscar Wilde's disgrace. The odious Marquess of Queensberry had arrived at the theatre on the opening night carrying a bouquet of carrots and turnips with which he intended to humiliate Wilde, and was refused entry, thereby setting in motion the sequence of events which was to end in court. To his credit, George Alexander refused to give evidence at the trial, but following the conviction, he removed the playwright's name from the billboards, understandably perhaps, given the scope of Victorian hypocrisies. Less forgivable was his apparent snub to Wilde, whom he saw in France after the release from prison and did not stop to acknowledge. He regretted this. At the ignominious auction of Wilde's effects at his home in Tite Street, Alexander bought the acting rights to *The Importance of Being Earnest* and *Lady Windermere's Fan*. When the plays were revived, he went to visit Wilde to offer friendship and help, and made him voluntary payments in lieu of royalties. Later, he bequeathed the acting rights to Wilde's sons. Henry Irving, too, was one of the few to send the chastened man a message of welcome on his release.

Charles Hawtrey, on the other hand, approached Lord Queensberry's solicitor Charles Russell and offered damaging information about Oscar Wilde's habits and young friends, and on the night of his conviction he and his collaborator Brookfield held a victory dinner with Queensberry in celebration.[28] He was elected a member of the club in 1921, knighted in 1922, and died in 1923. He was later revealed to have fathered an illegitimate child by Ellen Terry's niece, a fact worth mentioning only to counter his assumption of superior morality. Fortunately, George Alexander did not live to witness any of this, having died of consumption in 1918.

He would have been even more distressed by the fate of his exquisite theatre. The St James's closed down in 1957 and was set for demolition. Practically the whole of the acting profession turned out to march in the streets in protest, but to no avail. The theatre was wantonly destroyed and replaced by a singularly ugly office-block.

---

28 Ellmann, *op.cit.*, pp 415, 449

William Shakespeare (1564–1616) Terracotta by Louis François Roubiliac 1742

James Winston (1773–1843)

Engraving by Thomas Cheesman after
Samuel de Wilde 1807

*Charles Kemble (1775–1854) as
Macbeth in Macbeth*

Oil on canvas by Andrew Morton 1836

The Garrick Club House, 35 King Street.

Detail from Tallis's London Street Views No.79,
King Street and New Street, published by John Tallis 1838–40

Charles Mathews (1776–1835)
as *Fond Barney, Mr Wiggins, Buskin, the Drunken Ostler and Himself*
Oil on canvas by George Henry Harlow 1814

Charles Mathews (1776–1835)
as Sir Fretful Plagiary in The Critic

Oil on canvas by Samuel de Wilde 1813

Thomas Potter Cooke (1786–1864) singing
Ben Backstay Tinsel print based on a
tuppence-coloured published by Orlando
Hodgson c.1832

Edwin Forrest (1806–1872)

Oil on canvas by Thomas Sully 1839

William Charles Macready (1793–1873)
as Macbeth in Macbeth

Staffordshire pottery
by Thomas Parr c.1852

James Robertson Anderson (1811–1895) as Ulric in Werner

Lithograph by R J Lane 1838

Charles Kean (1811–1868)
Albumen photograph by Martin Laroche c.1857

Playbill for a performance of The Merchant of Venice at Windsor Castle 1856

Charles Kean (1811–1868) and Pattie Chapman (c.1830–1912) as Shylock and Jessica in The Merchant of Venice Albumen photograph by Martin Laroche 1858

Charles Kean (1811–1868), John Ryder (1814–1885) and H Butler (fl.1851–1857) as Richard, Bolinbroke and Carlisle in Richard II Albumen photograph by Martin Laroche 1857

Samuel Phelps (1804–1878) as Cardinal Wolsey in Henry VIII
Oil on canvas
by Sir Johnston Forbes-Robertson 1878

Samuel Phelps (1804–1878)
Carte de visite photograph by unknown
c.1870

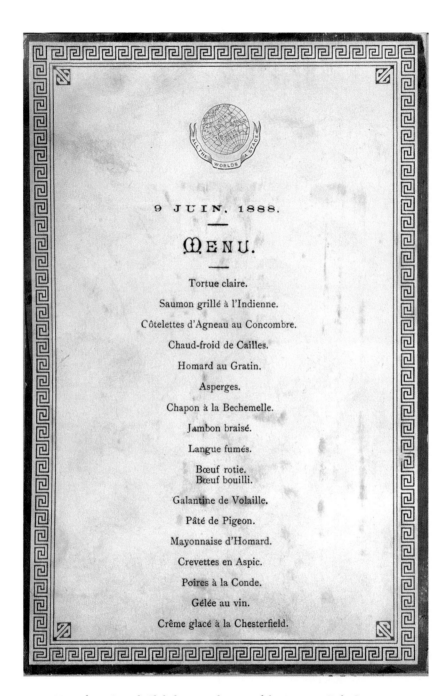

9 JUIN, 1888.

—

Menu.

—

Tortue claire.

Saumon grillé à l'Indienne.

Côtelettes d'Agneau au Concombre.

Chaud-froid de Cailles.

Homard au Gratin.

Asperges.

Chapon à la Bechemelle.

Jambon braisé.

Langue fumés.

Bœuf rotie.
Bœuf bouilli.

Galantine de Volaille.

Pâté de Pigeon.

Mayonnaise d'Homard.

Crevettes en Aspic.

Poires à la Conde.

Gélée au vin.

Crème glacé à la Chesterfield.

Menu for a Garrick Club dinner in honour of the Augustin Daly Company,
Sir John Hare (1844–1921) in the chair 1888

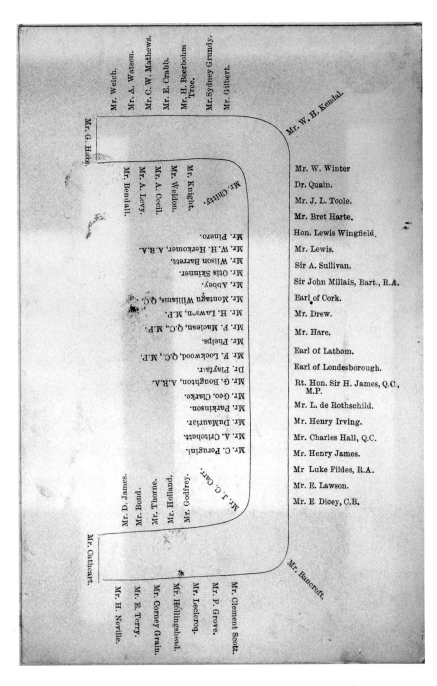

Mr. Welch.
Mr. A. Watson.
Mr. C. W. Mathews.
Mr. E. Crabb.
Mr. H. Beerbohm Tree.
Mr. Sydney Grundy.
Mr. Gilbert.

Mr. W. H. Kendal.

Mr. G. Hare.

Mr. Bendall.
Mr. A. Levy.
Mr. A. Cecil.
Mr. Weldon.
Mr. Knight.
Mr. Chitty.

Mr. Pinero.
Mr. W. H. Herkomer, A.R.A.
Mr. Wilson Barrett.
Mr. Otis Skinner.
Mr. Abbey.
Mr. Montagu Williams, Q.C.
Mr. H. Lawson, M.P.
Mr. F. Maclean, Q.C., M.P.
Mr. Phelps.
Mr. F. Lockwood, Q.C., M.P.
Dr. Playfair.
Mr. G. Boughton, A.R.A.
Mr. Geo. Clarke.
Mr. Parkinson.
Mr. DuMaurier.
Mr. A. Ortchett.
Mr. C. Perugini.

Mr. W. Winter
Dr. Quain.
Mr. J. L. Toole.
Mr. Bret Harte.
Hon. Lewis Wingfield.
Mr. Lewis.
Sir A. Sullivan.
Sir John Millais, Bart., R.A.
Earl of Cork.
Mr. Drew.
Mr. Hare.
Earl of Lathom.
Earl of Londesborough.
Rt. Hon. Sir H. James, Q.C., M.P.
Mr. L. de Rothschild.
Mr. Henry Irving.
Mr. Charles Hall, Q.C.
Mr. Henry James.
Mr Luke Fildes, R.A.
Mr. E. Lawson.
Mr. E. Dicey, C.B.

Mr. J. C. Carr.

Mr. D. James.
Mr. Bond.
Mr. Thorne.
Mr. Holland.
Mr. Godfrey.

Mr. Cathcart.

Mr. Bancroft.

Mr. H. Neville.
Mr. E. Terry.
Mr. Corney Grain.
Mr. Hollingshead.
Mr. Leclercq.
Mr. F. Grove.
Mr. Clement Scott.

Seating plan for a Garrick Club dinner in honour of the Augustin Daly Company,
Sir John Hare (1844–1921) in the chair 1888

Top Left: *Sir Squire Bancroft* (1841–1926) Oil on canvas by Hugh Goldwin Riviere 1900

Top Right: *John Lawrence Toole* (1830–1906) Oil on canvas by The Hon. John Collier 1887

Bottom Right: *Sir Henry Irving* (1838–1905) Oil on canvas by Sir John Everett Millais 1883

AFTER THE SUPPER.

COPYRIGHT, ENTD. STAT. HALL.

*After the Supper: Sir Henry Irving (1838–1905), John Lawrence Toole (1830–1906)
and Sir Squire Bancroft (1841–1926)*

Albumen photograph after a drawing by Phil May c.1890

Sir Herbert Beerbohm Tree
(1853–1917) as Svengali in Trilby
Watercolour by Albert Morrow
c.1895

Sir Herbert Beerbohm Tree
(1853–1917) as Falstaff in the Merry
Wives of Windsor Photo-gravure
published in Modern Shakespearean
Celebrities by Virtue & Co c.1902

Sir Herbert Beerbohm Tree (1853–1917) as The Duke of Guisebury in The Dancing Girl
Cabinet photograph published by Barraud c.1891

Hamlet
Scene 5 Act 1st
Cliffs at Elsinore

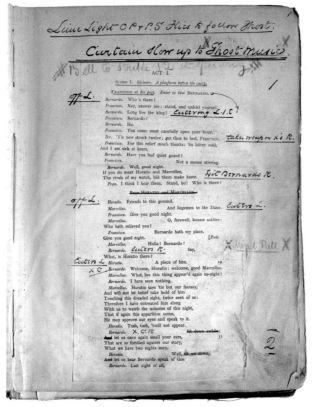

Top: *Hamlet. Act 1 Scene 5. Cliffs at Elsinore. As played by Mr. Irving, Lyceum Theatre, 200 nights*

Watercolour set design from the Lyceum Theatre prompt book, attributed to Hawes Craven 1874

Bottom Left: *Hamlet. Act 1 Scene 1. As played by Mr. Irving, Lyceum Theatre, 200 nights*

Page from the Lyceum Theatre prompt book 1874

Mᴿ HENRY IRVING

Sir Henry Irving (1838–1905) as Matthias in The Bells
Cabinet photograph by the London Stereoscopic Co. c.1871

Sir John Martin Harvey (1863–1944) as Richard in Richard III
Oil on canvas 1925

7

MORE ACTOR - MANAGERS

The other actor-managers flourishing at this same moment of creative fertility exerted very diverse influence. Indeed, it is difficult to imagine four men more unlike in motive and style than Charles Wyndham, John Martin-Harvey, Frank Benson and Johnston Forbes-Robertson, each of whom left his individual mark.

Oscar Wilde admitted that he had in mind for *The Importance of Being Earnest* Charles Hawtrey and Charles Wyndham. In the event, neither of them was cast, but Wyndham would have carried it off with aplomb. He and Hawtrey were the finest light comedians of their day, inheriting the tradition of Elliston and of David Garrick himself, who famously observed that any fool could make his name as a tragedian, but that comedy was a serious business. Wyndham perfected the style of amused nonchalance which made audiences feel so comfortable that they almost knew him as a friend. He trained to be a doctor, and actually went to the United States to serve in the Federal army during the Civil War as resident surgeon, taking time off occasionally to appear on stage, that being his abiding hobby. In 1869 he played in *The School for Scandal* in New York and on his return to London took charge of the Criterion Theatre, where he resided as actor-manager from 1877 to 1899, producing and acting in dozens of pleasant, if not distinguished, entertainments. His most famous role was as Garrick in Tom Robertson's play of that name, in which he appeared for the first time in 1886 (twenty-two years after its *première* at the Haymarket) and subsequently made it so much his own that he was frequently called upon to revive it. He even played it in German in Berlin and other cities, following which the Criterion Theatre was filled with the laurel wreaths with which he had been presented on tour.

His enduring legacy, however, is architectural rather than thespian, for it is he who in 1899 built Wyndham's Theatre in Charing Cross Road, the last theatre to be built with a perfect picture-frame stage, which he inaugurated, predictably, with a new production of *David Garrick*. Shortly thereafter he also built the New Theatre behind it, in St Martin's Lane. The Management of both passed to his widow in 1919 and subsequently to her son and stepson Howard Wyndham and Bronson Albery, remaining very much a family affair. The New was re-named the Albery in recognition of this, and is now the Noël Coward.

Wyndham's impersonation of Garrick is immortalised in the portrait of him which hangs on the left wall of the bar. He had been elected to the club in 1886 and knighted in 1902.

His contemporary John Martin-Harvey waited much longer both for his election (1919) and his knighthood (1921), but he had perforce to be a patient man, for his career had been painfully slow to take off, and his managements woundingly reluctant to give him a chance to prove himself. Having joined Irving's company at the

Lyceum at the age of nineteen, he then languished loyally for fourteen years in walk-on parts, watching, learning, never once complaining, and working out for himself that he would one day inherit Irving's mantle. To this end he seems to have adopted Irving's manner and demonstrated convincingly that to be a great actor you have to behave like one. His hand waved imperiously, his entrance into a room asserted the right to attention, and his vowels were ever grandly rounded. He was almost a relic even when in his late thirties, for his style, declamatory and grandiloquent, evoked an earlier era. He and Charles Wyndham were magnetic opposites both in style and substance.

When Forbes-Robertson came to give his historical début as Hamlet in 1897, with Mrs Patrick Campbell as a rather unorthodox Ophelia, Martin-Harvey was cast as Osric (another small part!) but Forbes-Robertson declared this to be "a perfect embodiment of that affected dandy, quite the best I ever remember to have seen."[1]

Finally, he was given the opportunity to manage the Lyceum in Irving's absence in America, and he put on an adaptation of Dickens' *Tale of Two Cities* which he and his wife had worked on themselves, specifically as a vehicle for his special talents. It had been his wife's idea in the first place, and they together devised the plotting and scenes, seeking assistance with some of the dialogue. The result was entitled *The Only Way* and Martin-Harvey gave his first performance in the leading part of Sydney Carton in 1899. He became so identified with this role that he was still playing it forty years later at the age of seventy-six.

This was not, however, the summit of his career.

---

1 Johnston Forbes-Robertson, *A Player Under Three Reigns* (1925), p 173

After playing Hamlet himself, plus Henry V, Richard III and Petruchio in *The Taming of the Shrew*, none of them destined to mark an epoch, he appeared as Oedipus in Reinhardt's production of Sophocles' *Oedipus Rex* at Covent Garden for three weeks in 1912, the first actor to play the part since Betterton more than two hundred years earlier. It caused a sensation and was the talk of London for many years afterwards, as long as there were survivors who had seen it, the performance described by Macqueen-Pope as "savage in its stark horror".[2] At last he had found the part for which his dated, thunderous delivery of long and difficult speech was ideally suited, for he knew, as they had always known in the old school, that theatrical effect depended upon voice control and the march towards *crescendo*. It was William Charles Macready all over again.

According to Hesketh Pearson, Martin-Harvey's especial quality was the ability to create atmosphere. "By merely looking over his shoulder", he wrote, "he could make you feel that something sinister was behind him; by a simple movement of his hands, he could suggest tension; by an inflection of his voice he could generate fear or sympathy or romance."[3] What he could not do was to impersonate a perfectly ordinary human being, who behaved as if he might have a bus to catch, which is of course what Wyndham excelled in. Thus when he came to play in Shaw's *The Devil's Disciple* it was awkwardly clear that he was in the wrong place, speaking lines by the wrong author.

Far more significant in the long sweep of theatrical history, however, and with especial regard to the rediscovery of the original Shakespeare, one of the principal themes

2 Kalman Burnim and John Baskett, *Brief Lives* (2003)
3 Hesketh Pearson, *The Last Actor-Managers*, p 52

of this narrative, were the careers of Frank Benson and Johnston Forbes-Robertson, the former for his heroic work in bringing the plays of Shakespeare to masses of people who had never seen any of them before, the latter for giving the world, at last, the first flawless Hamlet.

On the face of it, Frank Benson was the most unlikely person to become an actor at all, but he was obsessed by Shakespeare, and driven by an unquenchable ambition to make the plays available to everyone. He said it was his "hobby", and there are generations of schoolchildren who learnt from him that Shakespeare was not a boring indecipherable study, who are therefore in his debt, as well as the inheritors of his work in Stratford-upon-Avon, not to mention the scores of actors who learnt their trade with him and ingested his enthusiasm.

He was first and foremost a sportsman, and a very good one at that. As an undergraduate at New College, Oxford, he ran the three-mile event and beat all records. But at the same time he and some friends mounted a production of *Agamemnon* in Greek which was to change the course of his life. With characteristic candour and self-deprecation he said that he was supposed to have been studying Greek for thirteen years and had never yet read through a play, so he might as well try. He played Clytemnestra. The performance ran for an hour and three-quarters without a break, and apparently held the audience spell-bound, despite most of them not understanding a word of it. Praise came from all sides, including from Tennyson, Gladstone, Browning, George Eliot, Millais, and the reputation of this young man even reached the Lyceum Theatre in London. Henry Irving invited him and a colleague to come and see a performance of *The Corsican Brothers* and go back-stage afterwards. In the dressing-room Irving addressed them thus: "You young men did splendidly. Ah, if only I had had the opportunity in my young days that you have in yours! Why do you not band together in your troupe, work, study and become a company, the like of which this age has not seen? Should any of you determine to adopt the stage as your profession I shall be only too glad to render you any assistance I can."[4]

Encouraged by this, Benson assembled a group for an amateur performance of *Romeo and Juliet* in London, which found no favour at all with critics but earned the respect of Irving, who promptly offered him a job at the Lyceum, his first part to be Paris in that same play. Bram Stoker took him aside and warned him that he wanted technique, which could only be gained by work, work, work. "I'll tell you something else", he said. "I have seen some of the cleverest amateurs, really good on a small stage, hopelessly ineffective on a larger one." An old actor in the company called Walter Lacy went further. "You can't act for nuts at present", he said. "You don't know the rudiments; but you've got power, you've got acting in you and, by God! Sir, hardened old stager as I am, you carried me away sometimes and made me pipe my eye."[5]

His father, who had not been pleased that Frank should choose such a rum profession, nevertheless did not stand in his way and gave him £500 to start him off. Even without this, the boy would have continued, for he was irrepressible and so bold as to be cheeky. One of the delights of his *Memoirs* is that he can look back upon his younger self with good humour and self-mockery. Reporting for duty

4 Frank Benson, *My Memoirs* (1930), pp 127-128
5 *ibid.*, pp 146, 151

at the Lyceum he was given a cheerful welcome by Irving: "Glad to see you, my boy; hope you will be comfortable", which draws this charming comment: "He does not realize, I thought, that I have come to teach him how to act." After the first week he comes to see that acting is not quite as simple as he imagined, but still wondered why "the management was so blind as to keep me as Paris instead of letting me play Romeo, and Irving the Apothecary."[6]

It would turn out that it was not Benson's acting skills which would make his contribution to the theatre so historic. In point of fact, there are indications they were pretty slim, and one suspects he was well aware of this, or he would not have been able to laugh at himself so freely. One who would over the next few years see all his performances in the great tragic roles said they were enjoyable but incomprehensible. "He mouthed the lines until they were meaningless, sang them until they were indistinguishable and bawled them until they were deafening…He had nearly every fault of which an actor can be guilty: when he spoke verse he ranted, and when he spoke prose he rattled."[7] Moreover, he would in his career give so many performances in a week that he would get them mixed up, transposing lines from one play to another, as he never really studied them with care. This might seem surprising for somebody who adored Shakespeare so obviously, but is the better explained when one notes that his admiration was founded entirely upon excitement, and not at all upon scholarship.

It may be that he took to heart the advice given by Fanny Stirling, an old actress who was well-known as the

6 *ibid.*, pp 170, 173

7 Pearson, *op.cit.*, pp 34, 38

best Nurse in *Romeo & Juliet*, who said, "You will never be an actor until you have learnt to get through your part though the snow comes through the roof; with an audience consisting of only two or three drunks, who are not listening; while the sparrows twitter and flutter round the auditorium before settling to roost in the flies; while rats trot across the footlights carrying off your pet powder-puff in their mouths. You have got to learn how to act though none of the company except yourself are sober; when no one gives you your proper cue; when you have not had a square meal for a month and will probably get no salary on Saturday; when you are sent on to play a part of two or three hundred lines with one night's study, and no proper rehearsal. When you can do this, and not dry up; but hold an audience, great or small, drunk or sober, stalls or gallery or Royal Box, whether the play is good or bad, and your part actor-proof or impossible, then and not till then may you call yourself an actor."[8]

Sage words from the proverbial old trouper who had spanned the generations back to 1830. Benson would not have to endure anything quite as trying as this litany, but he would devote his life to getting the play on come what may and so would know what she meant. After leaving the Lyceum one year later he set up his own F R Benson Company in 1883, his father helpfully buying props, costumes and scenery, and set about touring the country for the rest of his working life. He produced and acted in thirty-five of Shakespeare's plays (all except *Titus Andronicus* and *Troilus and Cressida*), an achievement unmatched by anyone else before him, carrying on the pioneering work of Samuel Phelps but with this distinction that, while

---

8 Benson, *op.cit.*, p 190

Phelps had his permanent home at Sadler's Wells, Benson was always on the move, always packing, always rehearsing new recruits, always venturing to distant corners of the country. He was also the first to attempt a complete, uncut version of *Hamlet*. From 1886 he gained the confidence of the powerful Flower family in Stratford-upon-Avon and for twenty-six years gave the annual Shakespeare Festival of plays during the summer months at the Memorial Theatre there. There can have been few theatre-goers in the early years of the twentieth century who had not at some time or another seen a Benson production.

His love of sports never left him. Indeed, it was incorporated into the ethos of his company, and when he listed his preparations for a career on the stage he included boxing, fencing, wrestling and single-stick (a form of fencing with only one hand). His idea of relaxation was to spend half an hour at an open window swinging dumb-bells, and he was perfectly happy to go for a swim between a matinée and evening performance. In such an atmosphere of athletic prowess it was no wonder that the moments best remembered by schoolchildren at a Benson display were the duels and the fights, with battle-axes and swords glinting and smashing, all rehearsed with glee and zest and brought to a perfection of fitness. For himself, he was able to jump over tables and hurl himself through windows on stage, make headlong descents down a rope and carry weights which would have broken another man's back. He even proposed that "the actor should, as a general rule, stand much as a fencer stands at attention, only less constrained, and the feet wider apart, the body three-quarter face to the audience."

The company teased him that he acted more with

muscle than with mind, but they supported him whole-heartedly. Cricket mattered to him so much that he sometimes phrased his contracts with new actors as, "To play the Ghost in Hamlet and keep wicket", or "To play Laertes and field cover point." But never was there an actor-manager more fondly treated by his fellow-actors. As he was kind and sweet-natured to the point of foolishness, so they would do anything for him in return, even to volunteering a cut of 50% in salary to help him through difficult times. "He was often financially embarrassed, but the people who advanced money to tide him over found it impossible to remind him of what he owed them."[9] He became a member of the Garrick Club in 1893 and in 1901 founded an acting-school from which graduated many of the actors who would grace our stages in the first half of the twentieth century, who proudly called themselves The Bensonians. One of them was Isadora Duncan, who made her stage début dancing in the camp scene of his *Henry V*.

The honours bestowed upon him came with a touch of friendliness and fondness which was itself rare. He was made a Governor of the Memorial and a Trustee of Shakespeare's Birthplace, and finally given the Freedom of the Borough of Stratford-upon-Avon, only the second actor to be so honoured, the first being David Garrick in 1769. This was in recognition of his avowed aim that every play of Shakespeare's be presented on the stage of the Memorial Theatre in keeping with the intentions of the founders. "Thank God", said the stage-carpenter after the next First Night, "there's another bloody king disposed of."

Best of all, when he appeared as Julius Caesar at Drury Lane in 1916 to mark the tercentenary of Shakespeare's

9 Pearson, *op.cit.*, p 36

death, King George V summoned him to the Royal Box. He was still in costume as the corpse of Caesar, with sunken eyes and blue lips and a long night-shirt, but the King had decided there and then to confer a knighthood upon him. Somebody was hastily sent out to the theatrical costumiers Simmons to fetch a sword, and Sir Frank Benson rose from his knees having been knighted with a stage-prop. To this day, he is the only actor-knight to have been dubbed in a theatre.

A throng of thousands was at the station to greet him when he returned to Stratford-upon-Avon, and they dragged his carriage, horseless, through the streets in celebration.

* * *

Johnston Forbes-Robertson never felt easy being an actor. He flinched at the sight of his name on a bill-board, and after retirement honestly confessed that "I was not temperamentally suited to my calling." He went so far as to claim that he had never been on stage without longing for the moment when the curtain would come down on the last act, and that rarely did he enjoy himself for a moment. His nerves, generally regarded as necessary to a good performance, were to him "nought but a shackling handicap."[10]

And this was the man whom colleagues, critics and public declared to be probably the first actor ever who was able to speak the poetic words of Shakespeare with the fluidity and tone which they demanded. Audiences

10 Johnston Forbes-Robertson, *A Player Under Three Reigns* (1925), p 288

found themselves exalted by the conviction carried in the lusciousness of his voice, as if he alone had found the way to release the truth inherent in the verse. "For sheer beauty Forbes-Robertson's delivery of Buckingham's farewell speech remains something of a sacred memory", wrote George Arthur. "The impression, night after night, left on the audience whose eyes were riveted on the actor as they drank in the intonations of his matchless voice, was that one of the noble army of martyrs had already crossed the dark river and was speaking from an unseen world."[11]

The reluctant actor nevertheless treated his voice with great respect and understood what a vital element it was in dramatic technique. When a young actress sought his advice in the 1920s and gave a private audition for him, he concentrated his remarks on her voice. He told her to sit at a piano every day, decide on a note in the middle of her voice, strike it on the piano, then speak some line of verse to it, firmly, vocalising it without singing it. After that, she should do exactly the same with the next higher note on the keyboard, and so on to the octave, always repeating the same line. She should use a different line of verse each day, but not miss a day of the exercise. This, he said, would improve her tone and inflection. Such was his own control, that in the cavernous Drury Lane Theatre he could be heard clearly at the back of the top gallery, when apparently speaking in a whisper. Something of the richness of this instrument can just be detected on distant recordings.

The young man's destiny took a detour when he went on stage, for his background and social upbringing had prepared him to be a painter. His father had written an

---

11 Sir George Arthur, *From Phelps to Gielgud* (1936), p 164

authoritative history of painting from Cimabue to Turner, his mother was an accomplished artist, and as a child he had modelled for Rossetti. When Ellen Terry first met him, it was as an aspiring painter, "a dreamy, poetic-looking creature in a blue smock", and throughout his career he continued to paint portraits, often of his fellow-actors, whenever he could snatch some time off. One of his biggest, commissioned by Irving, was of the church scene in *Much Ado About Nothing*, when the marriage ceremony between Claudio and Hero is interrupted. This majestic and imposing picture now hangs at the Players' Club in New York, and of the thirty or so figures depicted one can discern Ellen Terry, Forbes-Robertson himself as Claudio, William Terriss and Henry Irving. (In a typical display of Irving's warm generosity, he insisted on paying double the agreed fee because the picture was double the expected size).

Charles Reade, having re-discovered Ellen Terry and persuaded her back to the stage, recruited the young artist to join his cast, whereupon he promptly fell in love with her grace and golden hair (he was ever of a romantic disposition). Following that, he was part of the stock company from Manchester which supplied the cast for a revival of Samuel Phelps' production of *Henry IV, Part Two*, in which Phelps doubled as the King and Justice Shallow. This was the crucial turning-point, for Forbes-Robertson took the part of Prince Hal. During the very first rehearsal of their scene together, Phelps realised that this new actor was not of the common run. "Young man", he muttered, "you know nothing about this part; come to my dressing-room tonight at seven o'clock." Knocking nervously at the door that evening, Forbes-Robertson need not have worried, for he found "a gentle, kind, and considerate tutor", who, while dressed as Bottom for his role in half an hour's time, went patiently through the Prince Hal part offering much valuable insight. More than that, a firm professional friendship was instantly formed, and Phelps took the novice with him on almost all his subsequent engagements, encouraging him and following his career with avuncular interest. For his part, Forbes-Robertson responded warmly to Phelps' integrity, his contempt for seeking favour with the press and his social reserve; they were in fact two of a kind, separated only by years. It is fortunate that Forbes-Robertson painted a full-length study of his mentor a few months before he died in 1874, in his final role as Wolsey, and even nicer that, while it was still being done, Squire Bancroft sent word that the members of the Garrick were getting together to buy it. The news made the old man beam with joy. Forbes-Robertson made no secret of his belief that he owed everything to the teaching and the influence of Samuel Phelps.[12]

His next move was to join the Bancrofts at their Prince of Wales Theatre, where he applauded, with relief, their habit of delivering the actors' salaries to their dressing-rooms; he had been known to go without pay for three weeks rather than submit to the ordeal of queuing up in a beggarly fashion, another indication of his fastidious, courteous personality. And in 1882 he joined Irving at the Lyceum for the first of several seasons, which culminated in his taking over the management during Irving's absence in America in 1895. Characteristically, he was hesitant about assuming this responsibility, both because he might not be up to the challenge and because he did not care

---

12 Forbes-Robertson, *op,cit.*, pp 67-70

for the business of making and losing money. It was also typical that he allowed himself to be swayed by others, notably by Mrs Patrick Campbell.

The opening production was *Romeo and Juliet*, with himself and Mrs Pat in the leads. It was a bad choice. There were rumours that he would have opened with *Hamlet* were it not for Mrs Pat's insistence on playing Juliet. One can only imagine her petulance and obduracy, and his quiet chivalrous acquiescence, hiding behind the polite observation that she "was very ill and in great pain", but the imagination is justified by her subsequent outrageous behaviour when he did come to play Hamlet two years later. In the meantime, he closed this first season with *School for Scandal*, again with Mrs Pat in the more suitable part of Lady Teazle.

When offered the Lyceum again in 1897, he demurred, not having the funds to support such a venture, but Horatio Bottomley offered to back him, and Irving told him what to put on. "Play Hamlet", he said. "Do you really mean that?" replied Forbes-Robertson. "Yes", he said, "and I will lend you the scenery and properties." Still, his doubts lingered. He told Ellen Terry that he thought everyone was sick of Hamlet, that the part had been played to death. She very reasonably pointed out that a violinist would not decline the opportunity to play a sonata by Beethoven on the grounds that it had already been played by other violinists. "It was mainly due to the encouragement of Irving and Miss Terry that I ventured on a revival of *Hamlet*", he wrote, again with that charming hint of self-disparagement; it was not for him to presume himself fit for such heights.

The morning after the first night of this historic

production, Irving interrupted his preparations for the American tour to invite Forbes-Robertson to his room. He was sitting with the morning papers in front of him. Slapping his hand on the newspapers, he exclaimed, "Well, you've done it! And now you must go and play Hamlet all over the world." After a long chat, he ushered the younger man to the door, and opened it for him in deference. Placing a hand on his shoulder, he said, "Well, the readiness is all."[13]

One of the reviews on the table was by George Bernard Shaw, who noted that Forbes-Robertson was at last a match for Shakespeare's art, which he both delighted in and understood. "He does not utter half a line; then stop to act; then go on with another half-line; and then stop to act again, with the clock running away with Shakespeare's chances all the time. He plays as Shakespeare should be played, on the line and to the line, with the utterance and acting simultaneous, inseparable and in fact identical. Not for a moment is he solemnly conscious of Shakespeare's reputation or of Hamlet's momentousness in literary history: on the contrary, he delivers us from all these boredoms instead of heaping them on us." That is a remarkable assessment, for it represents the kind of Hamlet we expect today as a matter of course, and yet when Forbes-Robertson played the part in this way in 1897, *being* Hamlet rather than *acting* him, it came as a total revelation. The whole town stood in amazement, and the interpretation was immediately acclaimed the greatest ever. Writing half a century later, Hesketh Pearson was still in awe. "I have seen some thirty Hamlets", he wrote, "including the 'stars' in every London revival of the play

13 *ibid.*, p 172

between 1905 and 1950, but Robertson's was far superior to all the others and there was no second-best: there was simply Forbes-Robertson – and the rest."[14] A few years later when he was playing the part in New York, all the other actors in town begged him to do a special morning performance, when they would not themselves be working, and the Knickerbocker Theatre was crowded for the ensuing occasion with professionals. "That I cherish with a grateful memory as the most eventful episode in my theatrical career", he wrote.[15]

On the other hand, Mrs Patrick Campbell as Ophelia was very trying. With exquisite politeness he described her performance as "original and unconventional", when what he meant was provocative and unnerving. For all her native brilliance, Mrs Pat was monstrous to work with, wilfully committed to treating the art of acting as something frivolous (referring to 'Amlet the Dine' in public for example), an attitude which was bound to grate with the earnest Forbes-Robertson. Frances Donaldson says that she treated those who fell under her spell to "systematic torture", making fun of them, deriding what they most valued, savaging them relentlessly. Ian Forbes-Robertson, the stage-manager during *Hamlet*, took her aside and told her, "You know Mrs Campbell, you are killing my brother."[16] And for four years, she was his leading lady.

Together they created the title roles in *Caesar and Cleopatra*, which Shaw had written specifically with him in mind, affording a unique opportunity to see "a great classical actor interpreting to perfection a self-inspired

14 Pearson, *op.cit.*, p 1
15 *op.cit.*, p 229
16 Frances Donaldson, *The Actor-Managers* (1970), pp 133-134

classical part."[17] This, however, was no match for his most successful production, a trite and shallow piece, now forgotten, called *The Passing of the Third Floor Back* by Jerome K. Jerome, which he put on at the St James's Theatre following a long holiday abroad to recover from Mrs Pat. He and his wife, the actress Gertrude Elliott, were both enraptured by the high moral purpose of the plot, which they would naturally find attractive after the ordeal of Mrs Pat, and this consideration dictated their decision more than any professional judgement. It is the story of a stranger who moves into a boarding-house in Bloomsbury, peopled with unhappy and jaded folk, and whose beneficent personality effects a profound change in them all, bringing them peace and love and contentment. This simple tale, mocked by some critics, was held by audiences to be both ennobling and refreshing, nobody daring to puncture the stillness in the theatre until the curtain came down on the Stranger's last words: "I came because you wanted me."

Forbes-Robertson received hundreds of letters from playgoers who confided that their personal troubles had been alleviated by exposure to this play, and however simplistic the moral message of it might be, one can well imagine that the man's own probity and integrity would easily inform his interpretation, and with that disarming, comforting voice, he might appear something of a secret confessor to the subconscious. At any rate, he went on playing it for the rest of his life, so many times that he grew tired of it; the play's admirers would have been shocked to hear him exclaim in the wings one night, just before his first entrance, "Christ! Will they never let me give up this *bloody* part?"[18]

---

17 Pearson, *op.cit.*, p 5
18 Hesketh Pearson, *Extraordinary People* (1965), p 173

In 1912 he decided to retire, with a Farewell Tour to America, final performances at Drury Lane, and at various provincial theatres where he was known and honoured. His knighthood was conferred in 1913, but the accolade he most appreciated was a telegram from his friend and colleague Herbert Beerbohm Tree, the warmth and generosity of which are palpable beneath words of ordinary delight. "On this important night I should like you to know", he wrote, "with what admiration and sympathy I send you my heartfelt congratulations on your great achievement and splendid termination of your dignified career. All our stage is proud of you. May you live many years in our united esteem and grateful memory of the public. God bless you, my dear Johnston."

Twenty years later, and four years before his death, the club gave a dinner in his honour, at which Lord Buckmaster, the Lord Chancellor, said, "I like best to think of Forbes-Robertson as a man who helped to reveal to us the wonder and the glory and the power of the greatest Englishman that ever wrote."[19] There is not a man or woman in the profession, then or now, who would disagree.

* * *

Two more actor-managers complete this fertile period straddling the turn of the century and up to the Great War, although neither of them left his mark on a classical role. They were rather of the paradoxically eccentric style already established by Hawtrey and Wyndham, eccentric because they made a fetish of being normal. They contrived to look as if they were actors by accident, which is very

19 Geoffrey Wansell, *The Garrick Club* (2004), p 74

clever indeed. They shone and glittered quietly. They are Seymour Hicks and Gerald du Maurier.

Hicks began his career at the age of sixteen and by the time he reached twenty he was with the legendary J L Toole, who was Henry Irving's closest friend and confidant despite (or perhaps because of) being quite opposite in character and professional skills. He was both the finest 'low' comedian of his day, performing in his own theatre on the Strand, and an irrepressible practical joker in private. Irving had turned to him to find a job in his company for his son Laurence, and there Laurence encountered the high-spirited and lively Seymour Hicks, who never seemed to have two pennies in his pocket. The pair set about writing an adaptation for the stage of Sheridan Le Fanu's *Uncle Silas*, with the encouragement of Irving himself, who however balked at financing a commercial staging of it. All the same, the experience set Hicks on his dual career as playwright and actor-producer, for he eventually wrote and mounted no less than sixty-four plays. Also, he never forgot Irving's kind words, and it was personal wish as well as professional pride which urged him to locate and purchase, fourteen years later, the chair upon which Irving breathed his last in Bradford.

He was remarkably versatile, being adept in straight drama as well as musical comedy, and frequently topped the bill in music-hall. But his real contribution was to build and manage the Aldwych Theatre in 1906, followed in 1907 by the theatre in Shaftesbury Avenue which was first called the Hicks, then the Globe, and is now the Gielgud. He married the actress Ellaline Terriss, daughter of William Terriss (another Irving connection), and they frequently starred together in plays that he had written;

none of them have survived the evolution of taste. When the Great War broke out, Seymour Hicks took a company of entertainers out to France, for which he was awarded the Légion d'Honneur, but he was not knighted in England until 1935. His membership of the club spanned fifty years, from 1899 until his death in an utterly changed world, in 1949.

While Hicks was working at the Globe, Gerald du Maurier reigned at the Wyndham's, starring in dozens of productions for twenty-five years from 1910. He had hardly struggled to get there, for his father, the *Punch* cartoonist and novelist George du Maurier, had asked John Hare to take him on in a small part in 1894, after which he worked with both Forbes-Robertson and Beerbohm Tree, in the latter case taking a part in the hugely successful adaptation of his father's book *Trilby*. From there he moved to the Royalty, under the whimsical and emotionally dangerous management of Mrs Patrick Campbell. Like everyone else, he endured more than enjoyed the collaboration. His daughter Daphne du Maurier was obviously recalling his stories about her when she wrote, "You adored her and hated her in turn. You sat at her feet and worshipped, or rushed from her presence slamming the door and calling damnation upon her name. She was disturbing and possessive and impossible…There was no peace with her, no quiet moment; it was either heaven or hell, ecstasy or despair."[20] On the other hand, she took a great deal of trouble to teach him technique, and much of what later became recognisable as his unique style was, by his own account, due to her tuition.

Du Maurier's first major success was in J M Barrie's

---

20 Daphne du Maurier, *Gerald: A Portrait* (1934)

The Admirable Crichton, in which he created the juvenile lead. But the role which fell into his lap almost as a family present was that of Captain Hook in Barrie's *Peter Pan* in 1904 (the year after his election to the Garrick). Barrie was very seriously fond of du Maurier's elder sister Mrs Llewellyn Davies and wrote the story for her five little sons. That the boys' uncle Gerald should play the terrifying Captain Hook (as well as Mr Darling) when the play was staged was a matter of course; it was like a family parlour-game played out in public. It was wildly effective, "a bogey of fear who lives perpetually in the grey recesses of every small boy's mind", and so convincing that children were carried screaming from the theatre. What du Maurier achieved with this *grand guignol* creation was a starkly accurate parody of the melodramatic excesses of the recent past, which he had been doing privately at home even as a boy; his uncannily spooky imitation of Irving at his worst (or best!) had always been a favourite.

In 1905 came du Maurier's incarnation of the gentleman-crook in the title role of *Raffles*, in a style as far removed from the snarl and thunder of Captain Hook as it is possible to imagine. This was to define his career and his reputation for years to come, perhaps forever, and to open a debate as to what constitutes real 'acting' on the modern stage in an up-to-date story. In this play du Maurier perfected the technique of making his entrance on stage look natural, as if the audience were not there and he was in his own home. He strolled on, walked about, smoked his pipe, held conversations with other people on stage, and strolled off again. He excelled in this manner because he quite deliberately made it his own, the relaxed demeanour, the easy repartee, the graceful English gentleman. He did not quite invent the *genre*, but he did make it his own garden, so that everyone else in light comedy would be measured against him. The public loved him for it, because they trusted him, they believed he was true; the critics appreciated it for the subtle control which it concealed; and other actors celebrated him without reserve, for they knew how difficult it really was to seem to be doing nothing.

Sir George Arthur said that he was "incomparable", dismissing the facile insult that he did not act at all, but merely behaved in a certain way. "Never was criticism wider of the truth", he wrote. "Gerald du Maurier was, from the crown of his head to the sole of his foot, one of the most 'theatrical' actors of his day. He did not, as so many people, cheaply commented, 'walk through' his parts; rather would he, with consummate art, get an intensely dramatic effect while deluding the audience into regarding as a quite casual natural movement a gesture which had been planned and rehearsed with the utmost care and patience in front of a long looking-glass."[21] Those who tried to imitate him merely appeared artless and lazy, which is why Frances Donaldson is quite right to maintain that he "made a vital contribution to the development of acting."[22] The pity only is that the contribution was so invisible, and devoted to a list of such unmemorable roles, as to pass unnoticed. The fact was, he could play any part he chose in any of his own productions and carry it off with equal aplomb; the technique was inherited by scores of actors who had brushed against his influence at Wyndham's Theatre.

---

21 Arthur, *op.cit.*, pp 219-220
22 *op.cit.*, p 176

There was one more Barrie play in which the du Maurier style was deployed to more searching purpose. This was *Dear Brutus* in 1917. The leading role was of a man exposed, his hopes and ideals revealed as chimeras, impossible of realisation. It is a play about disappointment and despair, and at last the 'throw-away' technique was shown to be pregnant with relentless honesty. According to his daughter, he was brave to attempt this, for he had none of the protection that the old style of declamatory bombast naturally afforded. The performance was "very moving and very terrible; he concealed nothing, and laid himself bare to the gaze of the world with a ruthless disregard of his own privacy, putting himself in pillory, to be looked upon by the curious as though in some sudden and desperate need of salvation."[23]

During the Great War he was active in many ways, by entertaining soldiers, by joining up with them, and by reviving a patriotic play by his brother Guy called *An Englishman's Home*, said to be the most effective piece of propaganda ever written. He was also President of the Actors' Benevolent Fund. For all these reasons he was knighted in 1922.

With one late-flowering exception in an actor whose remarkable power would resurrect the ethos of the actor-manager in the middle of the century (Wolfit), Gerald du Maurier was the last of the breed, those tireless men with a noble history of devotion to their calling and to the excellence of theatrical production stretching back an entire century. Flourishing at the same time, or at least overlapping one another, it is tempting to indulge the imagination and watch Tree, Irving, du Maurier, Bancroft,

---

23 quoted in Donaldson, p 178

Alexander, Wyndham, Hicks and Forbes-Robertson all dining together at the Garrick Club, planning the future of the London stage in desultory and inventive conversation between courses. Alas, there are no records of who spoke to whom at any one ordinary dinner in the week, but there is plenty of anecdotal evidence of du Maurier dining with Tree, and of Forbes-Robertson chatting to Irving, together with the historical certainty that all these men frequented the club regularly. We can but surmise that the building was indeed, to some degree or other, the forum for discussion about the future of the English stage, the ways in which Shakespearean production should be improved, and the earnest desire of all of them to promote the idea which had been cherished by Macready and Phelps, that one day a truly National Theatre should be established in London.

8

GRANVILLE-BARKER AND GIELGUD

At least we know what Forbes-Robertson would have said on the subject, for he wrote it down. While virtually every other major European capital city had its National Theatre, some of them for more than two hundred and fifty years, London was doggedly deprived because the English (that "nation of shop-keepers") had always been more interested in trade than artistic pride. The philistines prevailed. "Unfortunately, the English spirit is such that any national encouragement of the fine arts would be sternly opposed", wrote Forbes-Robertson. Then a shy optimism edged its way in. "Those, however, who know and understand how important is the Drama as an inspiring influence, watch hopefully for a better time, and there are signs in various directions that the people are slowly beginning to understand the educational value of the spoken word upon the legitimate stage."[1]

There were within the club other actors who held a different view. Here's what Charles Wyndham had to say on the matter: "A National Theatre, if it is to be in fact what is indicated by the name, would be a type of institution alien to the spirit of our nation and our age, which has always believed in, and relied on, individual effort and personal competition as a healthier stimulus than the motherly or

---

1 Johnston Forbes-Robertson, *A Player Under Three Reigns*, p 172

grand-motherly fostering of a State nurse."[2] In other words, it's against the British 'way of life' and smacks of socialism. We can be sure that conversation around the Long Table was at least lively.

Wyndham's attitude had long been the common one, with the result that, since the cancellation of the monopoly held by the two Theatres Royal, Drury Lane and Covent Garden, which had each been an 'unofficial' National Theatre with unsatisfactory and often tawdry consequences, it had indeed been left to "individual effort" on the part of the few to undertake responsibilities which should have fallen to society as a whole. The monopoly of the patented houses had been swept aside in 1843. Almost immediately, one man took upon himself the task of establishing a theatre and repertoire worthy of the nation; Samuel Phelps, from 1844 to 1862 had miraculously succeeded in mounting Shakespearean productions in the most unlikely neighbourhood of Islington, transforming Sadler's Wells into the de facto National Theatre of the day. At more or less the same time, and with an entirely different concept, Charles Kean was showing his historically accurate scenery-shows at the Princess's Theatre, from 1850 to 1859. Their example had prompted some to foresee the coming of a truly national institution in time, although they might have despaired had they known how long it would take.

In October 1876, the Lord Mayor of London held a banquet for the theatrical profession at which the toast was to "The Shakespearean Drama", and Phelps was invited to respond. Managing to stifle his natural shyness, he took the opportunity to point out that something important had

---

2 *Daily Telegraph*, 26 March, 1908

been achieved at Sadler's Wells. "If that could be done by me as a humble individual", he said, "why could it not be done by the Government of this country? Why could not a subsidized theatre, upon a moderate scale of expense, be added to the late educational scheme, by which children are forced somehow or other into school? I maintain, from the experience of eighteen years, that the perpetual iteration of Shakespeare's words, if nothing more, going on daily for so many months in the year, must and would produce a great effect upon the public mind…If I could find any member of Parliament (which I fear is hopeless), I would willingly devote what little of life remains to me, to point out the way in which this could be done, and I would willingly give evidence in the House of Commons to prove the truth of Shakespeare's educating powers."[3]

Alas, he died two years later, never to be consulted on the matter. In the meantime, of course, yet another house had assumed central place in the theatrical life of London. From 1871 to the end of the century the Lyceum was, in the public mind, *the* National Theatre if ever there were to be one, and this, again, was due to the effort, vision and energy of one man – Henry Irving. He knew perfectly well that the Lyceum would not last forever, and that his successor might not share the same purpose, so he too gave eloquent voice to the notion of a real National Theatre in 1878, the very year of Phelps' death; no doubt he was aware of what Phelps had said at the Lord Mayor's Banquet, and wanted to lend support to his colleague (who had, after all, originally inspired his wish to be an actor) on behalf of the profession. The occasion was a paper read

---

3 Shirley S Allen, *Samuel Phelps and Sadler's Wells Theatre* (1971), p 310; a longer excerpt is also in John Coleman, *Memoirs of Samuel Phelps* (1886)

at a meeting of the Social Science Congress. "Is a National Theatre desirable?" he asked. "Is its establishment upon a permanent basis a possibility?"

Irving answered his own questions in this way: "With regard to its desirability, I have little, if any, doubt. In this country, artistic perfection of a high ideal is not always the road to worldly prosperity; and so long as open competition exists there will always be found persons whose aim is monetary success rather than the achievement of good work. In order that the stage may be of educational value, it is necessary that those who follow its art should have an ideal standard somewhat above the average of contemporary taste...To effect this some security is necessary. If the purifying and ennobling influence of the art is to be exercised in such a manner as to have a lasting power, it is necessary that the individual be replaced by something in the shape of a corporation, or by the working of some scheme by its nature fixed and permanent."

He went on to posit the startling notion that, once established, the theatre would have to be fully independent. "A 'National Theatre' implies an institution which, in its nature, is not either limited or fleeting. Such a scheme must be thorough, must rest upon a very secure basis, and must conform to the requirements of art, polity, and commerce...Once established under proper guarantees, it should be allowed to work out its own ideas in its own way. Art can never suffer by the untrammelled and unshackled freedom of artists...Our art alone has yet no local habitation, no official recognition, no political significance. Should the scheme of a National Theatre be carried out, great results might follow."[4] It was a speech

---

4 Geoffrey Whitworth, *The Making of a National Theatre* (1951), pp31-33

of remarkable prescience, given what would eventually evolve.

Another influence came to bear with the establishment of the Elizabethan Stage Society by William Poel in 1894. Poel was an actor as well as manager of the Old Vic, and although he did not ostensibly promote the idea of a National Theatre, the example he set gave extra vigour to the idea and was to have such profound resonance that, when the National Theatre finally opened nearly a century later, its stage would be more or less the one Poel had envisaged. He had precise and clear ideas of how the Elizabethan theatre looked, and held that Elizabethan drama could best be appreciated in Elizabethan conditions. With a minimum of scenery, simplicity of staging, the removal of the proscenium arch and a stage which protruded into the auditorium to be surrounded by spectators on almost three sides, he abolished at a stroke the Victorian obsession (particularly in the hands of Charles Kean) with elaborate trappings. The effect was to free Shakespeare's text from the imprisonment of excessive detail, to offer a clean and spare space in which the verse could soar, and to concentrate attention on the content of the words alone. To this end, he taught that the actor must identify the key word in any speech, and structure his delivery and rhythm around it. He also made sure that each scene followed naturally upon the preceding one, without unnatural breaks in the action. Poel used the same approach with Marlowe, Middleton, Beaumont & Fletcher and Ben Jonson, and there is hardly an actor or director of the twentieth century who does not bear the signs of his influence.

The first of these is without question the most important. The actor who played the lead in William Poel's production of *Richard II* for the Elizabethan Stage Society in 1899 was Harley Granville-Barker, aged twenty-two. The experience marked not only his own life and career forever, but formed in him an ambition for the future of the English stage to which he would devote his energies with heroic endeavour. His own projects as actor and director flourished apace; Shaw selected him to create the role of Marchbanks in *Candida*, and he also appeared in *Captain Brassbound's Conversion*, *Mrs Warren's Profession*, *Major Barbara* and *Man and Superman*, always in leading parts. When he took up management of the Royal Court Theatre, he produced a clutch of modern drama which was revolutionary at the time, with plays by Ibsen, Galsworthy and Schnitzler, as well as his own play *The Voysey Inheritance*. Following that, he established a repertory system at the Savoy Theatre producing Shakespearean drama in the Poel style, with simplicity and poetic clarity. They were considered to be utterly fresh and beautiful, certainly the best representations of Shakespeare since Phelps, and audiences swarmed into the Savoy to be enraptured. He was elected to the Garrick Club in 1908.

All the while, however, Granville-Barker was engaged on a task with much grander and more historical repercussions. In 1907 he and the critic William Archer published *A National Theatre: Scheme and Estimates*, a volume of both meticulous analysis and passionate advocacy. "It is essential to break away, completely and unequivocally, from the ideals and traditions of the profit-seeking stage", they wrote. A putative National Theatre "must impose itself on public notice, not by posters and column advertisements in the newspapers, but by the very fact of its ample, dignified, and liberal existence. It must bulk large in the social and intellectual life of London…It must be visibly and unmistakably a popular institution, making a large appeal to the whole community…It will be seen that the Theatre we propose would be a National Theatre in this sense, that it would be from the first conditionally – and, in the event of success, would become absolutely – the property of the nation."[5]

This was visionary indeed, and the vision had never before been promoted with such zest. And the authors' concern was not merely with the drama itself, but with the well-being of the actors also (that doubtless being Granville-Barker's input). The National Theatre would enable actors to be constantly employed, in major roles in some productions and in minor ones in others, no one performer to be valued above all others, but to work as a team. "The artistic advantage to the actor arising from a variety of employment is generally admitted, yet not fully realised", they wrote. "Beyond all doubt, the suppression of the old stock company by the long run system has done a very real service to the stage. It has encouraged a finish, both in play-writing and acting, which the older conditions never allowed. It has broken a tradition of slovenliness…. Being cast only for parts for which his personality is obviously suited, [the actor] is tied down to one line of work, never attains any suppleness or versatility, and at last becomes stale and uninteresting, even in the parts to which he is so closely confined. Constant mechanical repetition of one type of character hardens his peculiarities into mannerisms. Even if his performance of a part be not mechanical from the outset, the intolerable monotony

---

5 William Archer and H Granville-Barker, *A National Theatre: Scheme and Estimates* (1907), p xviii

involved in seven or eight repetitions a week soon grinds all spontaneity out of it; and it is not only his performance of that part that suffers, but his capability for others."[6] Mere actors had never before enjoyed such attention or been valued with such consideration.

Support for the notion of a National Theatre came from an unexpected source, the Secretary of State for the Colonies, at that time Mr Winston Churchill. At a banquet in honour of Ellen Terry at the Hotel Cecil, Churchill said that "we" (perhaps the Government?) did not do much in England for the dramatic art. We left it to shift for itself. We were content to let it be governed and guided, to ebb and flow hither and thither, merely by chance and caprice, and to regulate it, so far as the nation was concerned, only by commercial considerations. This, he thought was a great pity, and in a perfectly Churchillian phrase he pointed out "self-sacrifice and not self-interest was the parent of the arts." Granville-Barker's immediate response to this address was to send round to Churchill a copy of the book which he and Archer had written, with a covering letter asking mischievously that he keep it handy for reference whenever the subject comes up, as it would one day, in the House of Commons.[7]

Next came a letter to *The Times* from John Hare, pouring cold water on the idea that Shakespeare should be memorialised by a statue (as had been suggested). "Shakespeare has, it seems to me, raised the most indestructible monument to his genius by the works he has left us", he wrote, "and it requires no blocks of stone or marble to keep his memory green. But I venture to think

6 *ibid.*, pp 32-33
7 Whitworth, *op.cit.*, pp 58-59

that the opportunity has offered itself to associate the name of our national poet, who has enriched the literature of the world and brought imperishable glory to the stage of his native land, with the founding of a national theatre."[8] The momentum gathered.

The House of Commons debated the idea for the first time just five years later, when a private member's bill was introduced on the resolution "that in the opinion of this House there shall be established a National Theatre, to be vested in trustees and assisted by the State, for the performance of the plays of Shakespeare and other dramas of recognized merit." By coincidence, but very appropriately, the debate took place on Shakespeare's birthday, 23 April, 1913, seventy years after the law had been passed to abolish the monopoly of the patented theatres. The MP who proposed the motion, a Mr MacKinder, said at the conclusion of a long speech, "I believe that a small grant made by the State would have the effect, in not a long term of years, of stimulating drama throughout the country by, in the first place, cultivating the public, in the second place by training actors, and in the third place by holding up a high standard. I believe that these are functions in which the State may legitimately take the lead, and with that object I have brought forward the Motion that I now beg to move." Generous mention was made of Granville-Barker's example. "We know that he has produced plays which in the ordinary commercial run would never have seen the light, and has educated the public", said Mr Ponsonby. Even Parliament acknowledged that Granville-Barker was the champion and leader of a movement which was no longer solely the subject of gossip among actors. "The day

8 *The Times*, 10 March, 1908

is past, I think", continued Ponsonby, "when the arts are merely looked upon as trivial and frivolous adjuncts to our ordinary life."

There was, inevitably, much opposition, on grounds which echo with wretched familiarity even today. It was said that to establish a National Theatre would interfere with our liberties; that the existing West End theatres already provided for all our needs; that the public was not greedy for Shakespeare and the classics as a whole, for they catered to a minority taste; that it would be an academic exercise, stuffy and well-meaning but dull. Most infuriating of all was the insidious assumption that it did not really matter one way or the other, and that one ought properly to spend time on more important issues. This philistine attitude brought forth from John Martin-Harvey a splutter of indignation at a subsequent conference. "I do not think children need educating", he said, "drama is inherent in them – Shakespeare they take to as a duck to water. It is the *poor* and the children who support Shakespeare...it is the working classes...who need the beauty in their lives which great drama brings to them. It is the most extraordinary thing to me that no Government has ever had the vision to perceive the necessity of *beauty* in the lives of the poor." He did not say so directly, but he might just as well have been celebrating the example set by Samuel Phelps in Islington half a century earlier.

George Bernard Shaw made the same point with characteristic bluntness. People sometimes asked him whether the English people really wanted a national theatre, he said. Of course they did not. They never wanted anything. They had got the British Museum, the National Gallery, and Westminster Abbey, but they never wanted them. But once these things stood as mysterious phenomena that had come to them they were quite proud of them, and felt that the place would be incomplete without them.[9]

Not surprisingly, the motion was defeated in the House of Commons. For the moment, with the advent of the Great War and its hideous harvest, the great idea was submerged; yet it survived in abeyance and its day was but postponed.

* * *

A number of young actors and future Garrick members were already making their names before the First World War, most notably one who was hugely influenced by William Poel and Granville-Barker, and who would one day form part of the team ultimately responsible for the foundation of the National Theatre. This was Lewis Casson, a strikingly handsome actor with a fine, melodious voice who, after a début in *The Winter's Tale* joined Granville-Barker's company at the Royal Court Theatre and was in the original cast there of Shaw's *Man and Superman*. Following that he played a season at the Gaiety in Manchester, where he met and married a newcomer called Sybil Thorndike; thereafter their careers marched in tandem. He served as a major in the war, was awarded the Military Cross and sent home wounded.

A contemporary was A. E. Matthews, always known as 'Matty', who astonishingly had already forged a successful career in the nineteenth century after starting as a call-boy at the Princess's Theatre in Oxford Street in 1886 and had

---

9 Whitworth, *op.cit.*, pp 155, 208, 210

even appeared with Ellen Terry. The astonishment arises from the fact that he was still working in my lifetime some seventy years later. His specialty was farce and witty light comedy, in which, like Hawtrey, he appeared to be doing very little but actually controlled every second. In 1920 he was Algie in *The Importance of Being Earnest* in New York. Since he never appeared in Shakespeare and had no great contribution to make to the national theatre movement, he cannot easily be fitted into the themes of this narrative, but in old age he was a cherished member of the Garrick Club, which alone suffices, and, as we shall see, in the era of the film industry a very popular perennial.

Felix Aylmer made his début in a bit part with Seymour Hicks in 1911, and he, too, subsequently felt the influence of Granville-Barker, in whose Shakespeare productions he acted at the Savoy; he would later confess that he did not enjoy playing Shakespeare and he, like Matty, would much later feature in many film roles. Aylmer had also worked with both Beerbohm Tree and Fred Terry, thus connecting the distant past with the burgeoning future, for Fred Terry had been with Squire and Mrs Bancroft in his early years, and was the brother of Ellen Terry. His most famous part was Sir Percy Blakeney in *The Scarlet Pimpernel*, which he first played in 1905 and with which he became so identified that he is the inevitable actor who comes to mind as soon as the play is mentioned. The links between theatrical eras are rendered even stronger by the realisation that one of Fred Terry's other sisters had just had a grandson, born the year before *The Scarlet Pimpernel*, who would be known to us as John Gielgud.

In some ways the Great War was a watershed in the theatre as in every other aspect of English life, for the styles and tastes which would come to fruition once it was all over would reflect both the yearning need for undemanding but gleefully witty entertainment on the one hand (notably supplied by Noël Coward), and a fierce and open pride in the maturity to which English acting genius was steadily aspiring. The depth, sophistication and ambitious reach of this genius would be apparent in the post-war years with the emergence of two titans; John Gielgud's first appearance on stage came in 1921, and Laurence Olivier's in 1922.

* * *

John Gielgud's first appearance in public was not on stage, but in a setting which could hardly have been more theatrical. When the solemn burial of the Unknown Soldier took place in Westminster Abbey in 1919, and the entire nation united to lament the wasted lives of so many young men, pupils at the adjacent Westminster School played their part. One of them was fifteen-year-old Gielgud, who served in the ceremony as an usher's attendant. It was a good start.

As a member of the Terry theatrical dynasty on his mother's side the urge to perform might have been innate. It was further enhanced by an inheritance from his paternal great-grandmother, who had been the finest Shakespearean actress in Lithuania, and there is a village there which still bears the family name (almost) – Gielgaudskis. The family had migrated to Poland, so that John's father, despite working on the London Stock Exchange, was in fact Polish, introducing another strain which he would one day draw upon for his insights into Chekhov. His father assented to his obvious desire to become an actor, provided that he could prove capable of earning his living by the time he was twenty-five. This he would do with time to spare.

While taking lessons with Lady Benson, who had her own acting school in the same neighbourhood as the Gielgud home (she was the actress wife of Sir Frank Benson), he went to the Old Vic as an unpaid extra in *Henry V*, produced by the idiosyncratic Robert Atkins who knew him only as "that boy in the brown suit". After that, he went to RADA and found himself, again as a drama student lent to a professional production, following Felix Aylmer around the stage as an orderly. There followed a season at the Oxford Playhouse, appearing in Congreve's *Love for Love* and Chekhov's *The Cherry Orchard*, in which he played Trofimov; Chekhov was still relatively unknown in England, and so the king of critics James Agate went to Oxford to see it. He wrote, "I suggest that *The Cherry Orchard* is one of the great plays of the world, and young Gielgud as Trofimov is perfection itself." He was still only twenty, and the name so unfamiliar that the university paper referred to him as 'Mr Gielgerd' and a local journal, even worse, transformed him into 'Joan Gillseed'.[10]

Back in London, however, the name would soon resonate widely. He understudied, then took over from, Noël Coward in *The Vortex*, followed by *The Constant Nymph* and a short, unremarkable engagement in New York. Then he launched properly into classical parts with a season at the Old Vic playing Romeo, Antonio and Richard II. From now on, Gielgud's career would be a kaleidoscopic panoply of different roles, many glorious, some better left

10 *The Ages of Gielgud* (1984), ed. Ronald Harwood, p 31

unnoticed, but at any rate all too numerous to inform a tedious list. His legacy is best served by highlighting those roles in which he made history, and which linger in our collective memory. The first of these must be Richard II, which he first played at the age of twenty-six and would later return to with such firm authority that there are those who maintain this was a finer portrayal than his immortal Hamlet. One who saw it at the Old Vic was a woman called Elizabeth Mackintosh, who was so inspired that she sat down to write a new stage version of the story especially for Gielgud, which she called *Richard of Bordeaux*. As author she used the name Gordon Daviot, but she was already known for historical novels under another name, Josephine Tey. *Richard of Bordeaux* was destined to be "one of those plays that nobody liked except the public."[11] As soon as it opened at the New Theatre in St Martin's Lane, it made Gielgud into a 'star', to be followed in the street, pointed out in restaurants, endlessly photographed for souvenir postcards. He quite blatantly enjoyed every minute of it.

What was more important was the recognition that, shallow though the writing might be, Gielgud ennobled it with the intelligence of his acting. The now-veteran actor Esmé Percy wrote and told him, "Having been born in an age that now seems legendary, my memory houses many splendours, but your Richard shall be added to my first sight of Henry Irving…among the greatest and most poignant nights of my life."[12] Even the Chancellor of the Exchequer, Stanley Baldwin, saw fit to write a fan-letter. When the queues had subsided, and the cheers grown

---

11 Sheridan Morley, *John G: The Authorised Biography of John Gielgud* (2001), p 97
12 *ibid.*, p 98

quiet, the play itself was all but forgotten and was never revived in London for another actor. But it would always signal the moment of John Gielgud's first great impact upon the public consciousness.

Not, however, the most enduring. That distinction must belong to his definitive, haunting portrayal of Hamlet. He had first played it at the Old Vic under Harcourt Williams, when he already drew plaudits. In the first place it was such a novelty to see the part played by a young man, as we nowadays would take for granted that it must be, if it is accurately to suggest a man recently returned from university. Forbes-Robertson had been forty-four when he played it, and Irving thirty-six. Gielgud was just twenty-six, and with pensive, handsome mien allied to weariness of woe, he was extraordinarily romantic. James Agate wrote, "I have no hesitation whatsoever in saying that it is the high-water mark of English Shakespearean acting in our time. This actor is young, thoughtful, clever, and sensitive. His performance is subtle, brilliant, vigorous, imaginative, tender and full of the right kind of ironic humour." His great-uncle Fred Terry sent him an effusive letter: "I have in the past forty years seen many Hamlets, but none, I think, which Shakespeare himself would have liked as much as yours." Sybil Thorndike agreed. "Yours is the Hamlet of my dreams and I never hope to see it played better. I was swept off my feet into another world, and moved beyond words", she told him. Another actress, Diana Wynyard, told him that his performance had made her think about the play for the first time, and with this remark she hit upon the precise nature of Gielgud's genius in the role, a genius which would deepen with ever more insight as the years passed.

The 1934 production at the New Theatre was his own. He would re-visit the part and bring utter sublimity to it in 1944, and make a BBC recording in 1948 which has to find a place in every playgoer's library. For the moment, the 1934 performances are the ones that placed Gielgud on a peak, and the portrait photograph of him in the role at that time is world-famous and constantly reproduced. For the small but crucial cameo part of Osric, Gielgud employed a twenty year-old novice called Alec Guinness, who proceeded to watch him from the wings every night and declare that the portrayal was "definitive".[13] When it was all over six months later, Guinness wrote to say that he had never been happier. "I am not a very gay or happy person by nature", he said, "but I find the confidence you have in me a great source of happiness. I want to write this because it's one of those things which mean a lot to me, but I find very hard to speak." That rings very true, as Alec's Garrick Club colleagues would years later testify that it was difficult to persuade him to say anything personal at all; Gielgud's influence upon him must indeed have been powerful to elicit such praise.

The novelist Rosamund Lehmann wrote out of the blue to tell him, "I felt all through the production that this was exactly what Shakespeare would have wanted." More pertinently, there were very perspicacious observations from George Devine, who would in a later age become a highly influential actor-director at the Royal Court Theatre, but was then a young student who had two years earlier secured Gielgud to direct *Romeo and Juliet* for the Oxford University Dramatic Society. "The general spread of culture and knowledge in our time", he wrote, "makes

13 *The Ages of Gielgud*, p 61

it unnecessary for Hamlet to underline everything as he goes along. What you are doing is crediting us in the audience with a kind of intelligence…and I do think you have shown us the future of Shakespeare instead of, as usual, the past."[14]

In retrospect, the next venture was pregnant with symbolism. *Romeo and Juliet* would provide him with two classic roles, for he could alternate Romeo and Mercutio with another actor and thereby add some spice to the entertainment. Having cast Peggy Ashcroft for Juliet and Edith Evans as the Nurse, he offered the Romeo/Mercutio dual role to an up-and-coming young actor who would contrast with him in a different style of romantic appeal, one Laurence Olivier. It was to be the beginning of a gentle rivalry which would last half a century, respectful on Gielgud's part, a trifle jealous on Olivier's, but thankfully spared that intensity which characterised so many of the nineteenth-century competitions between titanic egos. The difference between them was apparent immediately, Olivier passionate, athletic and vibrant, Gielgud poised, careful and poetic. The trouble was, the critics still for the most part preferred Gielgud's measured rhapsody to Olivier's undisciplined emotion. One of them put it like this: "As Romeo, Mr Olivier was about twenty times as much in love with Peggy Ashcroft's Juliet as Mr Gielgud was. But Mr Gielgud spoke most of the poetry far better than Mr Olivier. Yet, I must out with it, the fire of Mr Olivier's passion carried the play along in a way that Mr Gielgud's could never quite manage."

Olivier never entirely forgave the slightly older man for his clear superiority as a speaker of verse, despite Gielgud's

---

14 Morley, *op.cit.*, pp 112, 115, 116

innate generosity of spirit, and they would never again appear on stage together. Privately he would admit that, were it not for John Gielgud's example and challenge, he might never have become a classical actor at all. But his ambition was charged by this experience, and it was clear to the public that the newcomer was going to be real competition for Gielgud's ascendancy.[15]

It was likewise clear that this ascendancy was built upon the triple foundations of style, formidable though invisible technique, and an utterly seductive voice. As for the style, Gielgud gave the impression that he was the first actor ever to be subservient to the words he was speaking and to be totally indifferent to his own ego; he was never 'showing off'. The speech mattered, the man himself was merely the instrument through which the words unlocked their meaning. The critic Michael Billington put it this way: "He has a matchless feeling for the architecture of a speech, taking a series of lines on a single breath and building to a thrilling crescendo. But, within that, there is a rare sensitivity to the weight and sense of each particular phrase." Another critic, J.C. Trewin, also detected this uncanny archeological attention to a sentence. "Style is not a physical affectation", he wrote. "It is bred of natural elegance of mind, and unblurred response to the word." Gielgud himself agreed that his approach was specific. "I try to study the sound, shape, and length of words as they are written on the page. In a verse speech (and often in a long prose one, too) I am constantly aware of the whole span of the arc – the beginning, middle, and end of the passage."[16] He in fact submitted to the internal

---

15 *ibid.*, pp 120-123, 124, 126
16 *The Ages of Gielgud*, pp 15, 110

logic and magic (notions not antithetical in his case) of the lines rather than let the lines artificially imprison their meaning in a straightjacket of form. Elsewhere he said, "It's like swimming, you know. If you surrender to the water you keep up, but if you fight it you drown."[17] He allowed the iambic pentameter to do the work, happy with the inference that Shakespeare knew what he was about and required no flashy actor to help him say what he wanted to say. The humility of this approach had the extraordinary effect of introducing the audience to Shakespeare himself, almost in an intimate manner. One could hear Shakespeare thinking, watch the thoughts forming; the words were the life of the man held before the audience.

This very personal, conspiratorial style inspired spectators to collaborate with Gielgud in re-creating what had been in the writer's head. It was "complete contact with the deep imaginative sub-concious inside the mind of the beholder", according to Ralph Richardson.[18] Indeed, it was Richardson, who would be one of Gielgud's most enduring friends (but not, alas, a member of the Garrick) who pointed out in characteristically blunt fashion the nobility of imagination in Gielgud's acting. "I could come on and say, 'I'm from the Gas Works, I've come to read the meter', and I think that people would believe me," he said. "But it's strange that John Gielgud, whose acting I admire extravagantly (I think he is one of the greatest actors living) could not come on and say, 'I'm from the Gas Works, I've come to read the meter.' People would not believe that he came from the Gas Works. Then the other curious thing is that, at the end of The Tempest, John has come on and said,

---

17 Lewis Funke and John Booth, *Actors Talk About Acting* (1961), p 7
18 Bryan Forbes, *That Despicable Race* (1980), p 286

'I am the Duke of Milan' and you believe it. He *is* the Duke of Milan, absolutely splendid. Now, I have played in *The Tempest* and I have said, 'I am the Duke of Milan', and no one has believed me for one moment."[19] This is much more than identification with character; it is familiarity with the writer's mind. Donald Sinden put it this way: "He speaks Shakespeare's lines as if he had written them himself; we understand them because he understands them; if we do not, it is our fault, not his."[20]

How he made the audience share his insight was through superlative technique. Like most other actors he examined himself minutely to discover the truth of his reactions, and said that he concentrated on the memory of when he saw somebody dead for the first time in order to give Hamlet's famous soliloquy its resonance – he was thinking how the person had looked in death and found himself reliving the reflections of that moment, through the medium of Shakespeare's words. "It is the private curse of all good actors that they develop abnormal powers of self-observation", wrote Richard Bebb.[21] His technique was constantly on the move, honed and polished and re-tuned in rehearsal, so often that other actors found it difficult to keep up with his quicksilver mind. Simon Callow has made a useful analogy with culinary art. "For me a rehearsal room is like a kitchen," he writes, "where you combine ingredients as they come to hand, testing, tasting. Finally, you apply flame, and the thing grows; exactly how, no one knows."[22] This was the fascination as well as the mystery

---

19 *ibid.*, p 246

20 Donald Sinden, *A Touch of the Memoirs* (1982), p 61

21 Richard Bebb, *Tragedians of the City*, talk broadcast on BBC, 12 April 1972, and published in the *Journal of Recorded Sound*.

22 Simon Callow, *Being An Actor* (1984), p 105

of Gielgud's technique; he had conquered you before you even knew you were prey, and found yourself thinking the way he (and Shakespeare) wanted you to think, without knowing quite how he had done it.

The technique had also to be further developed and altered in performance, to match the tone and flavour of the audience (no two audiences being alike, as every actor will tell you). It was, he said, "a continual adjustment, like putting screws in a wireless." It was easier if one could pretend after a while that the audience was not there, in order to achieve that relaxation without which all technique is so much irksome baggage. "Relaxation is the secret of good acting", he said. "Young actors when they are nervous tighten up as soon as they start. This tension sometimes is effective, but it is terribly exhausting and only briefly effective."[23] What was required was a kind of virtuosity in breathing and phrasing.

The gift of a relaxed technique enabled the third prong of his art, his exquisite voice, the freedom to make melody with vowels and consonants and to rescue the verse from threat of strangulation by false emphases. It was said of Charles Kemble that one could not imagine "so much charm in words as mere sounds" and that his technique enabled him to give a "perfect, most musical delivery of the meditative passages."[24] In the case of John Gielgud, that delivery made of his voice the most perfect instrument for verse-speaking of any actor in history; there were those who still preferred the voice of Forbes-Robertson, but they were outnumbered as the years passed. The critic Kenneth Tynan famously described Gielgud's voice as

23 Bertram Joseph, *The Tragic Actor* (1959)
24 *ibid.*, p 312

having had an east wind blown through it, Trewin called it a Stradivarius controlled by a master, and Alec Guinness coined the beautiful phrase, "like a silver trumpet muffled in silk".[25] The odd thing is that using the voice as a musical instrument does not, as a non-actor might suspect, isolate it from sense, render it affected and remote; it is not at all like chanting or like Mrs Bancroft's "bell with a wooden tongue; it makes a sound, but there it ends."[26] With Gielgud's masterly control, musical discipline revealed meaning and truth of character with rare clarity. "He doesn't simply speak verse: he *acts* it", wrote Michael Billington. And so, it is slight praise to celebrate his voice as if there were nothing else, and no tribute to their novelty for some modern actors to mumble and shuffle their way through the poetry in a wilful attempt to shake off Gielgud's imperishable legacy; they merely confirm it. And there are plenty of recordings which testify that this was the pinnacle to which all Shakespearean acting had been striving through the centuries, reached not through the old panache, but with quiet, thrilling intelligence.

* * *

Meanwhile, the momentum towards the goal of a genuine National Theatre was not allowed to slacken, and a small but crucial advance was made when a formal question was put to the Prime Minister, Ramsay MacDonald, in the House of Commons on 22 July, 1929, to this effect: "Would he, in order to promote the artistic sincerity and dignity of Great Britain and to encourage the best elements in the

25 *The Ages of Gielgud*, p 57
26 J A Hammerton, *The Actor's Art* (1897), p 26

British Theatre, consider the establishment of a national theatre on lines somewhat similar to those followed in many European countries?" MacDonald's reply was distinctly encouraging. Far from dismissing the idea in the usual way, he expressed "a great deal of sympathy" and let it be understood that, should further concrete proposals be forthcoming, the Government would consider them seriously.[27] The indefatigable Granville-Barker immediately rose to the challenge with a new book in 1930, essentially an expansion of his original plan published twenty-three years earlier, in which he for the first time proposed an actual position by the River Thames. "The site facing the river between County Hall and the Surrey Approach to the new Charing Cross Bridge, is about all that one can wish for", he wrote. "A National Theatre could hardly be better placed. A National Opera House could find a place opposite." If we replace the suggested Opera House with a Concert Hall, we have a pretty close picture of what would eventually be built on the South Bank some thirty years later.

Granville-Barker was prescient in yet another detail. Boldly, he maintained that there should not be one theatre, but two theatres under the same roof, to enable the stable of actors to be fully employed most of the time and for their work to be refreshed by experimental drama as well as the classics. It was the only way in which the financial challenges could be squared with reality, and he went into searching analysis of the way in which the theatre could be made to pay for itself, enumerating a possible schedule of performances and parts shared. "The provision of two houses, by which the margin of idleness can be reduced

---

27 Geoffrey Whitworth, op.cit., p 142

to as near vanishing point as possible, is the obvious, is really the only remedy. There is none in the employment of actors who do not care if they stand idle and will do it cheaply, or whom nobody else will employ; this would be reduction in quality. Nor is there in the anarchy of a company with half its members for half the time occupied elsewhere."[28] This, too, would come to pass one day, and it would do so in large part because Granville-Barker was no mere theoretician, but an experienced actor who knew how actors worked best. He was by now retired in the country busy writing his *Prefaces to Shakespeare*, and his vision was as keen as ever.

He would also, within a few years only, have the joy of seeing this vision realised by John Gielgud in the West End, without a new theatre, without a government subsidy, without fanfare and virtually single-handed. Following his successful season at the New Theatre with *Hamlet*, *Romeo and Juliet*, and *The Seagull*, at which he was in effect the first actor-manager (though he did not call himself such) since the heady days of Irving and Beerbohm Tree, he followed with a new season at the Queen's Theatre. At both, he assembled a company of the finest actors among his contemporaries, determined not to be a central attraction by reason of his fame but to be part of a team. He directed some plays himself, and brought in the huge talents of Komisarjevsky and Michel Saint-Denis to direct others. At such a moment, in the opinion of Peggy Ashcroft, "John exerted one of the most important influences in our theatre that I can remember."[29] His ideal of a company of collaborative rather than competitive actors was

---

28 *ibid.*, p 184
29 *The Ages of Gielgud*, p 72

demonstrated immediately at the Queen's with his first production, a revival of *Richard II*, in which he broke away from his own earlier portrayals in both Shakespeare and *Richard of Bordeaux* to allow equal weight to every part. Peggy Ashcroft shone at her luminous best, and Leon Quartermaine (another Garrick member) as John of Gaunt made such an impression that his performance "had already become a legend by the time the curtain fell."[30] Then there was another young unknown in the team (himself a Garrick man one day) called Michael Redgrave.

Gielgud announced his philosophy in a semi-public manner with a letter to the *Daily Telegraph* in which he declared that "Britain's National Theatre should not waste money on a vast new building; it should not just limit itself to Shakespeare and popular hits, and, thirdly, it should unite Sadler's Wells, the Old Vic, and the Stratford Memorial Theatre as interchangeable companies, all of whom would form a part of the National." In the meantime, he would invest his own money, the profits from his New York run as Hamlet, to create something akin to this ideal at the Queen's, and to ensure the highest possible quality of drama, he would allow eight to nine weeks of rehearsal time for each play, which was truly revolutionary.

The second play in the season was *The School for Scandal*, in which Gielgud played Joseph Surface. Laurence Olivier would generously assess this as "the best light comedy performance I have ever, or ever shall, see", but the production by Guthrie was rather too close to farce than Sheridan could ever have intended. There followed *The Three Sisters* directed by St Denis, so purely Chekhovian that its translator, Constance Garnett, who had been working

---

30 Giles Brandreth, *John Gielgud: An Actor's Life* (2000), p 68

on English versions of Chekhov for twenty years against much apathy and even some hostility, told Gielgud that she had always hoped and longed for a proper production of his plays in England. "At last", she said, "this has been achieved, and I just want to thank you for the great pleasure of seeing my dreams fulfilled." Guthrie admitted that this was "the most articulate and accomplished Chekhov that I have ever seen", and Siegfried Sassoon wrote to say that it was a magnificent, flawless achievement: "Thank you for an evening I shall never forget". In deference to his profession, Gielgud organised a special midnight matinée to which other working actors, who could not otherwise have seen the production, were invited, and at the end of the run a special dinner was given for him at the Garrick Club in tribute to the stimulation which he had given to the London stage.[31]

The final play of the season was *The Merchant of Venice* in which he offered a deeply malignant portrayal of Shylock, in Peggy Ashcroft's words "a fairy-tale monster, defying sympathy."[32] It was not a well-timed interpretation perhaps, with news of Nazi persecution of German Jews filtering through to some assiduous newspapers, but more to the point, it was not the kind of part to which Gielgud could comfortably bring truth. As the *Times* perceptively pointed out, "He is as incapable of portraying evil as he is of understanding it as a director."

But it was emphatically not the success of this or that role which marked the season out as historical. It was the example of a group of actors who congealed and co-operated to make a 'family' or 'ensemble' (both Gielgud

31 Morley, *op.cit.*, pp 151, 152, 153, 155, 157
32 *The Ages of Gielgud*, p 73

and Ashcroft, for example, were in all four plays, and developed antennae which allowed them to act as one). One of his designers (three women collectively known as The Motleys) said that he "single-handedly put the English theatre back on the world map" and that "because of his innate modesty, it was to be Olivier, after the war, who took all the credit for doing everything that John had done before it."

His biographer Sheridan Morley (another Garrick member) asserts his place in theatrical history in the most energetic and whole-hearted manner, with a paragraph which bears repetition in full. "If, at the end of almost a century", he wrote, "John Gielgud is to be remembered for any single achievement, it would surely have to be the way in which he redefined and recreated the resident classical repertory company. Without his interest and involvement in every aspect of this, from casting to costumes, from production to publicity, it is doubtful whether either the National Theatre or the Royal Shakespeare Company would have come into post-war existence quite so heavily influenced by his pre-war work."[33]

---

33 Morley, *op.cit.*, pp 159, 65

9

WOLFIT AND OLIVIER

With the outbreak of the Second World War, other symbolic but profound steps advanced the nagging notion that there really ought to be some official recognition of the importance of the legitimate theatre to the national psyche. The first of these was the establishment, weeks before war was declared, of the Entertainments National Service Association, known by its initials as ENSA. It was founded by Sir Seymour Hicks and organised by the theatre director (and Garrick member) Basil Dean, who had done similar work organising music and drama in the First World War and now persuaded the War Office that presenting theatrical entertainment to soldiers in the field would not only offer respite from the toil of battle, and thus serve as domestic propaganda to boost morale, but would also give them the artistic nourishment they deserved. The idea that drama could enrich, and was the natural right of every citizen, was after all at the root of the long slow movement towards a National Theatre, and ENSA provided a mighty illustration of this very notion in actual operation.

Of course, with so many entertainers spread over such a vast area, the quality often appealed to the simplest tastes with precious little intellectual demand to be made, and the troops soon came to know ENSA affectionately as Every Night Something Awful. The sheer scale of the endeavour stretches belief. The first ENSA concert took place one week after the declaration of war, at Old Dene Camp in Camberley. By the time the last stage was dismantled in 1946, ENSA had given over 2 and a half million performances to audiences totalling over 500 million. The organisation undertook to visit every major theatre of the war, transporting mobile stages and pianos the while, issuing uniforms to actors and singers lest they should be mistaken for spies when captured (the comedian Tommy Trinder refused to wear one on the grounds that if he were captured he deserved to be shot). Moreover, there was a good number of serious dramatic recitals included among the cheerful trivia, and Garrick members who took part included Noël Coward, Bryan Forbes, John Gielgud, Jack Hawkins, Laurence Olivier and Paul Scofield; Donald Sinden performed for the sister organisation operating in the Middle East, known as MESA. With time, the serious work came to be appreciated by the troops with even more delight than the jokes, giving yet more proof of the universality of drama.

A second wartime influence was exerted by one man with relentless drive and conviction, the last actor-manager Donald Wolfit. Almost like a one-man demonstration of the indomitable will of the English, Wolfit was as determined to bring the works of Shakespeare to the fighting men at the front as Churchill was to fire their spirit; indeed, the soaring eloquence of the politician echoed the uplifting power of the playwright, each showing in his own way the power of the word. Wolfit was convinced in his marrow that Shakespeare was as much part of the war-effort as anything else, and felt it his duty to enlist the National Poet. Even before he took his company off to entertain the troops, he had refused to cancel his autumn tour as war drew near, and he continued to play even during the black-out, when it was difficult to see exactly where the theatre was. His most inspired idea was to offer Shakespeare to the besieged Londoners when they could get time off from the war, so he rented the Strand Theatre for a derisory sum and opened it every day between one and two o'clock in the afternoon to present excerpts from the plays, sonnets and prologues. He called it Lunch Time Shakespeare. Only the stalls were used, with sandwiches and coffee in the stalls bar, and air-raids or alerts were not allowed to interrupt a performance, one of the cast announcing, "The warning has just gone. We shall proceed. Will those who wish to leave do so as quietly as possible".[1] Scarcely anyone moved. There were times when bombs fell and the walls shook, but Wolfit went on. The press made him a hero, with headlines such as "Shakespeare Beats Hitler", and together with Myra Hess giving her piano recitals at the National Gallery, he embodied the resistance of the Cockney Londoner.

Donald Wolfit's faith in the mission of the theatre to touch any audience in any circumstance was rewarded later, when his company performed *Hamlet* before troops in Europe and Field Marshall Montgomery told him afterwards, "This is what I have said the men have wanted for a long time." Later still, as they left Port Said after performances of *Hamlet, Much Ado*, and *The Merchant*, two thousand troops lined the ship's rails to give them a mighty

---

1 Donald Wolfit, *First Interval* (1954), pp 200-201

send-off, waving and cheering till they were out of sight.[2] This, together with the rapturous receptions he had been accorded in provincial theatres all over Great Britain, helped to encourage those who were still struggling to convince governments that the theatre mattered. "Had it not been for his courage and enterprise, a whole generation of young theatregoers would have grown up during the war without having seen a Shakespeare play on the stage."[3]

Donald Wolfit frankly identified with the underprivileged and looked with scorn upon those he considered pampered. He had not been born to the stage, nor had he come to it blessed with advantages. Short, burly even when young, moon-faced, with no chin, a big but rough speaking voice, and a broad Yorkshire accent which he had to struggle to get rid of at the beginning of his career, James Agate once described him as an "amiable gorilla."[4] What he lacked in beauty he more than made up for in fire and energy, in instinct and a sense of wonder at where he was and what he was doing. He had been an ordinary lad completely in love with the stage and destined to make it his home, but the journey had been long and strewn with obstacles, so that when, after an apprenticeship in Sheffield, he found himself offered the chance to join the famed Old Vic Company, he took it with mixed excitement and resentment. His huge ambition desperate to be assuaged, he knew this was a step to eventual greatness; on the other hand he was to share the space with people who had not had to work at all, in his view. On the top of this list was Gielgud, definitely to be numbered among the pampered,

2 Ronald Harwood, *Sir Donald Wolfit C.B.E.* (1971), pp 139-140, 147, 150, 188, 190
3 Norman Marshall, *The Other Theatre*
4 James Agate, *Ego 5 (1935-1948)*, p 80

a man whom he detested without concealment. He was Claudius to Gielgud's Hamlet, Tybalt in the famous production of *Romeo and Juliet*, Cassius to Gielgud's Mark Antony, always, it seemed, in the subservient role despite his being two years older; but then, of course, he had not been born into the Terry family, had he! It was therefore with extraordinary pride that he heard that the gallery were to present him with a laurel wreath, in accordance with their tradition, unknown to him, of honouring their favourite actor of the season. This was done on stage after his Cassius in *Julius Caesar*, and he hung on to the tatters of that laurel wreath for years afterwards. He knew he could connect with the crowd; he knew he spoke with their voice. That was to be his strength against the prejudices of fashion.

It was also at the Vic that he learnt from Harley Granville-Barker about staging, and from William Poel about voice projection and the proper phrasing of verse. As we saw in the last chapter, Poel insisted that the lines should flow with due attention to the key words in a speech, giving emphasis to draw out meaning, not plunder opportunities for vocal display. He "constantly corrected my vowel sounds, eradicated the false stresses and replaced them by new ones that were a revelation to me", wrote Wolfit.[5] He also observed with advantage the noble example of Ernest Milton, a Hamlet very much admired in his day, whose reputation has not survived the passage of years, save in the memories of other actors. As the result of these influences, he gradually developed his own style, or rather discovered the confidence to let it burst forth, since the Wolfit style had always been latent, awaiting release; it was part of the

---

5 Wolfit, *op.cit.*, p 142

man. It was a style that, in the words of his biographer Ronald Harwood, "would depend on a mighty inner power which was to swell to such enormity that the actor would have difficulty in containing it." It was a reservoir of vocal and emotional power which almost caught him by surprise when first exposed, and it was in the old-fashioned mode of "unashamed, unembarrassed passion" which tended to make the English uneasy and apologetic, except, that is, for the nineteenth-century English tragic actors; he was the exultant echo of an earlier tradition. Harwood again: "Wolfit was the latest in a long line of English actors who conformed to a similar pattern: men whose dramatic power was contained in a graceless physique; men whose style of acting was often questioned by their contemporaries but who overcame those reservations by the immensity of their projected passions." Men like Edmund Kean, in short. Donald Wolfit was becoming an actor out of his time, a virtuoso "in whom some ancient fire burned."[6] For many years his extravagant style would provoke mockery; eventually, when he gave it the part he was made for, it would excite only the most awed admiration.

Wolfit devoted almost his entire career to Shakespeare, with whom he felt an uncanny affinity. On some rare occasions when he deleted an awkward line, it was because he knew; "If I can't learn it, Shakespeare didn't write it", he said. At the Shakespeare Memorial Theatre he played many seasons of the greatest roles, then formed his own Donald Wolfit Shakespeare Company which toured the country from top to bottom, endlessly changing trains, living in conditions of real hardship, but determined on the solemn duty of making Shakespeare available to all.

6 Harwood, *op.cit.*, pp 100-101, 169, 226

Then came the war and the bombs and 'the show must go on', and performing for the troops. But it was at the Scala Theatre in London in 1944 that a Wolfit performance became legendary.

He would finally attempt to portray King Lear. "The time seemed opportune", he wrote. "If ever the sorrows of Lear, the cruelty and the blinding, staggering sickness of this great tragedy could be understood by the mind and heart of the people, surely the time must be now. Half our cities lay in partial ruins and there was worse to come… We were indeed on the open heath as a nation, defying the elements."[7] He tried it first in Cardiff, but knew that he had not been able to rise to the challenge; he felt like a swimmer avoiding the crushing waves. He would have to surrender himself to the part, unshackle the emotions wherein his strange acting talent resided. It happened on 12 April, 1944, in London.

The audience was unpromising, with only about sixty tickets sold. Wolfit prepared well in advance, surveyed the bare, defiant stage, and retired to get ready. Harwood describes the atmosphere that evening so potently that he must be quoted almost in full: "With forty-five minutes to go to curtain-up, he called for his dresser. In silence, the clothes were handed to him until the last heavy cloak sat upon the bent shoulders; the triple coronet was offered and he fixed it securely on his head, nodding and shaking as if with palsy. When the assistant stage-manager called five minutes to the rise of the curtain, Wolfit slowly descended to the stage, his dresser in attendance, carrying a silver salver upon which stood a moist chamois leather, a glass of Guinness and – rare in war-time – some peeled grapes.

---

7 Wolfit, *op.cit.*, p 211

Actors who happened to be waiting in the corridors stood aside to allow the little procession to pass; Wolfit nodded to them with an expression of infinite weariness. The silence backstage was oppressive."

"He waited in the wings, doing his best not to concern himself with the bustle of activity that precedes the performance; this, in itself, was unusual, for in other plays, no matter how large or wearying the part, he would be hissing last-minute instructions to the stage management, electricians and actors. But not this night; he stood perfectly still, with Rosalind [Iden], ready as Cordelia, beside him, occasionally glancing at her with a look that seemed to want to make sure that she understood the weight of all the world was upon his shoulders. He talked to no one; members of the company gave him a wide berth if they had to pass. He did not even enquire about the size of the audience; he might be expected to gaze through the peep-hole, but he did not; the house, in fact, was painfully thin, less than half-full. His stage-director ordered the actors to stand by. The house lights dimmed. Rosabel Watson received her cue, and the trumpet sounded. The curtain rose slowly."[8]

There followed a virtuoso performance which defies description. Somebody who was there told me, "Wolfit took off, and the heavens opened." When not on stage, he behaved with a strange remoteness, the tension in his back almost visible. He got through eight bottles of Guinness that evening. When on stage, he was gigantic. In the terrible scene in which the King turns upon his daughter Goneril and brings down the curse of Heaven upon her, wishing sterility into her womb, Richard Bebb said it made

---

8 Harwood, *op.cit.*, p 160

his flesh creep, and Donald Sinden that "you really thought he must have influence Up There." Wolfit clearly believed that he did, too. He lifted his arms high above his head, physically grabbed the curse from the skies, and then, with awful ferocity, hurled it at Goneril. "I thought, there will be a flash of smoke and Goneril will disappear", Sinden recalled. "Astonishing. I had never believed an actor could be that big."[9] He followed Granville-Barker's injunction that Lear *is* the storm.

Word passed round on the streets of London very quickly, so that on the second night the theatre was packed, with two hundred people standing, squeezing around the edge or squatting in the aisles. Many of these were in uniform, soldiers on leave. Yet this audience of untheatrical, unintellectual folk were spellbound by the combination of Shakespeare and Wolfit. Agate captured the moment in a review of historical significance. "It is certain that the audience surrendered to the stroke of something without quite knowing what. It left the theatre conscious of having been swept off its feet and not bothering to wonder why", he wrote. "I say deliberately that his performance on Wednesday was the greatest piece of Shakespearean acting I have seen since I have been privileged to write for the *Sunday Times*."[10] That word "deliberately" is a measure of the critic's wish to convey amazement. Jumping ahead a little, James Agate would also make an instructive comparison with Laurence Olivier's portrayal of Lear, supporting that distinction between the contrived, architectural style of acting and the fierce, unbridled style which trembles on the edge of danger. "Wolfit's Lear is a ruined piece of nature",

9 Bryan Forbes, *That Despicable Race* (1980), p 269
10 Harwood, *op.cit.*, pp 165-166; and Wolfit, *op.cit.*, p 219

he wrote. "Olivier's is a picture of ruins most cunningly presented."

Donald Wolfit had achieved his triple ambition to make Shakespeare live again, to demonstrate that ordinary people could respond to his plays, and to do his duty for his country in war-time. He had also conquered one of drama's most appalling challenges; if Hamlet belonged to Forbes-Robertson and Gielgud, henceforth Lear would be Wolfit's own, utterly unmatchable until Paul Scofield's soulful representation a generation later.

He had his eccentricities, of course. It was said that he ran his companies like a boot camp, the rest of the cast and crew cowering before him. He was autocratic and bullying, requiring others on stage to keep well clear of him lest his spotlight should be shared. "When I say at arm's length", he said, "I mean my arm as well as yours." When he was invited to play Othello as 'guest star' with another company in the provinces, he sent ahead a list of his conditions. One was that none of the actors should ever have appeared in that play before, and that the one cast as Iago should never even have played Shakespeare in his life. The notion of 'ensemble' acting, so recently and magnificently fostered by Gielgud, was poison to him; his more archaic tradition would not understand it. Of the dozens of stories told about him, one alone may epitomise the sense of self which he promoted. A junior actor who had to feed Macbeth with the cue, "The Queen, my lord, is dead", then retire to the shadows for the leading actor to reply "She should have died hereafter" and launch into the splendid "Tomorrow, and tomorrow, and tomorrow,/Creeps in this petty pace from day to day/To the last syllable of recorded time." Wolfit forgot that he had sacked the young man earlier that day, and that this was his last performance, so he was fed an alternative cue: "The Queen, my lord, is feeling very much better." I do hope it is true.

An actor who recalled those days told me, "You would never think of applying to join his company unless you and your family were starving. He was truly a horror, an absolute lunatic. Without the influence of his wife to keep him in control, somebody would have murdered him." The intensity of his rage could be terrifying. On the other hand, he was capable of kindness and care, sometimes allowing a small pension for a retired actor without the man's knowledge of whence it came. His unpredictability travelled with him like an advance tidal wave. Sometimes his make-up was bad because he had used entirely the wrong colours; his wigs were ill-fitting and shifted on his head; and even his own glorious performances he seemed determined to ruin with sentimentality, exaggerated effects and the terrible temptations of "ham". It is significant that the Lear he gave in 1944 had deteriorated within a few months into a shambles of melodrama and pose, the brilliance of his beginning having metamorphosed at his own hands. And suddenly, the next night, the genius would return and dazzle. Wolfit personified more than anyone the paradox inherent in great acting – that it could be magnificent or woefully risible; it could never be just adequate.

In 1942, after Lunch Time Shakespeare and before *King Lear*, he was elected a member of the Garrick Club, which he came to treasure with a fondness which surprised those who had only seen him perform. He was there regularly, a popular figure with members and staff, avuncular, warm, even cosy up to a point. Many years later, when the club celebrated the centenary of its move into the present building in Garrick Street, he voiced his feelings for the place in a moving speech. "I think perhaps that few of you realise what it means to an actor to be made a member of this club – how *terrified* we are of it all in the first years of our membership and what an *inspiration* it is to be allowed within these portals…it is a place with *magic* in it…for here sat Irving and Tree, Alexander and Pinero over *late suppers*…the brougham was fetched by the porter and one went home like a *gentleman* – as an actor should – full of wine and good fellowship."[11] Interesting that the ancient shabby reputation of actors should linger yet, even in its refutation, and absolutely fitting also that the refutation should come from one who felt keenly the wounds of any insult to his profession or to himself. Wolfit was ever the defensive upstart.

Although the war necessarily interrupted efforts to promote the National Theatre idea, it could not stifle them. Granville-Barker's advocacy had proven so strong that committees were formed and plans adopted. The most significant of these was the decision to amalgamate the Old Vic with the embryonic theatre, thereby giving the National house an already established identity. This was both a poetically satisfying idea, given the old Vic's history, and a practical one of great moment.

The Old Vic had been hatched from a very improbable egg. In 1880 the first female member of the London County Council, Emma Cons, had bought the freehold of the Royal Coburg Theatre in Waterloo Road with the intention of using it to provide clean entertainment for the layabouts and drunkards of Bermondsey. She was a ferociously keen

11 Harwood, *op.cit.*, pp 260-261

crusader, determined to rescue the fallen from the risk of moral turpitude. Renaming the theatre as the Royal Victoria Hall and Coffee Tavern, she offered wholesome lectures and readings sustained by coffee and buns. More significantly, she recruited the young actor William Poel to run things for her, with the results we know, for it was he who first lifted the theatre into the skies of high art with his 'pure' uncluttered stagings of Elizabethan Shakespeare. The theatre became very well-known, and in the Cockney manner the Royal Victoria Hall was quickly nicknamed the Old Vic. The name stuck.

Its future was assured, once again with impudent improbability, when Emma Cons appointed her equally pious and totally inexperienced niece Lilian Baylis as manager at the age of twenty-one. She became the guiding light of the theatre, its inspiration and artistic compass, for many years to come. From the endeavours of this bespectacled down-to-earth, simple and good woman arose not only the enduring reputation of the Old Vic, but the genesis of Sadler's Wells Ballet, later the Royal. The fact that she always addressed Queen Mary as "dear" says much to define her astonishing character. Thus, when Lilian Baylis lent the weight of her judgement and support to the National Theatre committee, they inherited a bonus of unquestionable merit.[12] On the committee which accepted the invitation from the Old Vic were Oliver Lyttelton (Chairman) and Lewis Casson, actor-member of the Garrick. We were in 1945, hostilities were over, and optimism was in the air.

Three years later, the new Government became the first to accept the principle of a theatre company to be

---

12 *ibid.*, pp 93-94

subsidised out of public funds. In reply to a question from Lyttelton in the House of Commons on 23 March, 1948, The Chancellor of the Exchequer, Sir Stafford Cripps, made this historic statement: "I understand that the L.C.C. are willing to reserve space for a National Theatre on the site which they propose to develop on the South Bank as a cultural centre, and to make the land available rent-free...The Government take the view that the establishment of a theatre to be operated under public auspices, which will set a standard for the production of drama in a setting worthy of Shakespeare and the British tradition, is a scheme to which the state should contribute. I am, therefore, proposing to ask for powers to provide a substantial part of the capital cost from public funds...My purpose in making this announcement at the present time, and in taking the steps I have stated, is to give assurance to the parties concerned so that they can proceed with their plans in the knowledge that they have the full sympathy and practical support of His Majesty's Government and of this House."[13]

It had taken nearly a century of example from actors and prodding from their allies to reach this culmination. Macready, Phelps, Irving, would have rejoiced; Wolfit, Olivier, Gielgud now stood in their place. All were Garrick men, and there was little doubt that, had it been in their power, they would have made Lilian Baylis a Garrick man, too.

The debates on the National Theatre Bill took place in the House of Commons on 21 January and in the House of Lords on 17 February, 1949. The motion that the Bill be given a second reading in the Commons was introduced

13 Geoffrey Whitworth, *The Making of a National Theatre* (1951), pp 237-238

by Glanvil Hall, Financial Secretary to the Treasury, with these stark, simple and resonant words: "This is a small Bill with a very great purpose", he said. All present on that day knew they were about to witness an event of artistic importance.

In the course of the ensuing debate Oliver Lyttelton on the opposition benches pointed out that Britain had made probably the greatest contribution in modern times to the drama, and historically more than any other nation, not excluding Greece. Before an attentive House he rose to a peroration which many confessed was the persuasive moment. "I have often been asked", he said, "as sponsor of this project, what is the necessity for a national theatre? This, of course, is a question which perhaps only the Secretary of the Philistine Society, if there is such a body, could appropriately ask. I usually reply in a rather conventional way by asking what is the need, come to that, for the National Gallery, for St Paul's Cathedral, Lycidas, or the Eroica Symphony of Beethoven. These works are not necessities in the sense that the President of the Board of Trade and others use the term when speaking about clothes, food, or houses. In fact, we only begin to enter the realms of art when we begin to leave the realms of necessity."[14]

He was congratulated on "his extremely fine speech" and told that "today is a red letter day in the history of British Government. It will go down to history as one of the days when a magnificent step forward was taken and a great scheme was promoted in a Bill by this Labour Government."[15] The Bill was duly adopted, and the Act of

---

14 *ibid.*, p 251
15 *ibid.*, p 255

Parliament published as the National Theatre Act, 1948. Granville-Barker's precepts, long in the stewing, had been followed almost to the letter. The impresario C. B. Cochran offered a postscript all his own. "State aid for the theatre is in the air", he wrote. "Why not start by giving Wolfit his own theatre?" Well, that did not happen, and one cannot help wondering that Wolfit would have insisted on doing everything his way and scuppered the project fairly swiftly; he was by nature impatient of committees. The Thames would flow a few more years yet before slapping against the walls of England's own theatre.

And when it did, there would certainly be the committee, with Olivier at its centre. In the meantime, Olivier made his mark with devastating effect in 1944, just months after Wolfit's Lear, so that two of the major performances of the twentieth century occurred within the same year. Olivier's was a revelatory portrayal of Richard III. As with Garrick, Kean and Irving before him, Olivier's sudden ascendancy was unexpected. He was not unknown, having played *Romeo and Juliet* with Gielgud nine years before, and a subdued Hamlet in 1937; but he had just returned from being a film-star in Hollywood, his hunger for fame and glory were well-known, and there was some prejudice against him. It was not felt that he would measure up to the demands of this great classical role; Gielgud had already established himself with Richard II and Hamlet, and his pre-eminence was thought to be unassailable. The doubters had not reckoned with Olivier's rogue ability to astonish, nor his demonic energy, what Kenneth Tynan called "his unparalleled animal powers". Nor, apparently, had he. The night before, he was still not sure how to attack the part and told his friend John Mills in the dressing-room that he was very worried, that it was going to be dreadful, that he simply did not know what he was going to do.

What he did do is history, and to quote Tynan again, "Olivier's Richard eats into the memory like acid into metal."[16] Another critic, W.A. Darlington, has left a detailed account of the actor's first entrance which so terrified the audience. Darlington expected the king to come limping on and go straight into "Now is the winter of our discontent" as many others had done. But no. Olivier "came in at the back, and made his progress downstage a thing of so many artfully contrived but deeply significant pauses and hesitations, of so much play of expression, that it seemed as if the time that elapsed before he spoke could be reckoned by minutes rather than seconds...Before the first line was delivered the actor had told us so much about the man he was impersonating that he had me (and, I could feel, the rest of the audience) sitting forward, tensely attentive, and quite certain that I was about to see the best Richard of my experience. And after the first speech I could, if it had been necessary, have written a notice."[17]

Some of those present were later to recall that they had been literally frightened *into* their seats by the opening speech and Olivier's overpowering depiction of unmitigated evil; that is, they drew back and pressed themselves against the seats, not drawing breath until the speech (twice as long as usual owing to Olivier's crafty addition of a passage from *Henry VI* and his equally sly adoption of Henry Irving's vocal idiosyncrasies) was over and he fixed them with that appalling leer through those icy eyes. Compared to Gielgud – an exquisite, finely-wrought, brooding, introspective

16 Kenneth Tynan, *A View of the English Stage* (1975), pp 15, 39
17 W A Darlington, *The Actor and His Audience* (1949),p 175

actor – Olivier was large, shattering, exploring unknown territories pungent with threat. Tynan wrote, "One thinks of Olivier in terms of other species, of panthers and lions; one thinks of Gielgud in terms of other arts, of ballet and portrait painting."[18] Never has the distinction been better expressed, and rarely have Dionysus and Apollo been better delineated.

Dionysus once again conquered theatrical space with Olivier's colossal performance the following year (1945) in *Oedipus Rex*. The high point in the drama came when Oedipus was finally made to realise that he had unknowingly slept with his mother and killed his father, and the audience watched, horrified, as the knowledge sank in. Richard Bebb describes the moment thus: "There was a long pause while the whole house held its breath. He stood perfectly still, threw his head back, and emitted from a distended throat two of the most blood-curdling screams that can ever have been heard in any theatre. They had the brightness of a high trumpet, and pierced every one of us like the sharpness of swords."[19] Tynan was also there. He knew what was coming, and waited for the rack to move into the final notch, "but I never hoped for so vast an anguish."[20] The scream, brilliantly caught in Irina Sedlecka's statuette, "must still be resounding in some high recess of the New Theatre's dome", he wrote. "Some stick of wood must still, I feel, be throbbing from it. The two cries were torn from beyond tears of shame or guilt; they came from the stomach, with all the ecstatic grief and fright of a new-born baby's wail." Olivier himself said he imagined the pain of a wolf whose tongue was stuck to ice.

---

18 Tynan, *op.cit.*, p 22
19 Catalogue to a series of statues by Irina Sedlecka, 1994
20 Tynan, *op.cit.*, p 27

Shortly afterwards comes the dreadful speech by the Chorus telling how Oedipus has stuck pins in his eyeballs not once, but several times. At this point Olivier appeared with blood streaming down his face from dark hollows, and one could hear the sound of seats banging as people left for the street; the St John's Ambulance Brigade were on duty every night, 15-strong, just in case.

These explosive performances confirmed Olivier's embrace of the stage as his natural habitat. Other Garrick actors of the same period had ventured into films and been swallowed by them. Leslie Howard, elected to the club in 1933, spent half his career in the United States, where he made several films before the second war. The most celebrated of these was perhaps the most widely-known film of all time, *Gone With the Wind*, in which, incidentally, three of the four leading characters were performed by English actors – Howard himself, Vivien Leigh and Olivia de Havilland. He made a number of appearances on stage in New York, including one as Hamlet which unfortunately collided with Gielgud's performance at another theatre in the same city. Howard did not emerge triumphant from the comparison. Returning to London, he devoted his talents to producing himself in a number of war films. Travelling on behalf of the British Council in 1943, his aircraft was shot down by enemy action.

The career of Michael Redgrave (elected in 1943) was interrupted both by films and by war. He had been one of the Old Vic's most promising young actors and a favourite of Lilian Baylis, appearing with Edith Evans in *As You Like It* and as Laertes to Olivier's Hamlet, until Alfred Hitchcock enticed him away for the film *The Lady Vanishes*. Having served as an ordinary seaman at the beginning of the war he returned to the stage briefly, but films came to dominate, with *The Browning Version* and *The Dam Busters* being most memorable, overshadowing a season at Stratford-upon-Avon where he played some heavyweight roles to considerable acclaim. In nice circularity, he was back at the Old Vic to play Claudius in the National Theatre's inaugural production in 1963, by which time he had received a knighthood.

Two Garrick men who crafted superlative careers in film were Alec Guinness and Richard Attenborough, the first skilfully combining screen and stage with alternate and equal success, the second more or less abandoning the stage for exclusive attention to film. Guinness's stage career was perfectly timed to secure a reputation for subtlety, then build upon it in cautious, considered steps. His début as Osric to Gielgud's Hamlet in 1934 earned immediate recognition, and this was followed by two roles in which he was judged impeccable. His Abel Drugger in Ben Jonson's *The Alchemist* was hailed as the best representation of that sly comical character since David Garrick two centuries earlier, and his Fool in *King Lear* was incomparable. Yet it was evident from the start that his finesse, his meticulous detail in characterisation, his avoidance of large theatrical effect, were ideally suited to the close intimate scrutiny of the film camera. Guinness's range appeared to be limitless, taking on dozens of different parts with dizzying success in scores of films, even playing nine different members of the same family in *Kind Hearts and Coronets*. It was a beautiful accident of timing that the maturity of the film industry coincided with this actor's most productive years – his art was minimal and suggestive, not flamboyant and obvious, indeed he was the very antithesis of Wolfit. He had a genius for eccentric comedy, always based upon close observation, as was shown best in *The Ladykillers* and *The Lavender Hill Mob*; his comedy was drawn from dissection and psychological study, to the degree that one swore one could watch the thoughts forming in his mind. This was never more sure than in his immortal portrayal of Fagin in David Lean's film *Oliver Twist*, as unapproachable in its way as Edith Evans's Lady Bracknell. Just as Dickens possessed the uncanny knack of creating characters that ever after inhabit the mind of the reader, as if injected therein, so Guinness's version of Fagin is lodged in the memory of all who see it. It is nice, if foolish, to reflect that Dickens and Guinness both being members of the Garrick, the writer would most certainly have applauded the actor's translation of his creation into life.

Alec Guinness's art was chameleon-like, able to change his face from within by concentration on deflecting the spectator's attention from what he was doing. He hardly ever looked the same twice, a specific talent he shared with Charles Matthews a hundred years earlier, so that his characterisations, soaked through with invisible detail, rendered his real self undetectable. Like Matthews, he could defy age, playing an old man as an old man would play him. And this inexhaustible malleability enabled him also to defy stardom. It is a wonderful paradox that Alec Guinness was one of the most famous actors in the world, adored by millions of youngsters as well as admired by seasoned film-goers in dozens of languages, and yet few, if any, would have been able to recognise him in the street or tell you anything whatever about him. According to Hazlitt, that is as it should be, and it would be difficult to argue the contrary. Despite immediate appearances,

Guinness was never a star; he was always an actor.

He was reluctant to admit who he was and wore his anonymity proudly. A frequent visitor at the club's Long Table, he would happily talk about anything, in quiet, measured tones, except acting, and a companion or guest who attempted to make a fuss of him would be offered a very polite but determined shoulder. This was due to more than shyness or reserve. It was as if he feared he would be asked to explain his art, which he would rather avoid as risking the dilution of it. He was ever on the defensive, terribly wary of the danger that somebody might seek to take advantage. But when he had learnt to trust, he was a very warm and generous host. The man and the actor were two entirely separate beings, in a way which remains rare in the theatre. A good friend in later years was Alan Bennett, who wrote two of his best parts for Guinness on his return to the stage.

Laurence Olivier overcame his unsatisfactory Hollywood adventure (while characteristically drawing from it lessons which would serve him well later – he was an eclectic collector of tricks), to make a film in England which would make him little less than a national hero. Winston Churchill conceived the notion of making a propaganda film to whip up patriotic fervour at a time of wearying resolve, and suggested *Henry V*. The Ministry of Information approached Olivier, who eagerly accepted the challenge (another of his defining professional traits) and not only starred in the film but directed it as well. His almost uncanny flair for capturing the centre of a character and writing it large enough for the public to identify without having to dig for explanations, was demonstrated again with startling effect. Just as his Richard III had been nailed down by the icy evil glare and the Irving intonations, so Henry V was depicted for all time by the wilful heroic exaggerations of his battle-cry, "Once more into the breach, dear friends". It is true to say that whenever one thinks of that speech one thinks of Olivier's delivery of it on screen; Shakespeare wrote it, yes, but Olivier made it immortal for millions of people who had never been to the theatre.

With ingenious subtlety he brought some film techniques in service on stage as well, notably with thrillingly obvious athleticism, but also with the camera's intensely intimate ability to look behind the eyes; to achieve this at a distance across the footlights was even unnerving. Both were demonstrated by his two portrayals of Coriolanus, another role he captured for himself, one before the war in 1938, and another twenty years later at Stratford-upon-Avon. The second displayed the lessons he had learnt in the cinema; the death-fall had him dangling by his ankles from a twelve-foot promontory, which must have been as fearsome to perform as it was terrifying to behold, and his interpretation of this immature, adolescent soldier-hero contrived to bring out Shakespeare's often unnoticed implication of sexual discovery in the toil of battle. The blatant proud virility of this Coriolanus was an expression of Olivier's visual style.

He was the perfect example of the actor's need to dominate and magnetise, and for this purpose to be self-centred. Wolfit, Irving, Tree, all knew that the audience had come to see *them*, and that if they underplayed the audience would feel a little betrayed. Olivier knew this, as if by instinct; he gave a show of power, a display of Dionysian abandon. His contemporary Gielgud harnessed the precisely opposite virtues of Apollonian control, feeling that art must derive ultimately from discipline. The difference between the two was never more clear than in their attitude towards blank verse. Harold Hobson said of Gielgud that "he sees the speech whole, ordered and regular in its music and architecture, and he presents it to us, not as Olivier does, luminous in one revealing detail, but in all its unbroken beauty."[21] The perceptive James Agate was rather more blunt. "Mr Olivier does not speak poetry badly", he said. "He does not speak it at all." That was because he did not *feel* the truth in the language; he grafted it on, even if the words resisted. And it worked.

Gielgud's fecundity and abundance of ideas made it imperative that he be properly directed in order to avoid his mind being clogged up with invention (and, conversely, rendered his own direction of other actors an endurance test, with every instruction undergoing endless repair). Peter Brook captured this best. "In John, tongue and mind work so closely together that it is sufficient for him to think of something for it to be said. Everything in him is moving all the time, at lightning speed – a stream of consciousness flows from him without pause; his flickering, darting tongue reflects everything around and inside him: his wit, his joy, his anxiety, his sadness, his appreciation of the tiniest detail of life and work, in fact, every observation once made is spoken…He is like an aircraft circling before it can land."[22] Irene Worth put it differently: "He simply talks faster than he can censor.[23]" This is the cause, too, of the hundreds of bricks which he dropped and which adorn every book of theatrical anecdotes; to include them here would require a chapter of extraordinary length.

---

21 *The Ages of Gielgud*, p 86
22 *ibid.*, p 102
23 *The Times*, 22 March, 1984

It is also worth mentioning, because sadly unusual, that Gielgud was the most modest and unselfish of actors. Of all the fine egos from Macready to Olivier so far covered in this narrative, he was without doubt the least grand, the most innocent; only Samuel Phelps comes anywhere near him in this regard. Far from surrounding himself with inferior performers the better to shine, when he managed his own companies at the Queens and the New Theatres he engaged only the finest talents and even subordinated himself to them; the theatrical experience mattered infinitely more than his personal success. A delightful story tells of his rehearsing a speech alone on an empty stage, when the only other person in the theatre was the charwoman mopping up the stage. She lent on her mop and said, "I don't think you should do it like that, dear", to which he responded, "Really? Oh God, how do you think I should do it?"[24]

Nor did jealousy ever stain him. He was quite uncompetitive, never keen on self-advertisement or self-promotion, and visibly distressed if his own reputation threatened to alienate others, whether they be fellow-actors or cab-drivers. This trait of personality would inform the best of his acting in the mellow years to come, in modern plays which it would have been impossible to predict for him earlier on. Olivier, too, would venture into dangerous territory, using the obverse of Gielgud's gifts – his need to shine.

Those unexpected changes of gear, for both men, were in the future. Meanwhile, Gielgud enlarged his Shakespearean repertoire with the small part of Angelo in *Measure for Measure* and with Leontes in *The Winter's Tale*,

---

24 *ibid.*, p 128

in which he examined the pathology of a man trapped by his own delusions with a depth which surprised all those who thought he was only a voice. Yet it was still the voice which hypnotised audiences in his solo recital performance, entitled *The Ages of Man*, which he played virtually all over the English-speaking world and which was duly recognised as the finest display of orchestral speech in the whole of the twentieth century. With only a lectern on a bare stage, Gielgud devised a singular entertainment in which, as Michel St Denis pointed out, he could present himself in three ways – as an actor, as a director indicating how these various roles ought to be played, and as a man talking directly to the audience between excerpts."[25] He was able to deliver speeches both from plays he knew well and from others which had not been in his repertoire, and hold audiences spell-bound without resort to any false additions. Michael Billington noted that he showed "the infinite pliability of the iambic pentameter and how, within a respect for the basic Shakespearean metre, one can achieve all manner of effects. Gielgud's verse-speaking is fantastically *supple*, totally unsentimental." He went on to write almost lyrically (for a critic), "Never shall I forget Gielgud on stage in *The Ages of Man*, Savile Row-suited and impeccably elegant, taking us to the extremity of emotion with nothing but Shakespeare's language and his own iron-clad technique to help him."[26] And he was not the only critic to be seduced. Philip Hope-Wallace said that it was "one of the most memorable evenings I have ever spent in a theatre. I find it hard to think that any other living actor could so deliver Clarence's dream speech - this was like great singing, paradoxically not to be analysed in words…

25 Morley, *op.cit.*, p 297
26 *The Ages of Gielgud*, p112

He was born, he grew up, he was even funny, and he died under our eyes. The anthology is sometimes a dangerous form, but I have seldom heard speaking which impelled us to listen so intently."[27] For what it's worth, I must agree; I was too young to witness his Hamlet, but this recital at the Theatre Royal Haymarket was at once an education and an entrancement.

Something of the quiet power simmering in these speeches can be discerned in two of his film roles. As Clarence in Olivier's *Richard III* Gielgud positively captures the film for himself in one touching scene before his execution, and as Cassius in the Hollywood *Julius Caesar* he appears to be the only actor who knows how to speak at all.

The Garrick Club was inordinately proud of him, both for his achievements and for his intensely clubbable nature, as a man full of fun and kindness. Members looked for opportunities to honour him with special occasions, although, to their shame, there were some who whispered that he deserved expulsion following a trivial incident shortly after his knighthood was conferred, which resulted in an appearance before magistrates. This brief hostility was quickly quenched. The knighthood itself was a cause for genuine public celebration, being announced twenty-four hours before the coronation of Elizabeth II in 1953 while Gielgud was appearing in *Venice Preserv'd* in Hammersmith. That evening, on his first entrance, the whole theatre rose to its feet. Paul Scofield, in the cast, recalled that "the audience rose to cheer him as never before…John's face was streaming with tears and the whole theatre was charged with high-emotional

---

27 Morley, *op. cit.*, p 301

excitement. It seemed as if the whole world was glad for him, and he was overwhelmed by this quite unexpected and clamorous revelation of public affection."[28] The scene was repeated a few months later, following the press reports of his court appearance. Gielgud was playing in Liverpool. At his entrance, the audience gave him a loud, standing ovation, punctured with shouts and cheers. It was a startling moment, confirming once more that the British public is always several steps more mature than its newspaper editors.

---

28 *ibid.*, p 235

10
FILMS AND TELEVISION

The period between the end of the Second World War and the eventual opening of the National Theatre saw the largest number of actors to be elected to the Garrick Club since its foundation. Given that this period coincided with the emergence of the British film industry as a significant artistic export, a good proportion of the actors now coming into the club were from the film world as well as the traditional stage. In the years from 1955 onwards, in particular, one might have found the Long Table substantially manned by a sprinkling of names unsuspected by the strollers in Covent Garden who habitually gaze at our Italianate building and wonder what on earth goes on in there. Not only might Olivier, Gielgud, Wolfit, Guinness be dining, but other august actor-managers like Anthony Quayle and John Clements, along with film-stars Alastair Sim, Jack Hawkins, John Mills, Marius Goring, Richard Attenborough, Rex Harrison, Kenneth More, supporting actors who seemed to be in everything, such as Campbell Singer and Raymond Huntley, stage and television actors like Michael Williams and Denholm Elliott, and those classical pillars who managed to steer through all three media with singular success, paramount among whom was Donald Sinden.

One might even have come across the veteran A.E. Matthews, born in the nineteenth century, whose early career flourished several chapters ago but whose fame in old age soared with his performance in *The Chiltern Hundreds* at the Vaudeville Theatre, making him a household name even up to his ninetieth year. The author of that play, William Douglas-Home, left a portrait of him in the *Dictionary of National Biography* which so perfectly describes the quintessential actor-member that it must be quoted in full. "Matty was a playwright's dream", he wrote. "The grand old man of the theatre without being remotely grand; the oldest actor acting with the youngest mind; the best-dressed member of the Garrick Club, even though he would travel by underground on a wet day in a deerstalker hat and a pyjama coat over his tweed suit and gumboots. He knew more about the technique of light-comedy acting than many of his colleagues, yet, such was his spontaneity, he succeeded in giving the impression that he knew nothing at all. On stage he was as selfish as any actor ever was but in private he was kindness personified. He was crotchety but he had a heart of gold. He was unpredictable, easily bored, perhaps a shade close with the drinks, but he had as much charm as any man in any other walk of life and he loved beauty in women and animals and he encouraged youth."[1]

Similar in style, at any rate professionally, was Rex Harrison; he and Matty both carried forward the tradition of acting-as-sleepwalking inherited from Hawtrey and du Maurier two generations before them. His early successes in Rattigan's *French Without Tears* and the film version of Coward's *Blithe Spirit*, respectively just pre-war and

---

1 *Dictionary of National Biography*

immediately post-war, were thunderously eclipsed by his deeply idiosyncratic portrayal of Professor Henry Higgins in the musical version of Shaw's *Pygmalion*, entitled *My Fair Lady*. When it opened at Drury Lane in 1958, an embargo was placed on any broadcasting of its music or dialogue until midnight the previous day, despite it having played in New York for two years already. As soon as Rex Harrison ambled his way vocally through the songs, talking them rather than singing them, it was obvious that the part could never belong to anyone else. In fact, he was a natural interpreter of Shaw, having played *Heartbreak House* and *The Devil's Disciple* with distinction, for Shaw's colloquial cadences perfectly matched Harrison's effortless chatter. He had likewise mastered the relaxed, discursive, reflective dialogue of Chekhov in the rarely-performed *Platonov*. But he steadfastly refused to have anything to do with Shakespeare. One is bound to admit that he was right to be stubborn on that point.

His contemporaries Anthony Quayle and John Clements were each stamped with quite different qualities. Although it was postulated in the last chapter that Donald Wolfit could be regarded as the final manifestation of the actor-manager, both Quayle and Clements carried on the tradition after him. Anthony Quayle in particular had an historical impact upon the production of Shakespearean drama at Stratford-upon-Avon. After a long career playing supporting roles with such dependability that he was in danger of being taken for granted, he was encouraged by both Gielgud and Guthrie and took over from Olivier as Henry V in an Old Vic tour before the war. The eight years he spent as director and leading actor at the Shakespeare

Memorial Theatre from 1948 transformed that delightful but parochial space into one of the world's principal stages, and brought back the fine triumphant days of Frank Benson. He achieved this entirely without public subsidy, but with a vision which excited audiences who longed to love their Shakespeare as a prized national asset. Quayle was the first to offer Shakespeare's history plays in chronological order, at the Festival of Britain in 1951, thereby knitting together disparate dramas to fashion one long historical tapestry. The idea was repeated by the Royal Shakespeare Company (which itself grew out of the Shakespeare Memorial Theatre) in their "Wars of the Roses" productions of 1964, but Anthony Quayle got there first and showed how it could be presented.

Returning to the West End stage he gave a performance in *Long Day's Journey Into Night* at the Piccadilly Theatre in 1958 which, for this writer at least, rose to a peak of theatrical experience that occurs only on a handful of occasions in one lifetime. The others in the cast were Gwen Frangçon-Davies as his wife, and Alan Bates and Ian Bannen as the sons. The anguish and horror of watching ambitions thwarted and hopes stifled, presented by a quartet of actors apparently suffocated by the emotions they themselves contrived to awaken, left me stumbling from the theatre into the street panting, shaking, shuddering, and close to primeval tears at the pity of it all. That indeed is a memory of acting to be cherished and protected.

John Clements made his contribution to actor-managing at the Chichester Festival Theatre, where he directed and performed in four plays every summer. He was as far removed from the Wolfit manner as it is possible to imagine, being unfailingly courteous and polite, but he did for Chichester the same as Quayle had done for Stratford, making the theatre a necessary excursion from London for anybody seriously interested in the drama as part of national life. As for the club, he was especially valued there for many years as a sage and experienced trustee.

Coeval with all these, and especially popular with his fellow-actors, was Robert Flemyng, whose career spanned sixty years from his creation of one of the leading young men's parts in Rattigan's "shimmeringly light and beguiling comedy" *French Without Tears* (alongside Rex Harrison), to a long run in Michael Frayn's farce *Noises Off*. He was also with Alec Guinness in Eliot's *The Cocktail Party* in 1949, and in a string of Shaftesbury Avenue successes, notably Nancy Mitford's translation and adaptation of *The Little Hut*. He was one of the few actors to be honoured for bravery in battle (Military Cross and OBE), but it was his selfless work on behalf of his profession, on the council of both Equity and the Actors' Charitable Trust, which earned him enduring gratitude. At the club he was "a marvellously convivial and uninhibited companion" with "an endearing modesty" and "infallible attractiveness."[2] The club held a dinner in his honour in 1994, the year before he died.

The huge success of uniquely British-style comedies made at Ealing Film Studios, together with epics of wartime heroism made by the J Arthur Rank Organisation, brought a new kind of actor-member to the Garrick, including some who had more or less forsaken the stage. The doyen of these was a singularly congenial and shy man, who regularly announced his imminent resignation from the club (nobody knew with how much sincerity) and who was more like a scholar than a film-star. Furthermore, this

---

2 *The Independent*, 24 May, 1995

was not by accident, for Alastair Sim had indeed begun his career as a lecturer in elocution at New College, Edinburgh, and finished it as an honorary Doctor of Law at the university there. In between, he became the most beloved and recognisable film actor in the country, with a sardonic style steeped in self-mockery and a measured manner of speech which seemed to suggest he was still bent on teaching his audiences how to pronounce words correctly. As with many actors in these pages, he is identified with one role which nobody else has been able to match, the title role in the film *Scrooge* (from Dickens' tale) which he made in 1951 and which continued to be shown every Christmas for years afterwards. His conversion to benignity at the end was so totally endearing that strangers were continually congratulating him for it. He made audiences feel good about themselves by guiding them towards a recognition of their own innate decency.

He could also make them laugh at their own foolishness by recklessly displaying his own, in an immortal partnership with Margaret Rutherford in films such as *The Happiest Days of Your Life* and *The Bells of St Trinian's* in which, appropriately, he played a school headmaster. The combination of her wobbling jowls and girlish giggles, and his suggestion of naughty thoughts with a sly smile proved irresistible. Alastair Sim had done stage work earlier in his career (starting with a walk-on in the notoriously bad *Othello* which Peggy Ashcroft gamely endured with Paul Robeson), but by an astonishing twist of circumstance the film-star who gave such innocent delight was, off-screen, the Rector of Edinburgh University. He had been elected rector in 1948, by a greater margin than any of his predecessors (including prime ministers), and was still rector when he played Scrooge. To the august assembly of academics and scholars as well as students who gathered to hear his address in Edinburgh, he said, "I admit that even to this day I enjoy being called an artiste, and if anyone likes to qualify it with some such adjective as 'great', 'incomparable', 'superb', then you can rely on me to finish the ritual by reacting with becoming modesty. But I shall know it is all nonsense."

His election merited front-page reporting in the London newspapers.

Jack Hawkins, who was to suffer the most insulting illness that can befall an actor – a throat cancer which took away his voice – had been cast by Gielgud as Algy in his pre-war production of *The Importance of Being Earnest* to tremendous effect, and was placed in charge of ENSA productions for the troops in India and South-east Asia during the war. But in peacetime he devoted himself wholly to the cinema, specialising in roles which demanded heroic fortitude and *sang-froid*, most notably in *The Cruel Sea* with Donald Sinden and *Bridge on the River Kwai* with Alec Guinness. He appeared trapped by his suitability for such parts, and was never able to explore a wider range. There was something of the understated English virility in him which almost *required* admiration rather than tepid appreciation. The presumption that the portrayal of stoicism came naturally to him was indeed proven by his continuing to work in non-speaking roles after the wretched affliction which stole his vocal chords; he would simply not cede conquest to a mere illness.

His friend and co-star in *The Cruel Sea*, Donald Sinden, went on to develop one of the most varied and venturesome careers of any actor in the twentieth century. His range from his early twenties into his eighth decade was such that he managed to straddle both the bold declamatory style of his nineteenth-century predecessors, whose spirit seemed to inhabit him and to fashion his voice, and the intimate, intricate miniaturism of close camera work, in which his eyes did the work and his detailed intuitive grasp of character always made the meaning clear. He could dominate the stage with a powerful presence and confident narrative flow, and also bend the screen to his subtle conceits, thus bringing together, in one man, ancient traditions and modern innovative techniques. There are few actors who could manage such a feat, making of himself a kind of vivid theatrical history in the flesh.

Some idea of Sinden's protean versatility may be inferred from three of the many roles upon which his reputation rests: Lord Foppington in Vanbrugh's *The Relapse* (1967), the lusty young medical student in the film *Doctor in the House* (1954), and a monumentally crushed majesty as *King Lear* (1976). One must defy the odds of finding three parts so dissimilar, yet he excelled in each with his own brand of formidable energy. The role of Lord Foppington, created by Colley Cibber in 1696, presented the challenge of mastering a rich Restoration style, and mastering the audience for it as well, since the long scene devoted to the fop's dressing requires an audience to be rigid with attention with nothing but vanity to hold them. He transformed himself from a prancing fool in undignified casual wear into the magnificent architecture of a self-adoring dandy, all with the help, of course, of a retinue of servants behaving as if they were party to the creation of a masterpiece. Sinden demonstrated his ability to conquer his audience, to make them obedient to his mood, even to determine when they should laugh and when they should not. It was a technique he said he was taught by Baliol Holloway, and which he himself admired most in the *farceur* Ralph Lynn in Ben Travers' comedies at the Aldwych. Sinden controlled the audience by forcing them to believe what he believed. As for the Restoration style, he said that the key to any part was to know how to walk and how to stand – the rest followed by inevitability.

Three occasions hover forever in my personal memory, the first his Richard Plantagenet in *The Wars of the Roses* in 1964 – all thunder and threat and clash of steel and personality, with hideous consequences; a scene from *Much Ado About Nothing* performed privately for members on the grand staircase of the Garrick Club with Judi Dench one evening in 1978; and the spectacularly hilarious revival of *London Assurance* in 1972. In this latter he played Sir Harcourt Courtley, newly arrived with all his urban sophistication and knowledge at a house in the country where he has been invited to stay. The last person he expects to find there is his son, so when he is introduced to him he greets him in a perfunctory manner, as befits a great man-about-town, and does not recognise him. But the audience does, and waits for the fact to penetrate beneath Sir Harcourt's fulsome costume. It seems to take forever. Sinden played upon expectations with such practised skill that he was able to keep them waiting for the penny to drop, and let them share in the illusion that he *hadn't* recognised his son, so confidently that he actually strode off-stage into the wings, to all appearances putting an end to the scene. By this time the audience could scarcely contain itself, and when some long seconds later Sinden came storming onto the stage again, pointing his finger and looking outraged, we knew he had finally realised and the house exploded. Few actors would have dared take the risk of such a protracted "double-take", but I, for one, had to get up from my seat and walk the aisle for some respite from laughter.

Sinden says he picked it up from a Laurel and Hardy film in which Hardy sees Laurel's photograph in the newspaper years after he was supposed to have perished in the trenches. The audience recognise the picture, Hardy does not. Until, minutes later, the camera is following him down a corridor when he suddenly stops as if tugged from behind, and we know from the heaving of his shoulders that enlightenment has struck.

Donald's quiet work on behalf of his profession, on Equity, the board of LAMDA, the British Theatre Museum and the Royal Theatrical Fund, was probably more extensive than that of any actor before him. And his knowledge of the history of British drama was beyond compare, as his ambulatory lecture among the portraits of the club, recently released on DVD, can testify; he knows all its ghosts personally. His film career even included tutoring Marilyn Monroe, which he did not much relish. But it must always be the first film, *Doctor In The House*, which stands as a monument to his ability to capture his audience. Seventeen million people saw the film in its first year of release, representing fully half the adult population of the country. (As the cast was fond of saying, why didn't the rest go?) He was knighted in 1997.

Another actor in the same film was Kenneth More, who nurtured an affection for the club so abundantly obvious that he seemed to regard it as home. This, of course, has happened to many of us, but everyone would have willingly conceded to More the right to be First Tenant, and when he sat at the head of the Long Table it was not only he who was pleased. This is how he put it himself: "If I only had enough money left in the world to pay the club subscription and nothing else, I would pay it...You never feel stagnant there; you are always plugged into life...The Garrick is really one of the main reasons why I would never leave England permanently."[3]

Kenneth More was the quintessential English film-star, able to suggest decency and resolve – those virtues which every Englishman claims for himself – in equal measure, and at the same time to rejoice in the sillier aspects of English humour. The first of these attributes was never more in evidence than in his portrayal of Douglas Bader, the pilot who strove to do his duty despite losing both legs, in *Reach for the Sky*, a film revered by every schoolboy in the 1950s; and the second came to play in the delightful and totally inconsequential film *Genevieve*, about a race from London to Brighton in classic old cars. With a chummy ease of manner which flew straight out of the screen, More was the one actor whom every film-goer wanted to know personally; his charm was palpable.

He demonstrated his ability to dig deeper in his one firm stage success as the bounder Freddie in Rattigan's *The Deep Blue Sea* opposite a radiant performance by Peggy Ashcroft, but thereafter concentrated on his film career until a television opportunity occurred to explore his latent range. This was Jolyon in the immortal BBC adaptation of Galsworthy's *Forsyte Saga* spread over twenty-four episodes,

---

3 Kenneth More, *More or Less* (1978), p 233

in which More evolved from a young man to a frail old gentleman, with consummate artistry. It seemed the entire country tuned in every week to see how Jolyon was getting on, and once again, it was More's obvious charm which brought the portrayal to life. It was odd to reflect that his first job had been as assistant stage manager at the Windmill, where the principal attractions were static naked ladies, and his first appearance on that stage was as a comedian's stooge. The journey from one to the other had been considerable.

Kenneth More, like Hawkins, Quayle and Clements, had seen active service in the war, but the one Garrick actor who could claim to have experienced that war at its most grim was Denholm Elliott, who was shot down in 1942 and spent three years as a prisoner at a Stalag in Silesia. As an actor, Elliott was superb, crafty and subtle, seeming not to care whether he was in work or not, but privately honing a technique which would make him capable of "stealing" a scene from any other actor one cared to name; in fact, one of them declared his ruling maxim to be, "Never act with children, animals or Denholm Elliott".[4] He had been with Sinden and Hawkins in *The Cruel Sea*, and Hollywood did not suspect the psychological precision of his characterisation, wasting him on shallow parts which he appeared to handle with eyes closed and nose pinched. He "excelled at seedy, dishevelled types, whose ill fortune was rooted in some private torment"[5], and finally found the role that his talents demanded in the shabby gentility of Mr Emerson in *A Room With A View*. Virtually all other actors selflessly admired him and even envied his apparently

---

4 *Dictionary of National Biography*
5 *ibid.*

effortless ability to detect truth in the smallest character part. He was, as far as I am able to discover, the only actor who took up the profession on the advice of a psychiatrist, as a cure for his kleptomania. Nothing was ever noticed to be missing after Elliott spent an evening at the club, so the cure must be judged to have been terminally effective.

Richard Attenborough was elected to the club in 1950 at the age of only twenty-six. Two years later he opened in a new play called *The Mousetrap* by Agatha Christie. I know because I was there (sitting under the roof for sixpence), and merrily predicted that it would not last more than a few weeks. Well, it did, and so did "Dickie", one of the club's most cherished members and another valiant defender of the arts. His film career started at the top, in *Brighton Rock* and *In Which We Serve*, but his most haunting performance was as the timid little man John Halliday Christie, a multiple murderer who boarded his victims behind the wallpaper and kept their pubic hair in a matchbox, in *Ten Rillington Place*. He showed how even the most sinister character, capable of the most vicious acts, can be damaged and ultimately rather pathetic. It was a portrayal which manifested considerable psychological understanding.

In time Attenborough acted less and directed more, with a dozen films earning international recognition, paramount among which must be *Gandhi*. Honours piled upon this unassuming man, often teased for his "theatrical" declarations of affection addressed to everyone in the profession, and many who were not, with the result that he accumulated the CBE, a knighthood in 1976, and finally elevation to the House of Lords in 1993. His charitable work was boundless, over many decades of dedication, and not only on behalf of actors.

Then there was Raymond Huntley, the polar opposite to Dickie Attenborough in any social situation. He appeared in nearly sixty films, always under the title, and in well over a hundred television appearances, the most famous being a long-running series based upon a fictional view of domestic Victorian life called *Upstairs, Downstairs*. He was the most dependable of actors, never ambitious for glory, happy to work quietly and retire to the club for a simple meal afterwards. He was also the man for whom the epithet 'laconic' might have been coined. Always in the same seat at the Long Table, to the right of Irving's chair at the head, he was happiest if one could pretend he was not there, as he gave the impression that conversation was an impertinence. He was overheard to mutter, "It is a sobering thought, that every time two men come through that door, at least one of them must be a member." I gave up trying to talk, until one day I sat next to him having attended a performance of the play he was then appearing in on Shaftesbury Avenue the night before. This, I thought, gave one the opportunity to engage in something resembling conversation. I told Huntley that I had enjoyed his performance. "Did you?" he grumbled. "I don't". I did not try again. He struck me as akin to the great Macready in temper, and yet it would be wrong to draw the obvious conclusion that people put up with him; on the contrary, everyone in the club was ruefully fond of him, as the resident grouch. Every gentleman's club must have a Huntley if its sense of humour is to survive.

John Mills appeared in over a hundred British films, making the history of post-war cinema almost a catalogue of his roles. He specialised as the ordinary man, devoid

Sir Johnston Forbes-Robertson (1853–1937) as *Leontes in The Winter's Tale*
Photo-gravure published in Modern Shakespearean Celebrities by Virtue & Co c.1902

Sir Gerald Du Maurier (1873–1934) and Arthur Lupino (c.1864–1908) as Mr Darling and Nana in Peter Pan

Postcard published by Ellis & Walery 1904

Menu for a dinner in honour of Sir James Matthew Barrie (1860–1937) and Sir Johnston Forbes-Robertson (1853–1937) at the Garrick Club 1913

Sir Charles Hawtrey (1858–1923), Charles Brookfield (1857–1913), Henry Kemble (1848–1907) and Lottie Venne (1852–1928) as Charles Shakleton, William, Mr Kershaw and Jane in Jane

Souvenir cabinet photograph and envelope
celebrating the 100th performance published by Bassano 1891

Sir George Alexander (1858–1918)
as Macduff in Macbeth

Cabinet photograph published by
Elliot and Fry c.1888

Sir Frank Benson
(1858–1939) *as Theseus in A*
Midsummer's Night's Dream

Photo-gravure published
in Modern Shakespearean
Celebrities by Virtue & Co
c.1902

4202 B ROTARY PHOTO E.C.   MR. GRANVILLE BARKER   FOULSHAM & BANFIELD.
AS "GENERAL BURGOYNE" IN "THE DEVIL'S DISCIPLE."

Top Left: *Harley Granville-Barker (1877–1946) as General Burgoyne in The Devil's Disciple*

Signed postcard by Foulsham & Banfield published by Rotary Photographic Co Ltd 1907

Bottom Left: *Sir Seymour Hicks (1871–1949) as Lucien in The Man in Dress Clothes*

Oil on canvas by Maurice Codner 1931

Alastair Sim (1900–1976)
Oil on canvas by Edward Seago
c.1960

Sir Alec Guinness (1914–2000)
Oil on canvas c.1949

Sir Felix Aylmer (1889–1979)
Oil on canvas by James Gunn 1962

Sir Noël Coward (1899–1973)
Oil on canvas by Edward Seago 1966

NEW THEATRE

ST. MARTIN'S LANE, W.C.2

Licensed by the Lord Chamberlain to HOWARD WYNDHAM

1934

JOHN GIELGUD
as HAMLET

Lessees
THE WYNDHAM THEATRES, Ltd.

Managing Directors
HOWARD WYNDHAM and BRONSON ALBERY

EVENINGS at 8

MATINEES: WEDNESDAY and SATURDAY at 2.15

HOWARD WYNDHAM and BRONSON ALBERY
present

SHAKESPEARE'S

HAMLET

Characters in the order of their appearance

Bernardo	GEORGE DEVINE
Francisco	PETER MURRAY-HILL
Horatio, *friend of Hamlet*	JACK HAWKINS
Marcellus	ELLIS IRVING
Ghost of Hamlet's Father	WILLIAM DEVLIN
Claudius, *King of Denmark*	FRANK VOSPER
Laertes, *Son of Polonius*	GLEN BYAM SHAW
Polonius, *Lord Chamberlain*	GEORGE HOWE
Hamlet, *Prince of Denmark*	JOHN GIELGUD
Gertrude, *Queen of Denmark, Mother to Hamlet*	LAURA COWIE
Ophelia, *Daughter of Polonius*	JESSICA TANDY
Reynaldo, *Servant to Polonius*	CECIL WINTER
Rosencrantz	RICHARD AINLEY
Guildenstern	ANTHONY QUAYLE
1st Player	GEORGE DEVINE
2nd Player	SAM BEAZLEY
3rd Player	ALEC GUINNESS
4th Player	IAN ATKINS
5th Player	RICHARD DARE
Norwegian Captain	PETER MURRAY-HILL
Fortinbras, *Prince of Norway*	GEOFFREY TOONE
A Courier	FRITH BANBURY
1st Grave Digger	BEN FIELD
2nd Grave Digger	LYON PLAYFAIR
Priest	CECIL WINTER
Osric	ALEC GUINNESS

Court Ladies: JEAN WINSTANLEY, ETHEL GLENDINNING, HERMIONE HANNEN, DORIS JOHNSTONE.

Courtiers, Ruffians, etc.: JOHN BOWN, PHILIP CLOWES, CEDRIC BOWDEN, PETER TRENT, IAN ATKINS, RICHARD DARE, GUY VIVIAN.

Soldiers: Messrs. STEWART, ROSE, GUNN, JOY, WHITE, HARWOOD, CHAPMAN, BROADLEY, NORMAN, WADE

The Play Produced by JOHN GIELGUD

Sir John Gielgud (1904–2000)
as Hamlet in Hamlet

Programme for Hamlet at the
New Theatre, London 1934

Top: *Baron Olivier (1907–1989) with Bernard Hailstone*
(1910–1987) and one of his two portraits of Olivier
Unknown photographer 1969

Left: *Baron Olivier (1907–1989) as Oedipus in Oedipus*
Bronzed resin cast by Irena Sedlecka 1998

Bottom Right: *Baron Olivier (1907–1989)*
Oil on canvas by Bernard Hailstone 1968

Top Left: *Kenneth More (1914–1982) and Susannah York (1939–) as Group Capt. Baker and Section Officer Maggie Harvey off screen in* The Battle of Britain

Unknown photographer 1969

Bottom Left: *Baron Olivier (1907–1989) as Richard in* Richard III

Pencil, chalk and wash on paper by Mervyn Peake 1945

WINES

—

Ch. Montrose, 1962

—

Quinta do Noval N/V

Signed menu for a Garrick Club dinner in honour of Sir John Gielgud (1904–2000)
on the occasion of his fiftieth year in the Theatre, 14 November 1971

MENU

Consommé Riche

—

Game Paté

—

Roast Saddle of Lamb
Roast Potatoes
Haricots Verts
Brussels Sprouts

—

Apple Pie and Cream
or
Welsh Rarebit

—

Coffee

Top Left: *Sir Lewis Casson* (1875–1969) Bronze by Liz Moore 1969
Top Right: *Jack Hawkins* (1910–1973) Bronze by David Rawnsley 1966
Bottom Left: *Marius Goring* (1912–1998) Bronze by unknown sculptor
Bottom Right: *Sir John Mills* (1908–2005) Bronze by unknown sculptor

Robert Morley (1908–1992)
Oil on canvas by David Poole 1976

*Sir Donald Wolfit (1902–1968) as Romeo
in rehearsals for a touring production of Romeo and Juliet*
Photographs by Michael Forbes 1939

Opposite Page, Top: *Sir Donald Wolfit (1902–1968) as Lear in King Lear*
Oil on canvas by R W Gick 1946

Bottom Left: Sir Donald Wolfit (1902–1968) Bromide print by Harold White 1942

Bottom Right: *Baron Attenborough* (1923–)

Bromide print by Godfrey Argent 1950 © National Portrait Gallery, London

Sir Donald Sinden (1923–) as Lord Foppington in the Relapse

Oil on canvas 1967

of flair or panache, who nevertheless was solidly reliable in a crisis, and was therefore cast time and again as the unpretentious hero in war-time. Noël Coward specifically wrote the part of Shorty Blake in *In Which We Serve* with Mills in mind. But his gift for characterisation was evident when he was afforded the opportunity to display it, as he did in two of David Lean's films, *Great Expectations*, in which he was the perfect Pip, and *Hobson's Choice* as Willie Mossop. He may have been the only actor-knight to have been born in a Dr Barnardo's Home, and to have begun his working career selling toilet paper.

Robert Morley, huge in both girth and personality, was notorious for making up the roles as he went along, with scant regard for what the author had intended; since he wrote many plays himself, he felt free to improve the work of others, and to tinker with the text according to the mood of the audience. His training took him back to the dawn of the century, for he had started in repertory under Frank Benson and it was there that he learnt that the pressures of coping with so many parts could be relieved somewhat by mingling them at will; Peggy Ashcroft said that he always seemed to be having so much fun, and he brought the same talent for mischief with him on his visits to the club.

Marius Goring was yet another actor with a unique distinction, or rather two. He was the only man able to perform with equal facility in French and German as well as English, once touring Europe as Hamlet in French, and touring Germany in German. Second, he was the only one to be made a Fellow of the Royal Society of Literature, by virtue of his having written, translated and adapted many plays for the stage and radio. He had trained under Harcourt Williams and been launched on his career by

Lilian Baylis, and despite manifold film parts (usually as sinister foreigners) his first loyalty remained with the stage. He was one of the founders of Equity, the actors' union.

Michael Williams was elected to the club on the same day as I, in January 1977. Next to the dozens of performances on which he built his fine reputation, especially perhaps the inspiring Henry V at Stratford-upon-Avon and that deliberately unnerving play *A Pack of Lies* in Shaftesbury Avenue, there were moments wherein he displayed the most polished and poised control over comic timing of his generation, recalling the celebrated mastery of James Nokes in the seventeenth century. In a political farce called *Out of Order*, in which he appeared with Donald Sinden, Williams used his mischievous face to brilliant effect in making a farcical situation even more intolerable, bewilderment passing into anguish passing into paralysing panic and terror. Similar skill informed his performance, again with Sinden, in *London Assurance*.

The deep rumble of Michael Hordern's voice, like tectonic plates shifting menacingly, is best heard on a rare recording of a musical fantasy called *The Butterfly Ball*, which he narrated with Judi Dench, her seductive mellifluousness pointing a sharp contrast, but his amazingly quirky performance in Tom Stoppard's *Jumpers* is lodged in countless memories as one of the great stage portrayals of the twentieth century. As the philosophy don George Moore, who had flourished at the turn of that century, Hordern was "forever debating with himself and occasionally with a tortoise". The same DNB entry points to his "anarchic brilliance in both comedy and tragedy, specializing as he did in morose clergymen, bizarre diplomats, dotty generals, and tetchy fathers."[6] In any of those categories, there was no one to compare with him.

If the above list appears rather like a catalogue, it is only because the post-war period was particularly rich in talent, and the British film industry was at a peak of achievement. Above and adjacent to all of them rose the parallel careers of Olivier and Gielgud, each of whom continued to develop and progress as if hungry for greater challenges. They both plunged headlong into experiments from which they might safely have fled, protecting already established reputations, were either of them cautious by nature. But they were both, in their separate ways, intrepid actors.

A revolution of historical significance was taking place in British drama, whereby drawing-room comedies which had been the staple of West End theatre all the way from Tom Robertson under the Bancrofts through to the "well-made plays" of Terence Rattigan and William Douglas-Home were rudely swept aside by "kitchen-sink" drama depicting the raw truths of working-class life, often written by working-class playwrights. The revolution even had its landmark date, 8th May, 1956, when the first performance of John Osborne's *Look Back in Anger* was given at the Royal Court Theatre. The immediate effect upon accepted subjects for drama, upon styles of performance, upon language permitted on stage, and especially upon audience expectation, was seismic. From that day onward, writers who embraced the new iconoclastic mood were collectively known as "angry young men", and actors accustomed to the comfort of tradition were wounded by their own hesitation; it is symptomatic that both Gielgud and Guinness turned down the opportunity to appear in

---

6 by Sheridan Morley

Waiting for Godot, now universally recognised as one of the masterpieces of twentieth-century drama. Laurence Olivier, on the other hand, was rather more adventurous.

John Osborne's second play, *The Entertainer*, told the story of a third-rate, hopelessly unsophisticated music-hall performer, whose act was embarrassingly tawdry and whose naïve obtuseness in continuing with a pointless career invited pitying sniggers. Olivier heard that Osborne was writing it, and enquired whether he might play the part. It was a brave move, for nothing in his career could have prepared him for it, and failure would have hurt him badly. What ensued was a marvellously shabby and honest portrayal of a man steeped in indignity and degradation, which Olivier built upon his famously meticulous observation of detail and a sure grasp of psychological truth. His suit was loud, tasteless, and weary from too much wear. His sickly collusion with the audience, tight with poor jokes and adolescent innuendo, was obviously fake and desperate. But more than that, he allowed the audience to see beyond the words and the tricks and find, in Michael Billington's apt words, "the total desolation of a man aware of his own essential hollowness and atrophied emotions. It was a world away from Macbeth, and yet Olivier invested the role with a similar arc of despair leading to the ultimate revelation of the character's terminal solitude." This was the actor on top of his art.

Very soon after this he was approached with the offer to take over a brand-new theatre in Chichester with a hexagonal open stage as director and manager (John Clements succeeded him there a few years later). His first seminal production at Chichester was Chekhov's *Uncle Vanya*, in which he himself played Astrov, and which again confirmed his prolific range. With his embrace of the new, and the experience of forming a company with administration and development added to the business of acting and directing, he was well on track for the ultimate trial of founder-director of a National Theatre.

Twelve years had elapsed since the debate in Parliament which formally promised government support for the scheme, and ten years since Queen Elizabeth the Queen Mother had laid a foundation stone at a point on the South Bank of the Thames which was then changed several times (she said it should have been placed on castors).[7] But there was never the money available to give the plan a necessary push towards realisation, and the new Chancellor, Selwyn Lloyd, pronounced that government could no longer undertake to provide funds. Having waited for over a century, the acting profession was not about to allow promises to be broken so easily, and actors rallied to protest, along with the Arts Council, against this cruel cynicism. When the London County Council, which had already assigned the site rent-free, further declared that it would share the cost of construction, the Government's resolve was shaken, and Selwyn Lloyd agreed there was a legal as well as moral obligation to see the plan through to fruition.

Thus in 1962 Oliver Lyttelton was appointed Chairman of the National Theatre Board, and Laurence Olivier offered the post of founder-director, which he accepted eagerly.

Still at Chichester, Olivier was able to assemble his new company from the actors he already had, with the addition of some relatively unknown names who would later reach

7 Tim Goodwin, *Britain's Royal National Theatre* (1988), p 9

the top of the profession. Encouraged, not to say bullied, by Olivier, the Board decided not to wait for the physical theatre to be built (just as well, since it would take another twelve years to get there), but to open the National Theatre Company at the Old Vic. And so, at last, the first production opened on 22 October, 1963. The play had, of course, to be *Hamlet*, with Peter O'Toole in the leading role. Kenneth More was offered the role of Claudius, but he lacked the confidence to tackle a classical role on such a public and historic occasion, and declined.

The success which attended the first productions under Olivier's leadership exceeded all expectation, and audiences came not only from all over the country, but from the world; the National Theatre was one of the reasons, henceforth, to visit London. The second production was a transfer of *Uncle Vanya* from Chichester, and the third a rare presentation of Farquhar's *The Recruiting Officer* with Olivier demonstrating his matchless skill in inventing "business" for a comedy role as Captain Brazen. He followed this with a performance as Othello which led one newspaper to declare that a ticket for this production was "the most difficult piece of paper to get hold of in Britain today."

It was certainly a bravura display of Olivier's own brand of 'method' acting, of imposing his very imaginative creation of a character upon a text which gave little justification for it. He prepared for it as for an Olympic event, training his body to develop muscular flexibility, learning how to walk with an unfamiliar gait, toning in the gymnasium for strength and physique. He trained his voice to lower an octave, and his make-up was severe and compellingly convincing. He conveyed the essence of tragedy by showing

Othello's narcissistic pride in stark colours before allowing us to watch it crumble under Iago's pernicious onslaught "leading, as he tore a crucifix from his neck, to an atavistic obeisance to the barbaric gods."[8]

Audiences, in general, were struck dumb with awe. Nobody had ever seen an Othello so overwhelmingly dramatic. They rose to their feet in celebratory respect. A special performance given for the acting profession was greeted with a stampede down the aisles towards the footlights to acclaim the master. When the production went to Moscow, it again caused an unstoppable explosion of admiration. I, however, sat there bemused and disbelieving. It seemed that this notoriously histrionic role had undone yet another great actor, as Olivier rolled and stumbled about more like a Jamaican immigrant than a noble Moor, his delivery of the lines distinctly negroid; it was an embarrassing example of actor's hubris, and one more likely to inspire mirth than miracle. He redeemed himself with a powerful display of agonised remorse at Desdemona's death, but the damage was done, and one realised at the curtain that the whole focus had been upon Othello, with Iago counting almost for nothing. This Othello belonged wholly to Olivier, hardly to Shakespeare.

The *Sunday Telegraph* published a notice by Alan Brien which gave voice to this minority opinion. "There is a kind of acting", he wrote, "of which only a great actor is capable. I find Sir Laurence Olivier's Othello the most prodigious and perverse example of this in a decade…he begins to double and treble his vowels, to stretch his consonants, to stagger and shake, even to vomit, near the frontiers of self-parody. His hips oscillate, his palms rotate, his voice skids

---

8 *Dictionary of National Biography*

and slides so that the Othello music takes on a Beatle beat."[9] As the D.N.B. disarmingly points out, this performance is "still controversial".

The National Theatre's first few years at the Old Vic under Olivier's leadership were arguably the most glittering and intellectually satisfying period in the whole history of British theatre. He made the Old Vic a place of intoxicating excitement, and it came as a fitting honour that he should be the first actor ever to be ennobled to the peerage, in 1970. The one honour he possibly enjoyed more, however, was the naming of the main auditorium in the new building on the South Bank after him. By that time he had relinquished his directorship, and his zeal for new challenges took him into a great deal of film and television work.

When Edmund Kean played Richard III in 1814, he was the first actor to use his sword to trace arcs in the sand outside his tent in the last act. That same sword had passed to Henry Irving, who gave it into the Terry family, whereby it eventually belonged to Gielgud. He then, in following tradition, solemnly gave it to Olivier on the occasion of his magnificent Richard III in 1944. The sword bore a generous inscription: "This sword given him by his mother Kate Terry Gielgud, 1938, is given to Laurence Olivier by his friend John Gielgud in appreciation of his performance of Richard III at the New Theatre, 1944." When asked, thirty-five years later, to whom he intended to bequeath it, Olivier tartly responded, "No one. It's mine."[10]

Shortly before Olivier's debatable Othello, Gielgud had also played the part at Stratford-upon-Avon in a

9 *Sunday Telegraph*, 1964
10 Giles Brandreth, *John Gielgud: An Actor's Life* (1984), pp 149-150

production by Franco Zeffirelli about which there was no debate necessary; it was universally judged to be dreadful, and the reason for that throws light upon the actor's own personality. Peter Hall claimed that his "extraordinary sweetness and innocence" made it virtually impossible for him to comprehend the deep blindness of Othello's jealousy. Much more to his taste was his first attempt at a truly modern play, Alan Bennett's *Forty Years On*, wherein he was required to reminisce about the past, all of which he had personally lived through, in a kind of intimate colloquy with the audience. Having already perfected the conversational style in *The Ages of Man*, his handling of this unusual role was pure delight. The real plunge into modernity came, however, with two plays that he shared with Ralph Richardson, David Storey's *Home* and Harold Pinter's *No Man's Land*. In *Home* the two actors talked amiably about disparate matters, leading nowhere in particular, often at cross-purposes and with passages of quiet reflection undisturbed by words at all, where the audience had to see what they were thinking, and gradually work out that they were themselves struggling to concentrate on the thoughts which hovered behind their eyes. The reason for their apparent vacuity only became clear after the interval, for the 'home' which formed the backcloth to their meanderings was a mental institution. With stunning understatement, they worked together like a piano duet, each preparing the way for the other. Harold Hobson: "At the very end, they stand, staring out above the heads of the audience, cheeks wet with tears in memory of some unnamed misery, weeping soundlessly as the lights fade on them. It makes a tragic, unforgettable close."[11]

---

11 Morley, *John G: The Authorised Biography of John Gielgud*, p 359

Similar silences permeated their next, and most glorious collaboration in *No Man's Land*. In this, as almost never before in his career, Gielgud had to construct a character from scratch, with very little help from the playwright, who himself admitted that Gielgud was engaged on "an act of creation rather than interpretation." The man was called Spooner, a shabby bohemian with a questionable past, in a shapeless suit, badly buttoned, unpressed trousers apparently held up with string or a tie, ill-fitting shirt, uncombed hair, spectacles, socks and sandals, altogether a bit of a mess, but with oddly fluent and at the same time purposeless sentences spat out through the cigarette-smoke. This "wonder of slept-in dishevelment"[12] was the master-stroke of an actor with genius in his soul. The Garrick Club gave a dinner in his honour not long afterwards, in the knowledge that, perhaps, he was unlikely ever to do anything better in his old age.

Amusingly, he had only ventured on to the National Theatre stage once, to play Oedipus in a production by Peter Brook. He did not look at all at home. The whole cast were dressed in matching sweaters and slacks "like a Bulgarian table-tennis team" (Alan Bennett)[13], and the rehearsals had been unorthodox to say the least. "The stunt that some directors have now of coming to do exercises and play games with you to know you better wastes an awful lot of time", he said. Nor did he care much for the theatre itself: "The atmosphere's cold, like an airport."[14]

Like Olivier, he too concentrated on small cameo parts in films and television, often to such effect that his was the

12 *The Ages of Gielgud*, p 146
13 *The Ages of Gielgud*, p 118
14 *The Times*, 22 March, 1984

only performance that registered in the nation's collective memory; they both appeared in the TV adaptation of Waugh's *Brideshead Revisited*, Gielgud actually contriving to make the character of Charles Ryder's father funnier and sharper than Waugh had done on the page. As he entered his nineties, he still seemed to be ready to learn and to hone his art, even as sadness enveloped him at the loss of all his contemporaries, whom he outlived by a considerable margin. The entire acting profession stood in awe of him, as they had of Irving a century before, and since Gielgud had been born only months before Irving died, he may with truth be said to have covered that century with his own career. The next generation of actors who are members of the club is with us still, and it includes many with already illustrious careers – David Suchet, Simon Russell Beale, Tom Courtenay, Peter Sallis, Geoffrey Palmer and more – but they will await a future edition of this narrative if we are neatly to finish with the year 2000, in which John Gielgud died, and one feels that they would all assent to the notion that the curtain should come down on him, the nicest as well as the most accomplished actor-member of the past hundred years.

He had read John Donne's poem "Death be not proud" at the funeral service for Olivier in Westminster Abbey in 1989. On his own death, as he got up from his dining -table and slumped into his driver's arms, the news was broadcast on radio and television stations the world over, but the service itself, in the village church of Wotton Underwood, was gently unpretentious and utterly private. Sir Donald Sinden read Donne's "No Man is an Island", Sir John Mills recited the poem "Do Not Despair for Johnny Head in Air" which he had first performed in *In Which We*

Serve, and Paul Scofield read the Shakespeare sonnet, "No longer mourn for me when I am dead". The simplicity was overwhelmingly sad and fittingly noble. Sinden wrote to the *Daily Telegraph* to say that "every actor regarded Sir John Gielgud as the leader of our profession. He spoke Shakespeare as if it were his mother tongue…For three centuries the theatre was dominated by three great actors: David Garrick in the eighteenth, Henry Irving in the nineteenth, and John Gielgud in the twentieth."[15]

John himself said, retreating from any fuss, "I have only been an actor, you know." The theatres of London did not agree; they all dimmed their lights, and many actors gave curtain speeches in celebration of his life before the audiences went home. Something important had occurred. Someone irreplaceable had been lost. They left the theatres in warm reflection.

---

15 The *Daily Telegraph,* 22 May, 2000

POSTSCRIPTUM

In the course of this story, I have attempted to identify three strands of development to describe the efforts of the Garrick Club, through the agency of those of its members who were actors, to influence the history of the drama in England. In all three I think we can now see that tentative plans made, even whispered, in 1831 when the club was founded, were encouraged and promoted by successive legions of members, through example as much as by suggestion, in each generation. The result is that all three strands of development had, by the year 2000, reached an apogee of success that our founders might have thought beyond their ambitions.

In no order of preference, for all three are of equal importance, the first may be the re-discovery of original Shakespearean text after far too many years of tolerating corrupted versions performed on the stages of the Theatres Royal Drury Lane and Covent Garden. This was made possible in the first place by the removal by Act of Parliament in 1843 of the monopoly previously enjoyed by these two theatres, but as always, it was the energy of individuals that carried the work, inch by inch, towards fruition. From the beginning William Charles Macready, the acknowledged great tragedian of his day, used his authority to elevate Shakespearean drama to peaks of intellectually satisfying intensity which it had not always known. Even he, however, did not consider that the public would be ready for anything but carefully crafted "acting" versions of the plays. It was Samuel Phelps who single-handedly rescued Shakespeare over a continuous period of eighteen years between 1844 and 1862, at, of all unlikely places, Sadler's Wells Theatre in Islington. Contemporaneously, Charles Kean plundered architectural, literary and pictorial sources in order to give Shakespeare visible verisimilitude, following years in which the plays had been presented in all the wrong costumes and against all the wrong backdrops. Some ten years later Henry Irving brought his own inimitable magic to add theatrical flourish to Shakespearean drama, to make of each play an event and a tonic that would not easily be forgotten. Johnston Forbes-Robertson carried forward Phelps's insistence on purity of expression and truth of characterisation, eschewing the feeble histrionic pleasure of centre-stage, while Herbert Beerbohm Tree continued Charles Kean's predilection for spectacular accuracy in staging.

It was not until the twentieth century that the actor finally recognised his subservience to the poetry, Gielgud carrying the torch of Forbes-Robertson and Olivier inheriting the panache of Irving, both, in their deeply different manners, bringing Shakespeare to the fore, while Wolfit did so with a brilliant idiosyncrasy which defied imitation. By the end of the century, and especially following the publication of definitive texts based upon every available scholarly source, productions habitually presented Shakespeare free of all intrusive fiddling. Every one of those actors engaged in this journey were Garrick members.

Second, the dream of a truly national theatrical company

to compare with those which flourished in European capitals was promulgated assiduously and repeatedly by these same actors over very many years, supported by others who relinquished acting for the directorial role, such as Harley Granville-Barker, until their collective zeal finally bullied Parliament into acquiescence, and the National Theatre rose in glory under the leadership of Olivier.

Third, the profession of acting has had to struggle to merit respect. Actors were considered unfit for society and were rarely acknowledged by gentlemen until the Garrick Club, with the specific aim of ridding London of this absurdity, opened its welcoming doors to a decent future. From being ignored, even disdained, in the eighteenth century, from having to queue with carpenters and errand-boys in order to receive payment for their work in the nineteenth, they grew in stature until the impossible accolade of a knighthood was bestowed on Henry Irving by a distinctly pleased Queen Victoria. Other knighthoods followed, capped by peerages for Olivier and Richard Attenborough almost exactly a hundred years later.

And the final stage in this progress? John Gielgud, having been already knighted and revered, became the only actor in history to be awarded by his sovereign with both the Companion of Honour and the Order of Merit.

The Garrick Club's actors have much to be proud of. The names of all of them are listed in appendix.

APPENDIX

ACTOR MEMBERS OF THE GARRICK CLU B 1831-2010

NAME AND DATES OF BIRTH & DEATH WITH YEARS OF MEMBERSHIP

A
—

Joss Ackland, C.B.E. (b.1928)
1975-1983; 1986-1995

Sir Timothy Ackroyd, Bt. (b.1958)
Elected in 1995

Brian Aherne (1902-1986) 1962-1986

Anthony Ainley (1932-2004) 1969-1980

Henry Hinchliffe Ainley (1879-1945)
1909-1934

John Alderton (b.1940) 1977-1990

Sir George Alexander (1858-1918)
1886-1918

Charles G. Allan (1852-1911) 1902-1911

Patrick Allen (1927-2006) 2001-2006

James Robertson Anderson (1811-1895)
1843-1895

Anthony Andrews (b.1948)
Elected in 1986

Nigel Anthony (b.1941) *Elected in* 2007

Ben Aris (1937-2003) 1989-2003

George Arliss (1868-1946) 1913-1946

Oscar Asche (1871-1936) 1915-1926

Arthur Askey, C.B.E. (1900-1982)
1978-1981

Hon. Delaval Astley (b.1960) 1999-2009

Baron Attenborough, C.B.E. (b.1923)
Elected in 1950

Henry Ayliff (1871-1949) 1943-1949

Sir Felix Aylmer, O.B.E. (1889-1979)
1937-1979

Allan Aynesworth (1864-1959)
1896-1959

B
—

Robin Bailey (1919-1999) 1987-1999

George Baker (b.1931) *Elected in* 1981

Michael Ball (b.1962) *Elected in* 2008

Sir Squire Bancroft (1841-1926)
1869-1926

Daniel E. Bandmann (1840-1905)
1868-1905

Leslie Banks (1890-1952) 1928-1952

John Bannister (fl.1879-1886) 1880-1886

Peter Barkworth (1929-2006) 1981-1986

Ivor Barnard (1887-1953) 1945-1953

Patrick Barr (1908-1985) 1954-1985

Wilson Barrett (1846-1904) 1883-1904

John Barron (1920-2004) 1978-2004

John Barrymore (1882-1942) 1924-1941

Peter Bartlett (1927-2007) 1993-2007

George Bartley (1782?-1858)
Original member-1834

Anthony Bate (b.1927) *Elected in* 1996

Sam Beazley (b.1916) *Elected in* 2004

Richard Bebb (1927-2006) 1987-2006

Kenneth Benda (1902-1978) 1965-1978

Albert Edward Benedict
(d.1915) 1907-1915

Christopher Benjamin (b.1934)
1994-1995

Peter Bennett (1917-1989) 1975-1989

Sir Francis (Frank) Robert Benson
(1858-1939) 1893-1939

Henry Thomas Betty (1819-1897)
1884-1897

Rodney Bewes (b.1937) *Elected in* 1982

Gerald Biron (d.1906) 1897-1903

Alfred Bishop (1848-1928) 1910-1920

Martin Bishop (b.1947) *Elected in* 2008

Denys Blakelock (1901-1970) 1946-1954;
1958-1970

Peter Blythe (1934-2004) 1985-2004

Derek Bond, M.C. (1920-2006)
1984-2006

Hugh Bonneville (b.1963) *Elected in* 1990

Dion George Boucicault (1859-1929)
1882-1929

Arthur Bourchier (1863-1927) 1885-1927

Peter Bowles (b.1936) *Elected in* 1988

Roger Braban (b.1931) *Elected in* 1998

Sebastian Breaks (b.1940) *Elected in* 1995

Jeremy Brett (1933-1995) 1973-1975

Richard Briers, C.B.E. (b.1934)
Elected in 1990

Jasper Britton (b.1962) *Elected in* 2007

Tony Britton (b.1924) *Elected in* 1972

Peter Broad (b.1954) *Elected in* 2007

Arthur Henry Bromley-Davenport
(d.1946) 1928-1946

Clive Brook (1887-1974) 1946-1974

William Graham Browne (1870-1937)
1908-1937

Nigel Bruce (1895-1953) 1929-1953

Jack Buchanan (1891-1957) 1938-1949

John Baldwin Buckstone (1802-1879)
1854-1870

Rowland Buckstone (1860-1922)
1909-1922

Hugh Burden (1913-1985) 1957-1985

Richard Burton, C.B.E. (1925-1984)
1960-1966

Anthony Bushell (1904-1997) 1947-1966

Henry James Byron (1835-1884)
1861-1884

C

Sir Michael Caine, C.B.E. (b.1933)
1971-1975

Charles Alexander Calvert (1828-1879)
1870-1879

Timothy Carlton (b.1939) *Elected in* 1995

Sir Lewis Casson, M.C. (1875-1969)
1954-1958

Arthur Cecil (1843-1896) 1867-1896

Jonathan Cecil (b.1939) *Elected in* 1988

John Chapman (1927-2001) 1991-2001

Sir Jeremy Child, Bt., (b.1944)
Elected in 1983

E. Holman Clark (1864-1925) 1906-1925

Sir John Clements, C.B.E. (1910-1988)
1943-1988

George Cole, O.B.E. (b.1925) 1954-1961

Giles Cole (b.1949) *Elected in* 1989

Henry Compton (1805-1877) 1853-1861

Sir Sean Connery (b.1930) 1968-1969

Tom Conti (b.1941) *Elected in* 1981

Thomas Potter Cooke (1786-1864) 1833-
1838; 1843-1861

Robert Coote (1909-1982) 1970-1982

Sir Tom Courtenay (b.1937)
Elected in 1968

Sir Noël Coward (1899-1973) 1966-1973

Brian Cox (b.1946) *Elected in* 1996

Michael Craig (b.1929) 1959-1970

Robin Craven (1906-1978) 1974-1978

Andrew Cruickshank, M.B.E. (1907-
1988) 1966-1988

Roland Culver, O.B.E. (1900-1984)
1951-1984

Finlay Currie (1878-1968) 1949-1968

George Curzon (1898-1976) 1928-1939;
1943-1976

D

Nigel Davenport (b.1928) 1982-1992

Geoffrey Davies (b.1942) 1995-1997

Rowland Davies (b.1941) *Elected in* 1979

Noel Davis (1927-2002) 1978-2000

Basil Dean, C.B.E. (1887-1978)
1939-1978

Maurice Denham, O.B.E. (1909-2002)
1964-2002

Sir William Henry Don, 7th Bt.
(1825-1862) 1846-1847?

Roy Dotrice, O.B.E. (b.1923)
Elected in 1970

Kenneth Douglas (1874-1923) 1910-1917

William Dowton (1764-1851)
Original member-1832

Sir Gerald Du Maurier (1873-1934)
1903-1934

Franklin Dyall (1874-1950) 1934-1950

E

Dennis Eadie (1875-1928) 1913-1928

Paul Eddington, C.B.E. (1927-1995)
1982-1995

Robert Eddison (1908-1991) 1950-1973

Peter Egan (b.1946) 1976-1992

Denholm Elliott, C.B.E. (1922-1992)
1954-1992

Clifford Evans (1912-1985) 1963-1985

F

Major Leslie Faber, M.C. (1879-1929)
1920-1929

James Bernard Fagan (1873-1933)
1920-1933

Douglas Fairbanks, K.B.E., D.S.C.
(1909-2000) 1974-1995

Charles Farley (1771-1859) 1831-1840?

William Farren (1825-1908) 1864-1874

Kenneth Farrington (b.1936)
Elected in 2008

John Fawcett (1769-1837) 1833-1837?

Charles Albert Fechter (1822-1879)
1863-c.1865

James Fernandez (1835-1915) 1888-1915

Peter Finch (1916-1977) 1954-1968

Frank Finlay, C.B.E. (b.1926)
Elected in 1978

Walter Fitzgerald (1896-1976) 1943-1976

Robert Flemyng, M.C., O.B.E.
(1912-1995) 1948-1995

Sir Johnston Forbes-Robertson
(1853-1937) 1888-1937

Norman Forbes-Robertson (1858-1932)
1901-1932

Matthew Forsyth (d.1954) 1948-1954

Edward Fox, O.B.E. (b.1937) 1980-1993

William Fox (1911-2008) 1974-2008

Charles V. France (1868-1949) 1938-1943

Clive Francis (b.1946) *Elected in* 1990

Raymond Francis (1911-1987) 1960-1987

Leslie French (1904-1999) 1967-1999

G

Sir Michael Gambon, C.B.E. (b.1940)
Elected in 1990

Leo Genn (1905-1978) 1943-1978

Paul Geoffrey (b.1955) 1991-1992

George Giddens (1845-1920) 1900-1920

Sir John Gielgud, O.M., C.H.
(1904-2000) 1970-2000

Julian Glover (b.1935) 1990-1993

Louis Goodrich (1864-1945) 1928-1939

Marius Goring, C.B.E. (1912-1998)
1949-1998

Bruce Graham (b.1948) *Elected in* 2010

Richard Corney Grain (1844-1895)
1884-1895

Harley Granville-Barker (1877-1946)
1908-1946

Martyn Green (1899-1975) 1952-1975

Richard Greene (1918-1985) 1954-1963

Hubert Gregg (1914-2004) 1964-2004

Hugh Griffith (1912-1980) 1952-1980

William Hunter Grimston (1843-1917)
1874-1917

George Grossmith (1847-1912) 1883-1912

George Grossmith (1874-1935) 1917-1935

Weedon Grossmith (1854-1919)
1906-1919

Sir Alec Guinness, C.H., C.B.E.
(1914-2000) 1948-1974; 1982-2000

Campbell Gullan (1881-1939) 1934-1939

Edmund Gwenn (1877-1959) 1924-1959

H
—

James K. Hackett (1869-1926) 1921-1926

Peter Haddon (1898-1962) 1946-1953

Tony Handy (b.1934) *Elected in* 2008

Nicholas Hannen (1881-1972) 1922-1972

Lawrence Hanray (1874-1947) 1943-1947

Hubert Harben (1878-1941) 1935-1940

Cyril Harcourt (1872-1924) 1916-1924

Lyn Harding (1867-1952) 1925-1943

Sir Cedric Hardwicke (1893-1964)
1931-1964

Gilbert Hare (1869-1951) 1891-1924

Sir John Hare (1844-1921) 1868-1921

John Pritt Harley (1786-1858)
Original member-1858

Robert Harris (1899-1995) 1952-1995

Sir Rex Harrison (1908-1990) 1954-1990

Giles Havergal, C.B.E. (b.1938)
Elected in 2006

Nigel Havers (b.1949) *Elected in* 1973

Jack Hawkins, C.B.E. (1910-1973)
1948-1973

Sir Charles Hawtrey (1858-1923)
1921-1923

Leslie Henson (1891-1957) 1948-1957

Charles Heslop (1883-1966) 1963-1966

Sir Seymour Hicks (1871-1949)
1899-1915; 1916-1949

Carleton Hobbs (1898-1978) 1963-1978

Stanley Holloway, O.B.E. (1890-1982)
1953-1982

Robert Holness (b.1928) *Elected in* 1998

Sir Anthony Hopkins (b.1937) 1994-1999

Sir Michael Hordern, C.B.E. (1911-1995)
1953-1995

Leslie Howard (1893-1943) 1933-1943

Roy Hudd, O.B.E. (b.1936) *Elected in* 1997

Barry Humphries, C.B.E. (b.1934)
Elected in 1979

Ian Hunter (1900-1975) 1934-1975

John Hurt, C.B.E. (b.1940)
Elected in 2005

I
-

Barrie Ingham (b.1934) *Elected in* 1995

Sir Henry Irving (1838-1905) 1874-1905

Henry Brodribb Irving (1870-1919)
1896-1919

Sir Gyles Isham, Bt. (1903-1976)
1925-1956

J
-

Gordon Jackson, O.B.E. (1923-1990)
1979-1990

Sir Derek Jacobi, C.B.E. (b.1938)
1982-1990

Michael Jayes (b. 1951) *Elected in* 1983

Peter Jeffrey (1929-1999) 1991-1999

Milton Johns (b.1938) *Elected in* 1982

Richard Johnson (b.1927) 2004-2006

Freddie Jones (b.1927) *Elected in* 1990

Richard Jones (1779-1851)

Original member-1839

Barry Justice (1940-1980) 1972-1980

K
—

Boris Karloff (1887-1969) 1960-1967

Charles Kean (1811-1868) 1833-1868

Robert Keeley (1793-1869) 1859-1869

Charles Kemble (1775-1854)

Original member-1854

Henry Kemble (1848-1907) 1878-1907

Stephen Kemble (b.1951) *Elected in* 1990

Edward Kempner (b.1957)

Elected in 1990

Frederick Kerr (1858-1933) 1920-1933

Geoffrey Kerr (1895-1971) 1941-1960

L
—

Walter Lacy (1809-1898) 1850-1898

Peter Land (b.1953) *Elected in* 1992

Matheson Lang (1879-1948) 1948-1948

David Langton (1912-1994) 1970-1994

Hugh Laurie, O.B.E. (b.1959)

Elected in 1995

John Laurie (1897-1980) 1954-1980

Gerald Lawrence (1873-1957) 1944-1955

Frank Lawton (1904-1969) 1942-1969

George Layton (b.1942) *Elected in* 2008

Richard Leech (1922-2004) 1974-2004

Dominic Le Foe (1931-2010) 1993-2010

Robert George Legge (1864-1905)

1887-1905

Nicholas Le Prevost (b.1947)

Elected in 1997

Eric Lewis (1855-1935) 1900-1917

Robert Lindsay (b.1950) *Elected in* 2000

Francis Lister (1899-1951) 1948-1951

Ian Liston (b.1948) *Elected in* 2009

Roger Lloyd Pack (b.1944) *Elected in* 1990

Terence Longdon (b.1922)

Elected in 1990

Lt.Col. Robert Loraine, D.S.O., M.C.

(1876-1935) 1918-1935

Charles Macready Lowne (1863-1941)

1910-1941

Patrick Ludlow (1903-1996) 1976-1996

Geoffrey Lumsden (1914-1984)

1980-1984

M
—

Patrick McGoohan (1928-2009)

1993-1999

John Lumsden Mackay (1867-1934)

1919-1934

Norman McKinnel (1870-1932)

1921-1932

Francis Henry Macklin (1848-1903)

1892-1903

William Charles Macready (1793-1873)

Original member - 1838

Herbert Marshall (1890-1966) 1927-1966

Sir John Martin-Harvey (1863-1944)

1919-1940

Raymond Massey (1896-1983) 1929-1983

Aubrey Mather (1885-1958) 1929-1953

Charles Mathews (1776-1835)

Original member - 1835

Charles James Mathews (1803-1878)

Original member-c.1838; 1874-1878

Alfred Edward Matthews (1869-1960)

1906-1960

Cyril Francis Maude (1862-1951)

1894-1951

Roger Maxwell (1900-1971) 1938-1966

Drinkwater Meadows (1799-1869)

1832-1860

Philip Merivale (1886-1946) 1935-1946

Sir John Mills, C.B.E. (1908-2005) 1945-2005

Dawson Milward (1870-1926) 1907-1926

Alec Monteath (b.1941) 1993-2007

Walter Montgomery (1827-1871) 1864-1871

Sir Roger Moore (b.1927) *Elected in* 1970

Kenneth More, C.B.E. (1914-1982) 1954-1982

André Morell (1909-1978) 1957-1978

Robert Morley, C.B.E. (1908-1992) 1948-1992

Clive Morton (1904-1975) 1958-1975

William Henry Murray (1790-1852) 1843-1846?

N

Laurence Naismith (1908-1992) 1954-1992

Owen Nares (1888-1943) 1929-1943

Henry Neville (1837-1910) 1865-1910

John Neville, O.B.E., C.M. (b.1925) 1970-1971

Jeremy Nicholas (b.1947) 2000-2002; *re-elected in* 2004

Derek Nimmo (1930-1999) 1972-1999

David Niven (1910-1983) 1944-1950

Eille Norwood (1861-1948) 1934-1939

O

Baron Olivier, O.M. (1907-1989) 1936-1989

Henry Oscar (1891-1969) 1952-1963

Peter O'Toole (b.1932) *Elected in* 1963

Brian Oulton (1908-1992) 1963-1991

P

Charles Lloyd Pack (1902-1983) 1974-1983

Geoffrey Palmer, O.B.E. (b.1927) *Elected in* 1988

Cecil Parker (1897-1971) 1940-1971

Richard Pasco, C.B.E. (b.1926) *Elected in* 1978

Nigel Patrick (1913-1981) 1952-1981

Samuel Phelps (1804-1878) 1874-1878

James William Pigott (fl.1882-1910) 1882-1908

Sir Nigel Playfair (1874-1934) 1897-1934

Robert Portal (b.1967) 1999-2002; *re-elected in* 2009

Tyrone Power (1797-1841) *Original member*-1841

Robert Pugh (b.1948) *Elected in* 2002

Q

Leon Quartermaine (1876-1967) 1915-1940

Sir Anthony Quayle, C.B.E. (1913-1989) 1944-1957; 1987-1989

John Quayle (b.1938) *Elected in* 1988

R

Basil Radford (1897-1952) 1948-1952

James Raglan (1901-1961) 1953-1961

Tristan Rawson (1888-1974) 1950-1959

Cyril Raymond (1897-1973) 1951-1968

Sir Michael Redgrave, C.B.E. (1908-1985) 1943-1974; 1983-1985

Alfred German Reed (1847-1895) 1887-1895

Thomas German Reed (1817-1888) 1859-1888

John Reeve jnr (fl. 1848-1852 1850-1852

George Relph (1888-1960) 1946-1960

John Rhys-Davies (b.1944) *Elected in* 2005

Ian Richardson, C.B.E. (1934-2007) 1976-2007

Edward H. Robins (1880-1955)
1935-1955

James Rodgers (d.1890) 1889-1890

Charles Cowper Ross (1929-1985)
1962-1985

Robert Roxby (1809?-1866) 1854-1866

Patrick Ryecart (b.1952) *Elected in* 1986

S

Robin Sachs (b.1951) 1991-1992

Peter Sallis, O.B.E. (b.1921)
Elected in 1978

Paul Scofield, C.H., C.B.E. (1922-2008)
1978-1980

David Shaughnessy (b.1957) 1981-1985

Sebastian Shaw (1905-1994) 1952-1994

Michael Shepley (1907-1961) 1943-1961

Alastair Sim, C.B.E. (1900-1976)
1943-1976

Ronald Simpson (1896-1957) 1938-1957

Hugh Sinclair (1903-1962) 1943-1951

Sir Donald Sinden, C.B.E. (b.1923)
Elected in 1960

Jeremy Sinden (1950-1996) 1978-1996

Marc Sinden (b.1954) 1986-1992

Guy Siner (b.1947) *Elected in* 1999

Campbell Singer (1909-1976) 1962-1976

Sir (Charles) Aubrey Smith (1863-1948)
1906-1948

Edward Askew Sothern (1826-1881)
1864-1881

Edward Hugh Sothern (1859-1933)
1903-1933

George Sothern (1870-1919) 1898-1919

Robert Speaight (1904-1976) 1937-1976

Trevor Spencer (1875-1945) 1929-1945

Ronald Squire (1886-1958) 1926-1936

Commander Sir Guy Standing, K.B.E.
(1873-1937) 1917-1932

John Standing (b.1934) 1975-1980

Athole Stewart, O.B.E. (1879-1940)
1920-1940

Arthur Stirling (1827-1898) 1867-1898

Nigel Stock (1919-1986) 1967-1986

Commander Henry Stoker, D.S.O.
(1885-1966) 1930-1966

Ken Stott (b.1954) *Elected in* 2010

David Suchet, O.B.E. (b.1946)
Elected in 1996

Lyall Swete (1865-1930) 1907-1930

T

Robert Taber (1866-1904) 1903-1904

Reginald Tate (1896-1955) 1948-1955

Conway Tearle (1878-1938) 1931-1938

Sir Godfrey Tearle (1884-1953)
1923-1953

Edward O'Connor Terry (1844-1912)
1884-1912

(Walter) Brandon Thomas (1848-1914)
1903-1914

Jevan Brandon Thomas (1898-1977)
1929-1932

Stephen Thorne (b.1935) *Elected in* 1996

Thomas Thorne (1841-1918) 1884-1909

Frank Thornton (b.1921) *Elected in* 1981

George Thorpe (1891-1961) 1943-1945

David Timson (b.1950) *Elected in* 2004

David Tomlinson (1917-2000) 1989-1990

John Lawrence Toole (1830-1906)
1864-1906

Harry Towb (1925-2009) 1988-2009

Sir Herbert Beerbohm Tree (1852-1917)
1884-1917

Frederick Treves, B.E.M. (b.1925)
Elected in 1991

Austin Trevor (1897-1978) 1943-1978

Spencer Trevor (1875-1945) 1929-1945

Ralph Truman (1900-1977) 1953-1977

John Turner (b.1932) *Elected in* 1984

THE ACTORS

U

Sir Peter Ustinov, C.B.E. (1921-2004)
1948-2004

V

Sydney Valentine (1865-1919) 1918-1919
George Vandenhoff (1820-1885)
1853-1856
James Villiers (1933-1998) 1975-1978
George James Vining (1824-1875)
1867-1875

W

Tom Ward (b.1971) *Elected in 2006*
Ian Wallace, O.B.E. (1919-2009)
1954-2009
James William Wallack (1795-1864)
Original member-1864
Lester Wallack (1820-1888) 1868-1888
Sam Wanamaker (1919-1993) 1993-1993
Herbert Waring (1857-1932) 1897-1904;
1905-1932
Harold Warrender (1903-1953)
1937-1953
Giles Watling (b.1953) *Elected in 1995*
Jack Watling (1923-2001) 1982-2001
Moray Watson (b.1928) *Elected in 1982*
Alan Webb (1906-1982) 1951-1956
Benjamin Webster (1798-1882)
1838-1882
Benjamin Webster (1864-1947)
1889-1947
Mogens Wieth (1919-1962) 1957-1962
Arthur Whitby (1869-1922) 1919-1922
Jeffrey Wickham (b.1933) *Elected in 1991*
Horace Wigan (1818?-1885) 1866-1868
Michael Wilding (1912-1979) 1960-1979
Edward Smith Willard (1853-1915)
1888-1915

Emlyn Williams, C.B.E. (1905-1987)
1940-1945
Hugh Williams (1904-1969) 1937-1939
Michael Williams (1935-2001) 1977-2001
Douglas Wilmer (b.1920) 1962-1977
Hon. Lewis Strange Wingfield
(1842-1891) 1864-1891
James Winston (1773-1843)
Original member-1843
Sir Donald Wolfit (1902-1968) 1942-1968
Arthur Wontner (1875-1960) 1916-1960
Edward Woodward, O.B.E. (1930-2009)
1984-2009
Benjamin Wrench (1778-1843) 1837-1843
Edward Richard Wright (1813-1859)
1853-1859
Sir Charles Wyndham (1837-1919)
1886-1919
Robert Henry Wyndham (1814-1894)
1873-1894

Y

Frederick Henry Yates (1797-1842)
Original member-1840
Charles Mayne Young (1777-1856)
Original member-1836
Roland Young (1887-1953) 1948-1953

INDEX